Thinking a

THINKING ABOUT MUSIC

An Introduction to the Philosophy of Music

LEWIS ROWELL

The University of Massachusetts Press   *Amherst*

Copyright © 1983 by
The University of Massachusetts Press
All rights reserved
First paperback edition, 1984
Second paperback printing, 1987
Printed in the United States of America
Acknowledgments for permission to reprint
material under copyright appear on the last
printed page of this book.

Library of Congress Cataloging in Publication Data
Rowell, Lewis Eugene, 1933–
Thinking about music.
Bibliography: p.
Includes index.
1. Music—Philosophy and aesthetics.   I. Title.
ML3800.R63   1983   780'.1   82-21979
ISBN 0-87023-386-6

For Unni

Contents

Preface

THIS BOOK IS for readers who are insatiably curious about music—
"students of music" in the broadest sense of the word. In this category I include those whose musical concerns are more humanistic
than technical, as well as those preparing for careers in music. *Thinking about Music* is not specifically addressed to musicologists or
philosophers, although I would hope that both may find something
of value herein. My only recommendation is that the reader be armed
with as diverse a set of musical experiences as possible, whether acquired through a lifetime of concert going, a record collection, amateur performance, or professional training.

In a library system of classification, *Thinking about Music* is apt
to be filed under the heading "Music—Aesthetics, history and problems of," and that is a fair description. In the ancient tradition of
philosophical literature, it might be termed an exhortation or an
isagoge—not an enchiridion. I do not outline *a* philosophy, *an* aesthetic, but rather a way toward such a philosophy. Personal opinions
can readily be detected here and there, but I have studiously avoided
any attempt to persuade readers to share them. And I regret to say
that I have not yet made up my mind on an alarming number of
major issues. Answers may come in time, but my immediate concern
is for the questions.

The expository sections are quite brief, and only rarely are they
accompanied by a full range of arguments. My aim has been to construct a systematic framework of thought to guide the reader's personal inquiry. The approach is often taxonomic, revealing my preference for understanding complex ideas by viewing them as clusters,

intellectual tapestries to be unraveled into their component strands. The lists that result are offered as an agenda for reflection, to be tested by readers against their own attitudes, beliefs, experiences, and values. I hope not for indulgence but for vigorous debate, and I shall be intensely disappointed if any reader fails to find some point on which we may agree to disagree.

Thinking about Music was conceived as a textbook, and I still think of it as such—perhaps in the sense that most such expository works are texts, generally for courses that either do not exist or are so few in number that they are overlooked by the commercial text-book market. I use it as a text in an undergraduate course ("Music and Ideas") at Indiana University, and it may prove useful in other similar courses.

The format requires little explanation. Three preliminary chapters set forth the field of inquiry and prepare for the set of historical chapters (4–7). After a pair of chapters devoted to various aesthetic "problems"—perception, detachment, meaning, values, et al.—the final two chapters present important alternatives to the traditional attitudes, beliefs, and values that inform the standard Western concert repertoire. Most of the book is indeed ethnocentric in that it assumes the values of Western civilization, but (I hope) neither deceptively nor offensively so.

Many intellectual and personal debts must be acknowledged. Of the many works listed in the Bibliography, my thought has been guided, in particular, by the writings of Monroe C. Beardsley, Władysław Tatarkiewicz, and Paul Weiss—the former two for their historical insights and the latter for his provocative and distinctive approach to the philosophy of art. Their influence upon this book has been profound and goes far beyond the numerous references to their works.

I also acknowledge with deep gratitude the contributions of many friends: J. T. Fraser, who was and is my guide in the study of time; Vernon Kliewer, for many helpful and friendly acts; Jon Kramer, for a penetrating review; Richard Martin and the entire production staff of the University of Massachusetts Press, for their encouragement and skill in preparing the manuscript for publication; Prem Lata Sharma and Prithwish Neogy, for their guidance in the arts of India; Ruth Solie, for a sympathetic reading and many valuable suggestions; Ric Trimillos, whose generosity in scheduling made the original manuscript possible; Allen Trubitt, for his constant support when it was most needed; Jim Tyler and Walter Maurer, who gave me tools; Larry Wallen, for an extraordinary contribution of time and friendship; and my original ten guinea pigs, but especially Bob Gjerdingen.

Thinking about Music

I Introduction: terms and themes

IT IS ALWAYS a good idea to be clear about just what it is that one is discussing, but in philosophy it is imperative. The first three chapters of this book are designed to set out the frame of reference for an inquiry: the first task is to present my understanding of what is included in the domains of music, philosophy, art, and aesthetics; the present chapter concludes with a set of basic propositions—themes that will be frequently sounded in the course of this book. Chapter two is a wide-ranging exploration of the types of questions the philosopher might ask with respect to music. Chapter three seeks to define music's place among the arts. After these rather lengthy but necessary preliminaries, the book proceeds to examine the history of ideas about music.

I propose to avoid for now the dangerous task of defining music. This may cause problems, but a definition (as the term implies) has a way of setting boundaries around a target word, and it seems desirable to allow my subject as wide a domain as possible. It will become clear that *music*, as commonly used, may refer to sounds, a piece of paper, an abstract formal concept, a collective behavior of society, or a single coordinated pattern of neurochemical impulses in the brain. It can be a product or a process. A definition that might satisfy most members of Western society may fail instantly when applied to non-Western musics or music written within the last twenty years. For now let *music* signify anything that is normally called *music*.

The literal definition of the word *philosophy* is familiar: from the

Greek *philo* (love) and *sophia* (knowledge, wisdom). A philosopher, then, is a seeker after knowledge, one who loves to exercise intellectual curiosity. Philosophy does not usually lead to definite answers (when it does, the results become a part of what we call *science*), because it generally deals with matters that cannot be proved by demonstration. The value of philosophy is asserted eloquently by Bertrand Russell:

> Philosophy is to be studied, not for the sake of any definite answers to its questions, since no definite answers can, as a rule, be known to be true, but rather for the sake of the questions themselves; because these questions enlarge our conception of what is possible, enrich our intellectual imagination and diminish the dogmatic assurance which closes the mind against speculation; . . .[1]

I would like to suggest four requisites for philosophy, although there are surely many more: a curious mind—without a questing mind, philosophical inquiry is tedious and pointless; an open mind, demonstrated by the willingness to suspend judgment and consider alternatives; the habit of disciplined thinking; and self-knowledge—awareness of one's beliefs, values, prejudices, and shortcomings. Mental activity and language are the *media* of philosophy: although mental activity obviously includes much that cannot be expressed in language (especially in the creation and perception of music), language continues to be the main way in which we communicate. Admittedly this poses special problems when applied to the nondiscursive, symbolic languages of the arts.

We demonstrate knowledge through various modes of understanding, only some of which involve language. Here are some ways in which musical knowledge can be obtained and/or demonstrated: through direct experience (with the phenomenon of music itself); by imitation through artistic praxis (doing) or *poiesis* (making); through mental reconstruction (during or after an artistic experience); in behavior (buying a concert ticket, choosing a profession); with a linguistic definition; by giving an analogy or metaphor; by giving an example; with dialectics (back-and-forth argument, as between Socrates and a disciple); by constructing a syllogism (the tightest form of logical reasoning, based on major and minor premises and leading inescapably to a conclusion that—granted the correctness of the premises—is thus demonstrated to be true).

Philosophers today hesitate to define the tasks of philosophy in terms of its traditional branches, but there is still some value in considering these domains:

metaphysics, that which is "beyond nature," the study of ultimates, including speculative cosmology. Music has a long history of association with this discipline.

theology, literally the study of God, generally interpreted more broadly today as the philosophy of religion

ontology, the philosophy of being (matter, existence)

epistemology, the philosophy of knowledge, how we can know reality

politics, ideally the philosophy of the public good

ethics, which deals with the good, moral philosophy

logic, which deals with the true

aesthetics, which deals with the beautiful (although, as will be shown, not all aesthetic questions turn on the issue of beauty). *Callistics* is the term that properly signifies a concern with beauty; *poetics* is the subbranch of aesthetics that deals with artistic creation. The word *aesthetics* comes from the Greek word meaning "to perceive, know, apprehend with the senses," so its proper application is to the philosophy of artistic perception.

The philosophy of art in general—and music, in particular—is generally acknowledged to be among the slipperiest branches of philosophy. There is thus all the more reason to develop terms carefully, apply them consistently, and give proper attention to technical problems of language.

Because art is the main province of aesthetics, many writers prefer to treat the philosophy of art and aesthetics as identical disciplines. I do not. Despite the obvious and large overlap between the two domains, I believe the distinction is worth preserving. The philosopher who addresses the arts considers many questions that lie outside the sphere of aesthetics; and similarly, many aesthetic questions are not at all concerned with works of art. Most of the world's musics are not art music (at least by some definitions), but aesthetic questions apply to all music. The following section will try to straighten out some of the confusion, although readers are invited (as always) to decide for themselves.

It is hard to formulate a definition of art that will satisfy everyone, but a start may be made by considering a carefully thought out definition by Sylvia Angus: "Art is the controlled structuring of a medium or a material to communicate as vividly and movingly as possible the artist's personal vision of experience."[2]

Even this short definition raises many debatable issues. One is whether art is a communication and, if so, how and what it communicates. Another is whether art can move, produce emotion. A third is whether art *is* carefully structured and, if so, by whom. A particularly treacherous question is just what does the word *experience* mean in this definition.

Most people will probably agree on most of the following points:

1 A work of art, although it may appear as a process, ultimately must be dealt with as an object, a thing.

2 It is separated, in some way, from the everyday world of things and experiences.

3 It is made—it doesn't just happen! It requires a human agent and a distinct act of creativity. The lovely tree that grows in one's back yard is not a work of art, although a Japanese bonsai tree is.

4 It requires a sensuous medium or material—sound, paint on canvas, words, the human body.

5 It is unique and cannot be replicated in precisely the same form (although it can, of course, often be reproduced in quantity).

6 It has excellence and the capacity to please.

7 It is created *for* human experience and must be perceived in some way through the sense(s) to which it is addressed.

8 It has unity and seems complete, unless damaged or abandoned in midstream by its maker.

9 It was created in response to a guiding idea, a vision of the whole. The process, though partly unconscious, is neither random nor haphazard.

With these statements as a background (whether one agrees with only some or all of them), consider the following definitions by Paul

Weiss: "A work of art is created by shaping resistant material into a new kind of space, time, or way of becoming. . . . The creation is guided by an idea, directed at an arresting prospect. In the course of that act deep-rooted emotions are expressed . . ."[3] and "A work of art is sensuous, concrete, embedded in a medium. There is no substitute for the experience of it. Every discussion of a work of art . . . will fail to capture its distinctive flavor and substantial being."[4]

Although such criteria do provide a basis for saying that a given object is or is not a work of art, there is seldom much point in saying so. It seems more profitable to determine whether something is good—or possibly even great—art, but here one enters the dangerous world of values which is the inescapable context for all discussions of art. Hippocrates said it best: "Life is short, art long, opportunity fleeting, experience treacherous, judgment difficult."[5]

It may be pedantic to split hairs about the precise domains of aesthetics and the philosophy of art, but there is little controversy over the meaning of the adjective *aesthetic:* an aesthetic object is an object that can be perceived with enjoyment, savor, even a thrill—it can be a tree, a leaf, a can of tomato soup, or a Beethoven symphony. The aesthetic experience is the act of perceiving, so vividly described in a famous passage by Berenson:

> In visual art the aesthetic moment is that flitting instant, so brief as to be almost timeless, when the spectator is at one with the work of art he is looking at, or with actuality of any kind that the spectator himself sees in terms of art, as form and color. He ceases to be his ordinary self, and the picture or building, statue, landscape, or aesthetic actuality is no longer outside himself. The two become one entity; time and space are abolished and the spectator is possessed by one awareness. When he recovers workaday consciousness it is as if he had been initiated into illuminating, exalting, formative mysteries. In short, the aesthetic moment is a moment of mystic vision.[6]

Reading the above paragraph, many readers may feel that they have been cheated because they have not experienced the heights of exaltation described, but surely everyone has recognized—perhaps to a lesser degree—the sensation of being caught up by a painting, musical composition, or play, and of being transformed by that experience. Two points may be added here: the experience does not always strike

6

us as pleasure (e.g., Picasso's shattering *Guernica*), and the experience is apt to be the most intense in an art other than the art one practices.

The single most vital precondition for the aesthetic experience is a special type of attitude, a state in which one is most receptive to intense artistic experience, characterized by critical attention. This attitude is likely to be present in but a small fraction of our encounters with art objects—other intentions, interests, or attitudes get in our way. We could scarcely call *aesthetic* the attitude of the department-store technician selecting fast and bouncy Muzak to speed shoppers through the store on Saturdays, the Casanova placing a record on the phonograph to accompany his intended seduction, the woman who hears the Bridal Chorus from *Lohengrin* and recalls her own wedding, the communicant who during Mass is only faintly aware of the muted organ music, or the basketball player who bounces nervously up and down, awaiting the end of the national anthem before a game.

Basic propositions

Music is a legitimate object of philosophy and thinking about music has a proper place among the inquiring disciplines. It is fashionable in some musical circles to advise against examining music too closely, on the dubious grounds that many who speak and write intelligently about music are unable to demonstrate their insights in performance. True, no amount of verbal discussion and analysis can substitute acceptably for the experience of music, nor should anyone expect it to do so. Although music and language have much in common, tones and words are not parallel modes of communication. In one way or another musical experience becomes mediated the moment it begins to be processed by the human mind. Whatever the reasons, our experience with music is often unexamined and based on unstated assumptions and values, despite the intensity of our musical convictions. Those who play and those who listen can benefit equally by asking—and trying to answer—the questions "What are we doing?" and "Why are we doing it?"

The activity of the philosopher and the critic is not the same. Criticism is applied philosophy: it is the job of the philosopher to think through those concepts that a critic has to have as a basis for his judgments. In theory there need be no discrepancy between their roles—a philosopher functions as a critic whenever he considers any individual work, and a critic cannot function at all without some general convictions on art (in addition to a formidable number of other qualifications). In each type of activity there is a risk: philosophers, if they remove themselves from the actual experience of art, risk becoming irrelevant and wholly theoretical; critics, if they fail to base their judgments upon informed analysis and defensible aesthetic principles, run the risk of incompetence.

The primary questions concerning music are those that involve being, knowing, and value. Discussions of musical aesthetics generally focus on values, but I would argue that questions of substance (ontology) and of how that substance can be known (epistemology) are the philosophical bedrock upon which all other questions ultimately depend.

The musical experience itself is a form of knowledge and a means of seeking truth. Music presents being to us in audible form, and our apperception of that being (insofar as it corresponds to the presentation) is a means of obtaining valid knowledge—of the world, of experience, of ourselves. The being of music is a being we can initiate, control, and terminate; with it we demonstrate that we are thinking and feeling creatures, perhaps the purest proof of our humanity.

The musical product (because it embodies important cultural values) constitutes a philosophical statement and can be read as such. This statement is frequently made with respect to some of the recent "minimalist" compositions of John Cage and others, but it is equally true of the music of Bach, Mozart, and Verdi.

Musical values are not absolutes. They are the products of culture and enjoy authority only within a given culture. As a social (or potentially social) art, music requires a community consensus to establish a value system, but within such a community of shared values it should be possible to obtain objective verification of the excellence of a given musical product or performance.

Most of music's unique features arise from the way in which music occupies and organizes its primary dimension—time. Time is a necessary condition for music, perhaps also a sufficient condition. I am not arguing the existence of music without sound, or without people, but both are imaginable. But I cannot imagine a music without extent of time. Some of the important problems of temporality in music will be explored in chapter three.

The sources of philosophy are not limited to the writings of the great philosophers. I contend that unconscious attitudes and beliefs, myths, sayings, and testimony from composers, performers, and listeners are equally valid as philosophical statements, although their analysis presents special problems. Both formal and informal philosophers have written and said many foolish things about music. We encounter the philosophy of music along a continuum from the most naïve speculation to the most abstruse technical argument, but the latter is no guarantee of either profundity or truth.

Philosophy should, as far as possible, be conducted using ordinary language and expressing ideas as simply as possible. Competent, disciplined, logical reasoning is surely an indispensable tool for philosophy, and no one will deny that one should use words exactly and economically. But technical jargon, semantically loaded terms, and extremely specialized meanings represent obstacles to the delivery of philosophy. And philosophy should be accessible to those who need it most. I willingly run the risk of being thought foolish, because many of the most vital questions about music can only be posed in naïve formulations.

The priority task for philosophy is (as Russell asserted) the framing of questions. Any attempt to arrive at ultimate answers will be futile unless one can be sure the right questions have been posed. The following chapter is just such an exercise in the framing of questions. My personal view is that one can, perhaps, agree which questions ought to be asked, but that each individual must find his or her own answers.

2 Meditations on a menuet

ANY MUSICAL WORK invites an almost inexhaustible assortment of relevant philosophical questions. As a case in point I propose to address the short menuet, K. 355, which Mozart wrote sometime between 1780 and 1790.[1] Any other piece would do, but this is unquestionably a work of excellence, easily accessible on recordings and in printed editions, and with some special qualifications. I pose a variety of questions—most with tentative answers and/or comments on the questions—which in fact are often more interesting than the answers. The reader may legitimately inquire why these questions were posed instead of others. The general order of the queries is controlled by a more-or-less systematic progression of ideas: from the objective to the subjective, and from the musical work to the listener to the external world.

Questions on the thing itself

1 *What is its substance?* In other words, what is the proper *being* of music—sound waves in the air, the printed score, the material (pressed vinyl, magnetic tape) on which it is recorded, electrochemical changes in the brain, the action of a piano as animated by the fingers? Can it be all of these at the same time? Is there an irreducible minimum to which we can point and say "In this Mozart's menuet exists?" We should, of course, take pains to separate what we take to be the piece itself from any particular performance or ex-

Wolfgang Amadeus Mozart, *Menuetto*, K. 355.

perience of it. How permanent is it? If all copies were lost, would it still exist once the last person had forgotten it?

2 *By what principles is it the way that it is?* Are there in fact any general principles or universals on which it depends? The problem of universals is an important one for philosophy and a source of many arguments. Personal universes vary in size, and what is valid for one may not be broad enough for another. There probably are a number of such universals valid for all music, and probably a smaller number valid not only for music but also for the other arts. A proposed set will appear in the following chapter.

3 *Does it change?* Or is it static? How fixed is the piece with regard to its material and/or form? How does it change in performance? Has it changed since it was originally conceived and first written down? This is yet another attempt to locate the irreducible minimum. The question is not trivial, because the work has certainly changed for all its performers and listeners over the years.

4 *What are its parts?* One can give a number of correct answers—we may be asking for a complete enumeration of all its components: 1,130 sounding tones, allowing for the turns and repeats (and surely this is one of the least important facts about the piece); or we may apply any one of an array of conventional analyses: it has forty-four measures, two main sections, a right- and a left-hand part, a melody and an accompaniment, nine phrases, a beginning, a middle, and an end.

5 *What are the dimensions within which it exists or which it manifests?* A sticky problem for music: we usually conceive of pitch and time as music's two major dimensions, and we speak of them in terms such as the *vertical* and the *horizontal*. A piece of music can indeed be represented on a line graph with pitch as the vertical and time as the horizontal axis. Timbre (tone color) is a third dimension, running off at a tangent that a mathematician would find possible to diagram. Are there others?

6 *When—and where—does the piece exist?* Only when it is played? Surely not. Can it exist within the mind alone? Probably. The location of music is another potentially interesting question, involving at its simplest a triangular relationship between source, transmission, and receiver(s).

7 *What are its qualities?* Presumably as opposed to its quantities (cf. question 4). It may be that all the properties of a musical

composition can be measured precisely, but that is not our usual way of experiencing a piece. Music has dynamic properties that change at complex and variable rates—of speed, of loudness. We habitually apply intersense modalities to music, describing it as *hot, smooth,* or *colorful.* Clearly this is a tricky problem, but musical descriptions are full of such language.

The question becomes still more problematic when we ascribe emotion or feeling to a composition. Is the quality of sadness actually resident in this work? Probably not, but see below—especially questions 23 through 26.

8   *Has it structure?* One of the most basic of all questions and one that may again be answered in various ways: by *structure* we may mean external shape, the sum of what we take to be its parts (cf. question 4), a complex interplay between deeply embedded structures and surface decoration, the still more complex interaction between tonal and thematic elements that musicians call *binary form,* or any number of other possibilities.

9   *Has it content?* What is it about? (About five minutes?) The serious question is whether music has subject matter—abstract tones and durations, themes, feelings, natural sounds, the depiction of actual events. Some prefer to deny the question, seeing no essential separation of form and content. Few other questions have been as hotly debated.

10   *Is it complete?* The question is not complicated in the abstract and is useful mainly as a basis for subsequent value judgments; and completeness has seldom been asserted as a negative criterion for music. But it is sometimes hard to say whether a musical work is complete or how it completes itself. Questions 43 and 44 are pertinent.

11   *Is it real?* Or a fiction, an illusion? There are interesting dimensions to this question: a certain amount of illusion is always present in art—strokes fuse into a line, tones are formed into what is perceived as a tune, paint on canvas is perceived as a representation. With such an intangible medium as music, we frequently wonder if our perceptions are accurate—frequently they are not! This is perhaps more of a problem for the auditor than for the thing itself, but it is legitimate to question the status of that which is received by our senses.

12   *Is it genuine?* A slightly different question that raises the

possibility of forgery. If Mozart did not write it, would it still have the same value for us and for society?

13 *Whose is it?* At first glance, it would seem that questions of property rights should be left for ASCAP and the lawyers, especially when money changes hands. But the problem cannot easily be dismissed. The peculiar relationship between a piece-as-written and a piece-as-performed suggests that both script and rendition represent creative investments. There is a parallel to the literary relationship between author and translator. And there is a wonderful story about a celebrated seventeenth-century Indian musician who used his skill in singing a certain *rāga* as collateral for a loan.

14 *What (or who) caused it?* Causation is always a major philosophical issue, so let us apply Aristotle's famous scheme of the four causes to our target piece:[2]

—material cause: sound waves, piano, pen and ink, vinyl, magnetic tape
—formal cause: menuet as a genre, "rounded binary" form, sonata, Classical style, major tonality
—efficient cause: Mozart, any pianist, engraver/publisher, a recording technician
—final cause: profit, pleasure, education, Mozart's need

While this scheme speaks for itself, one rather special musical problem may be mentioned—the status of musical instrument as "tool" and the degree to which the tool determines any of the properties of the musical work.

Questions of value

15 *Is it a work of art?* Surely it is, but a definitive answer would require evoking the several criteria we hold essential. We begin to move along a continuum from objective to subjective answers.

16 *Is it good?* And what properties must it (the piece, the performance) demonstrate in order to persuade me it is good? Each of us has a set of personal criteria, developed under the pressures of our education, our society, our experience—as well as our own mature preferences and our reasoning. But also: Is it a competent representa-

tive of its class, *menuetness*? Does it conform to the rules? Does it conform so relentlessly that it is not good?

17 *Will it do me good?* Inspire me, stimulate my emotions, channel my brain waves into regular patterns, heal me, comfort me, entertain me, further my education, make me value the good more highly?

18 Then we must ask: *Will it do me harm?* Appeal to my senses and thus blur my reason, cause me to lose my sense of proper proportion, make me soft, drug me, make me behave violently, keep me from doing my job, cause me to value it more highly than I should? The writings of formal philosophers from Plato on are full of suspicion of music's effects on the individual and society. I suggest that this strain of fear runs deep in many of us.

19 *Is it beautiful?* And what properties must it display in order to persuade me it is beautiful? Here we reach one of the most pervasive aesthetic issues. Among the criteria traditionally cited are these: harmony, proportion, clarity, intensity, unity, variety, completeness, consistency, mobility (for music), conflict and resolution. Perhaps these do boil down, as Beardsley suggests, to three main artistic canons—unity, complexity, intensity.[3] Readers who wish to pursue this question immediately may refer to the proposals of St. Thomas Aquinas in chapter six.

20 *Is it great?* Valuations of art works have frequently attempted to distinguish between positive and superlative, invoking such judgments as "monumental" and "sublime." Size, complexity, scale, and subject matter are among the criteria often mentioned. Or we may simply mean that the work is of surpassing excellence—in concept and/or execution.

21 *Is it in the public interest?* In other words, will it do us/them good? Since Plato's time philosophers have seldom neglected to remind us that music can have profound effects on society, as well as on the individual—usually couched in the old formula: "Old music benefits society by reinforcing the traditional values of orthodoxy, whereas new music subverts these values and undermines the stable society."

22 *What (if anything) does it mean?* And, more important, what do we mean when we say "What does it mean?" Meaning remains one of the basic issues in the philosophy of music, and a considerable portion of chapter eight is devoted to this problem, which

is far too complex to attempt even a brief exposition here. But the next four questions represent popular theories of musical meaning.

23   *Does it communicate anything?* And if so, what, from whom, and how? It is often taken for granted that music is a language, a "universal language" in some lexicons. Unquestionably some communication takes place when music is performed, but there has been little agreement on the nature of the message. The model for communication proposed by the linguist Roman Jakobson may prove useful:[4]

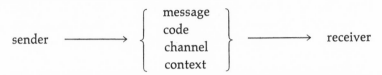

24   *Does it express anything?* If so, what and how? Only the verb has been changed. Those who hold that expression is a property of music might give the following answers for Mozart's menuet: sadness, purity, resignation, smiling through tears. Why?

25   *Does it imitate anything?* And again, what and how? Imitation (mimesis), one of the oldest theories of musical meaning, will be explored in chapter four. Those who take this position might give these answers: human emotion, sobs, bodily feelings of tension and release, smooth motion.

26   *Does it represent or stand for anything?* Is it, in other words, a symbol—of perfection, of revolution, a leitmotif (a boy playing Beethoven's *Für Elise* in Visconti's film version of *Death in Venice*)? Semiotic theories of musical meaning are in vogue today and deserve further elaboration—if music is a language, surely it is a symbolic language.

Questions relating more to the observer

27   *If it is real, how can I know so?* Can I trust my senses? How accurately do we perceive? See also question 11.

28   *Can I think music?* One can both think music and think *about* music. Every bit of mental activity in response to a musical stimulus involves some degree of mediation—thinking in words requires more, thinking in tones, less. The musician's ability to think in

music's own language strikes some laymen as mysterious, but their perception differs only in degree, not in kind. Active listening always features an act of mental reconstruction—what Hindemith called "coconstruction."[5]

29 *How are my own feelings and emotions involved with it?* Am I in a bad mood? Am I tired of practicing or analyzing this piece? Am I unusually receptive to it because of the way I feel today? Do I use it as a backdrop on which to project my feelings? Am I in the habit of associating freely in response to music—forming imagery, fashioning a mood, seeing a mental picture?

30 *Can my discussion of the work meet the demands of disciplined critical discourse?* This is a goal one seldom reaches, I suspect. One ought, ideally, to be a technically competent reasoner in discussing music (or any subject), and most of us would profit from a good course in logic. Philosophers are usually supremely competent at argument, but I do not get the impression that this expertise has made them skillful explainers of music.

31 *What prior assumptions have I made that direct and constrain my thinking?* Here it is best for me to give a personal answer, with reference to our menuet. My assumptions (and some of them are difficult to defend) include these: that menuets—by and large—are dainty, trivial, and tinkly; that D major is a "bright" key; that chromatic, slow music can be equated with sadness; that dissonance results in affect; and that musical structure consists of such things as step progressions, formal functions (statements, transitions, developments, restatements), tonal stability and instability. It is amazing with what a load of assumptions we approach almost any piece of music! Exploring them is usually a revelation. I recommend it.

32 *Must I possess any special or peculiar knowledge to assert that it is good, beautiful, or meaningful?* Is expertise required? Sometimes. Judgments that are based on a particular system of values require the judge to be competent; competence, in this case, includes both knowledge (of the values) and skill (in perception).

33 *What sort of perception, testimony, or evidence do I require in order to answer any of these questions?* Instinct, authority, tradition, audience response, assurance that a piece has passed "the test of time," record jackets, or critical reviews? If expertise is lacking, where do we place our trust?

34 *What kind of image of the composition can I construct within*

myself? This is a slightly more complex version of question 28, involving such issues as how music is stored in the memory, what sort of mental and physical activity accompanies the experience of music, expectation and affect.

35   *What is the relationship of the piece to the rest of society?* What are the special claims or interests of composers, performers, critics, teachers? Any single musical work affects thousands of lives in the most improbable ways. Because of a recent film, Ravel's *Bolero* has become virtually impossible to use as a teaching piece![6]

36   *Does it matter?* One should always reserve the right of the ultimate challenge to philosophy: "So what?"

Questions on the context of the piece

Is it important to know (and, if so, why)—

37   *when Mozart lived?* Some contend that external relations are (or should be) irrelevant to a musical work or any work of art. But this is surely too easy a position to take. Our knowledge of the piece's origin must color it for us in any number of ways, some of which are implied in the next questions.

38   *that the menuet is unusually chromatic for its period?* If all menuets are like this one, our questions may have been more properly addressed to the genre than to an individual work.

39   *that its structure was a common one in Mozart's day?* It helps, I believe, to realize that whatever is special about this menuet lies in its content, not its structure: a fine new wine in an old, much-used (but still serviceable) bottle!

40   *what Mozart's piano sounded like?* If we knew (and we have a good idea), it would give us a more precise notion of how to play the menuet—or at least to give a more historically accurate performance. If Mozart had lived to hear a modern piano, would he have preferred it? Most reconstructions of historical performance practice are technical improvements upon the original, but this is not to call them better. At the same time, our entire frame of reference for music—our scale of tonal, temporal, and dynamic proportions—has been permanently affected by all the music that has arisen since Mozart's era. There is no way for us to listen with the ears of Mozart's contemporaries, and it is useful that we realize it.

41 *that Mozart wrote bawdy letters to his cousin?* Seemingly the most trivial question of all. To me it is important that the same mind that gave birth to this music of the most exquisite refinement was also a mind that took delight in the most earthy language, puns, and coarse humor.

42 *that Mozart had become interested in Baroque counterpoint in the years 1781–82?* We know little about the origin of this menuet, but the internal evidence suggests that it could not have been written earlier. Our evaluation of any piece is colored by our knowledge: whether it is a student work, a product of mature mastery, innovative or conformist, or a product of old age. Is any critic of Mozart able to ignore the facts of the composer's incredibly rapid development and premature death?

43 *that this work might have been intended for inclusion in the piano sonata, K. 576?* It matters a great deal whether this menuet was intended to stand alone; some clearly were, others were not.

44 *or that it has no trio?* Stadler added a trio, presumably of his own composition, when he first published the menuet in 1801. Is the work complete without the usual trio and the conventional abbreviated reprise of the menuet? Surely no other composer's trio will do?

45 *that D major was a significant key for Mozart?* Certain keys appear to have distinct personalities in Mozart's music, as well as in the music of some other composers. This work seemingly contradicts the normal ethos of D major in Mozart—usually a brilliant, festive, diatonic key. And yet the expressive chromaticism may be all the more effective, given our knowledge of Mozartean D major!

46 *that Beethoven and later composers rejected the menuet in favor of the scherzo (as the lighter, dancelike movement in the sonata, quartet, and symphony)?* It seems unfair to drag Beethoven into these discussions, but the subsequent trends in musical style left the menuet as a self-contained representative of a closed historical era.

47 *that court dances of the seventeenth and eighteenth centuries often were transformed (as here) into highly stylized art music?* If we were to take this as salon music, we would not give it the attention it deserves; nor would we be likely to realize how far it stretches the mold.

48 *what Mozart intended?* The "intentional fallacy" is a standard item on any agenda of important aesthetic questions. I have knowingly fallen into this fallacy in questions 43 and 44, but for a

purpose. Certainly a composer's intentions are causal for his work and add to our knowledge. But evaluation becomes misdirected when it focuses upon such matters as the ease or effort with which a composer wrote a work, his religious fervor, or that his tears fell upon the manuscript as he wrote.

3   Music as art and artifact

How is music like—and unlike—the other arts? This chapter is an exercise in Aristotelian definition (*per genus et differentiam*): first, by examining various proposals for classifying the arts and some common features that they display, we reach a better understanding of music's proper genus (*ars*); then, by means of an analysis of certain of music's distinctive properties (time, tone, role, objectification), we assemble a partial list of the *differentia* that render music unique.

Classifying the arts

Music has not always been considered an art, nor have Western thinkers shown any tendency to agree on standard groupings of the arts until fairly recently. The Greek word for art was *techne*, and its meaning was closer to "craft, skill, technique." Aristotle, in a famous definition, stressed the cognitive aspect of art: "the ability to execute something with apt comprehension."[1] Art was as much a work of mind as a work of hand, a typically Greek antithesis that encouraged the distinction between the theoretical and the practical domains of any art.

As a consequence of this line of thinking, both poetry and music were excluded from the circle of the arts, because each was thought to be the product of inspiration and manic rapture. The poet and performer were viewed more as prophets, whereas the painter and architect were considered craftsmen and artisans. One was irrational, the other rational and worked according to a set of clear rules. As

Tatarkiewicz puts it, "Before the ancient idea of art became modern, two things were to happen: poetry and music were to be incorporated into art, while handicrafts and sciences were to be eliminated from it."[2]

Another important classificatory principle underlies the medieval grouping of the seven "liberal" arts: the trivium, or "three roads" (to eloquence)—grammar, rhetoric, logic; and the quadrivium, or "four roads" (to knowledge)—arithmetic, music, geometry, astronomy. This classification strikes us as strange today, mixing as it does science, art, and communication skills, but this and similar groupings of inquiring disciplines were regarded as encyclic, "forming a circle" that encompassed the knowledge that was considered essential for an educated person.

The Middle Ages thus promoted a somewhat schizoid view of music: *musica speculativa* was an intellectual discipline with a strong flavor of dilettantism, based on mathematics and allied with cosmological speculation, while *musica practica* occupied a much lower position. Such value judgments have often influenced classifications of the arts, e.g., into "major" and "minor" arts, although such divisions have varied over the centuries and in different cultures. Calligraphy, for example, has been consistently regarded among the major arts in traditional Chinese and Japanese aesthetics but as a minor art in Western civilization. The classification that we have devised for the "fine arts" is a recent product of Western thought, going back no farther than the mid-eighteenth century.[3] These are generally agreed to be poetry (and certain other literary genres), music, theater, dance, painting, sculpture, and architecture.

Virtually all the proposals for grouping the arts according to certain criteria have historical precedent. Here are several that seem useful:

—by medium, i.e., arts that use words, tones, stones, paint on canvas, or human bodies
—by the sense to which an art is primarily addressed, i.e., art one can look at, listen to, feel, smell, or taste
—by dimension, i.e., arts that use space, time, or any other dimension for their main sphere of operation
—by purpose, i.e., arts that are necessary, arts that are useful, and arts that entertain
—by residue. Proposed by Quintilian, this classification sepa-

rates the arts into (1) theoretical arts that leave no traces behind them and are characterized by the study of things, (2) practical arts that consist of an action of the artist without leaving a product, and (3) productive arts that leave behind an object.[4]
—by degree of determinacy. Painting and poetry can evoke determinate associations, music and architecture usually do not.

By far the most useful classification is by way of medium, although other criteria may be helpful for further subdivision. Max Dessoir's chart of the various artistic domains is a thoughtful and attractive formulation:[5]

spatial arts
motionless arts
arts dealing with
  images
	temporal arts
	arts of motion
	arts dealing with
	  gestures and sounds	

Sculpture Painting	Poetry Dance	reproductive arts figurative arts arts with determinate associations
Architecture	Music	free arts abstract arts arts with indeterminate associations

Paul Weiss, in *Nine Basic Arts*, has proposed one of the most stimulating schemes for classifying the arts, based upon the way in which each art is situated within its primary dimension—space, time, or "becoming."[6] One is asked to accept Weiss's controversial distinction between *musicry* (the composition of music) and *music* (the performance of music):

	arts of space	arts of time	arts of becoming
arts that enclose a created dimension	Architecture	Musicry	Music
arts that occupy a created dimension	Sculpture	Story	Theater
arts that are the dimension they create	Painting	Poetry	Dance

Illustration out of context does not do justice to Weiss's careful classification, nor can his full meaning be made clear without the aid of his very special definitions. Here, for example, are the two that most concern us:

"Musicry is the art of creating an emotionally sustained, silent, common time"; and "Music is the art of creating a structured audible becoming. . . . Music occupies a volume; it is spatial as well as temporal. But it is more as well. It is expansive, insistent, a sheer becoming in the shape of sound, produced by man. . . ."[7]

There is much to argue with in such a proposal, particularly the elusive concept of "becoming," but the value of Weiss's approach outlasts any individual objections. Some combination of medium and dimension appears to be the most natural and useful basis for artistic classification.

Composite or hybrid arts deserve some attention: opera is perhaps the most obvious example for the musician. From its beginnings around 1600, opera has been frequently proposed as the ideal fusion of the arts, and Richard Wagner's theory of the *Gesamtkunstwerk* (the "total" work of art), as set forth in *Oper und Drama*, celebrated the music drama as the embodiment of all the arts—music, acting, poetry, scenic design, dance, costume.[8] But in our discussion of such complex composites, we overlook the simple song and its fusion of text and music; the problems arising from the combination of words and music form a recurrent strand in the history of musical aesthetics.[9] Cinematography is a fairly recent synthesis of several arts and has received valuable discussion in the last few years. It is not hard to imagine other potentially successful hybrids.

There has been fairly general agreement on the present set of fine arts, but it seems unlikely that we have witnessed all possibilities. Can other, new arts arise? If, as has been suggested (and often deplored), Western society is evolving toward a state in which collective decisions may eventually replace most of those hitherto made by individuals, will there be a set of "arts of society?"[10] I believe there now exist prototypes of such societal arts, including the following:

instead of architecture, *city*—a harmonious, collectively designed total environment, e.g., Brasilia, Canberra, or L'Enfant's plan for Washington

instead of sculpture, *sculpture park*—Gustav Vigeland's Frogner

Park in Oslo, although executed by many hands, was the design of one mind; the sculpture park high above Lake Hakone in Japan is a better example.

instead of painting, *fence*—seemingly trivial in present form but suggestive of future possibilities

instead of poetry, *laws*—a throwback to an ancient Greek conception; I admit I do not see much excellence in what is now available!

instead of theater, *happening*—already well established as an art form

instead of dance, *rites*—many dance companies now feature collective improvisations; some type of urban dance or large-scale contest may be a possible next step. If some of these proposals appear to have their roots in popular culture, it is instructive to recall that many of the present arts began that way.

instead of music (and admittedly a problem), perhaps *festival*—many such "pieces" have already been planned and performed, although their general acceptance will require a much wider agreement on new musical values. This model will probably emphasize flexible guidelines, amateur participation, improvisation, and new attitudes toward time, space, and instruments. Formal collective composition has, as far as I know, been practiced only in the People's Republic of China, e.g., the *Yellow River Concerto*, which was reportedly written by a committee.

These proposals visualize an evolution from present models, but there is no reason to think that entirely new forms of art may not arise. It seems also possible that certain present genres of art may merge.

Common features of the arts

A poem is like a picture: one strikes your fancy more, the nearer you stand; another, the farther away. This courts the shade, that will wish to be seen in the light, and dreads not the critical insight of the judge. This pleased but once; that, though ten times called for, will always please. [Horace][11]

Horace's famous dictum "Ut pictura poesis" has long served as a slogan in comparative discussions of the arts. Critical interpretation of this passage has no doubt stretched its meaning far beyond what Horace had in mind, but the notion that the several arts display common properties and are amenable to analysis by means of a common lexicon has firmly taken root. In recognition that our use of language obviously *mediates* our experience of art, it is wise to remain aware that the problem is partly a verbal one; but, had we no language, would we not still sense similarities between (say) music and the other arts?

We are cautiously approaching the question of universals. It is arguable whether universals exist, and how widely valid a principle must be before we confer on it the authority of a universal. It all depends on the size of one's universe. To the scholar preoccupied with the music of Mozart, that composer's evolving style can constitute a universe. Some musicians will be content with a set of universals valid for the tradition of European art music, while others prefer not to recognize any principle as universal unless it applies equally to Western and non-Western music. The philosopher of art would prefer that such universals apply to the various arts. And given the possibility of space exploration and encounter with other civilizations, even this may not be broad enough. But—whatever one's scale of reference—if there *are* such universals, it is imperative that we identify them!

One must make a start somewhere. Consider the following set and the brief comments appended. We may observe at the start that most of these involve structural features and modes of organization—not material.

> *tonality:* the ability to create focus—Beethoven's D minor, color as a dominant hue in a painting, the apparent convergence of lines of parallel columns, a main plot theme or characteristic emotion (Othello's jealousy, Lady Macbeth's ambition, the "starcrossed" love of Romeo and Juliet)
>
> *tendency:* Whether they are natural tendencies—of the body, the look and feel of marble—or tendencies created by context (as in language and music), tendencies cause us to predict, feel expectation, and react when that expectation is gratified or frustrated.
>
> *pattern:* a decorative impulse that seems to be present to some degree in all the arts, whether visual, musical, verbal patterns or patterns of ideas

inception: All art works have beginnings, either in time or space or both, emphasized or disguised. We may not be present at its creation, so an art work may begin for us as we approach it. As I remarked earlier, art works are usually separated from the world of everyday experience—by frames, by silence, by performance in a special place in special costumes, by landscape, and by our attention.

closure: Art works also have ends and are usually felt to be complete, although our expectations of proper closure are tied to cultural notions—especially in the temporal arts. In the Western tradition, art works tend to be teleological, goal-directed, and end with a strong sense of finality. Quite the reverse is true for the arts of Asia.

interplay: Rarely is a work of art so simply organized that all of the important activity occurs in one area or along a single plane; we cannot fully experience a painting by looking only at its left edge, or a play by following the action and lines of a single character—or music simply by following the tune. The spectators must learn to shift their attention because the works themselves shift the locus of their activity. This is a good general definition of what is often called *counterpoint.*

silence: or its spatial equivalent, which we mistakenly call "emptiness." There are no empty spaces in the arts, nor are there true silences in music—any more than the air that we breathe is a vacuum. There are, however, areas of low—or no—activity and negative spaces. It is the "somethingness" that we usually attend to in music, not the "nothingness," and yet the uses of silence are numerous: silence may be mere punctuation or a minute interval between two articulated tones. It may be short or long, measured or unmeasured, interruptive or noninterruptive, tensed or relaxed. But in one way or another the silence becomes a part of the music.[12]

accent: the single touch, an individual highlight carefully placed— a color, a gesture, a stressed word, a tone "marked for our attention" in some special way.[13] Tonal (pitch), stress (loudness, sharpness of attack), and agogic (duration) accents are among those prominent in music.

beat: Regular pulsation is a common feature in many works of art, whether interpreted as an intermittent or continuous line, including the phenomena of rhyme and patterns of stress in the verbal arts. The most general term for this effect is *rhythm.*[14]

repetition: All the arts contain repetitions, although the tolerance (and perhaps the psychological necessity) for repetition is obviously much greater in music and dance than in poetry and other literary genres.

variation: The urge to decorate, to deviate, to introduce expressive change seems to be as basic to art as the urge to repeat.

hierarchy: Most works of art contain some type of explicit or implicit hierarchy—a many-layered structure that serves as organizing framework for the entire work. Even the simplest paintings, poems, compositions, sculptures, and dances appear hierarchical on closer inspection; they embrace a diversity of events from the clicks or dots of surface activity to the large-scale patterns that organize the whole work. Language itself can be viewed as a hierarchy. It seems probable that we implant this feature (like the preceding features) in our arts because we feel it as a pervasive characteristic of our experience.

Several other common terms can be applied successfully to a number of the arts: *texture, surface,* or *grain* is a useful concept for the plastic and tactile arts but requires careful definition when applied to music or literature. Very likely all the arts make use of *themes* embedded in some kind of *background,* and the systematic processing of these themes is usually called *structure* or *form.* If the work is not a single miniature unit, *sections* can often be delineated, with or without *transitions* between them. It is also useful to speak of *scale* in describing an art work so long as the term is not confused with its specific musical meaning—as the consecutive ordering of the basic pitch structure; but even this restricted use of the word is not inconsistent with the larger meaning if one compares a musical scale to the scale on a ruler or yardstick, or even the scale of a map: it is the basic set of proportions along which the art object is laid out.

Most art works have high points, *climaxes,* interspersed with areas of lesser tension or activity. *Development* is frequently used to describe the working out of the artistic themes or ideas, although here too some careful definition may be necessary. And most art works exhibit the alternation of *stability* and *instability*, produced by varying means. Other terms, though useful, carry widely differing meanings in different arts, e.g., *line*.

The term *line* signifies some kind of extension—straight or curved, long or short, continuous or intermittent, simple or complex, enclosing or separating, carrying a sense of force and motion, indicating a goal by pointing to it, possessing momentum or (at times) actual velocity. The connection of meaning between a visual and an audible line is quite apparent. A line of text is, of course, something altogether different, although it may serve this same linear function when set to music.

Harmony is one of the most important and controversial terms in the arts, extremely difficult to define in a way that is not highly abstract. The ancient concept of harmony, which we will explore in the next chapter, was as a balance or equilibrium between opposing tensions, a perfect though precarious relationship of part-to-part and part-to-whole. To the Greeks harmony required proportionate relationships that could be expressed in whole numbers, ideally in simple, superparticular ratios. Musical harmony could not be calculated on any other than a mathematical basis, hence the inclusion of music among the mathematical disciplines. The universe itself was seen as the perfect model for harmony and visualized as a set of concentric crystal spheres in harmonic proportion, each sounding its characteristic note.

Differentia

Our main concern is obviously for music. Although we will inevitably need to consider musical problems that have implications for the other arts, it is the special properties of music that present the greatest obstacles to our understanding. Only a few of these can be singled out for discussion.

Time: Time is the less explored of music's two primary dimensions; theorists of music have traditionally concerned themselves more with questions of pitch organization. The basic facts of beats, rhythmic patterns, meters, and meter signatures do not shed much light on the way in which music unfolds and is perceived in time. The very appearance of our rhythmic notation belies the dynamic mobility heard in music, and analysts have fallen into the habit of using spatial terms for temporal concepts.[15] We seem to find it easier to think and write about music as if it were a *state* rather than a *process*.

The concept of time has always been an elusive one for philosophers and scientists. It is generally realized that Newton's definition of "absolute, true, and mathematical time"[16] does not square with what has been learned in this century, and the many discrepancies between objective and subjective time measurements have been frequently pointed out. St. Augustine's famous lament expresses the dilemma: "What then is time? If no one asks me, I know; but when I am asked to explain it, I know not!"[17]

We know that time's two series (series A: before/after; series B: past/present/future) play a crucial role in the creation, perception, and memory of music. There is general agreement that the time of music is not the same as everyday clock time. It is a special, created time that shares many of the properties of clock time and a time that is socially accepted by performers and listeners. Here are a number of problems in time theory that are important for the concept of temporality in music:

1   *Is time atomistic or continuous?* Do "real" time and musical time consist of continuous durations or a series of intermittent events? If music is a succession of discrete stimuli, what is it that leads us to perceive it as *motion?* There may be many types of motions and rates of succession in the simplest piece of music—how is it that we mentally assemble these into a single time line? Most of us are convinced that we hear motion or "flow" in music; is it similar to the sequence of film frames in a movie? Is musical motion partly an illusion?

2   *How have metaphors for musical time captured some of its perceived properties?* Here are several:
   —a bamboo stem (Chinese), with its joints and nodes symbolizing the beats that articulate the continuity of music
   —a thread running through a necklace of pearls (Indian), another image of continuity by means of reticulation

—a wave (Zuckerkandl),[18] representing the crests and troughs of energy formed by beat patterns of regularly alternating strength and weakness

—a bowling alley (Zuckerkandl),[19] with time as the empty tunnel through which musical events are hurled

—an hour glass (Aristotle),[20] representing the present as the thin moment of passage between immense past and equally immense future

—a melody with the notes dissolved into one another (Bergson),[21] expressing the perceived continuity of music as the model for our perception of real time, *durée*

3 *Why is it that we perceive time passing at different rates?* Psychologists have established that eventful time seems to pass quickly, uneventful time, more slowly. What is the relationship in music between objective and subjective time? Do we find qualitative time represented in music—time with special moments?

4 *What is the "now" in music?* If we can perceive only a thin edge of the music as it passes through our field of hearing, why is it that our perception appears to stretch out until it includes whole phrases and themes?

5 *What is the special role that memory plays in apprehending music?* Musical perception involves one in a complicated process of attending to the present moment, relating this moment to both immediate and remote past (*retrodiction*, an exotic but useful term), and thus predicting its future (expectation).

6 *Does the time of music have any relationship to cultural notions of time?* Various cultures have thought of time as cyclical, modular, an irreversible and open-ended process, a straight line leading to a definite goal, or simply an illusion. The view of time embedded in Western music is that of the Judaeo-Christian traditional cosmology: time that begins with a decisive act of creation and moves in a straight line toward a final, apocalyptic event.[22]

7 *Can time be said to begin or to end?* Augustine rejected the question, "What existed before time began?," but it is a valid question for music. What is involved in beginning or ending a musical composition? How are feelings of motion, direction, energy, weight, and tonal tendencies initiated and successfully resolved?[23]

8 *Is there such a thing as timelessness, infinity, eternity?* Some recent compositions appear to be modeled after such a concept, sug-

gesting—by means of repetitive processes and other strategies—a state more than a process, *being* rather than *becoming*.[24]

9 *Does a musical work have but one time?* Or is there a possibility for multiple times in music and experience? Recent string quartets by Elliott Carter and Witold Lutosławski have explored this possibility with considerable success.[25]

10 *Can time bend?* What is there about musical time that not only allows it to be measured in terms of the rate of pulsations and the rate of eventfulness, but which also allows us to follow and enjoy changes in these rates of speed with perfect security?

11 *How multidimensional is the musical mind?* By what means is a composer able to fix a long time duration in his mind as if it were a single instant and freely mingle musical ideas in his subconscious? It is a feat of wizardry in which before, together, and after have no meaning until finally set down in a sequence that seems to us inevitable.

12 *Does the time of music have anything in common with the time of sport—"agonic" or contestual time?* Because the time of music is controlled by a set of rules and unfolds in a setting of social interaction, the comparison is appropriate. How do the time (and space) of music—as in a performance of a Beethoven symphony—correspond to the time and space of such sports as baseball, football, soccer, or basketball?

Tone: We mean here the nature of musical tone—not the organizing properties of tones in the realm of pitch. Tone is obviously a manifestation of musical space, but in a very special sense. Probably the two most basic tonal facts are our perception of them as "high" or "low" and the peculiar qualities that enable us to identify their source, as from a piano or koto. The technical, acoustic features of tone are seldom in the forefront of our consciousness, i.e., that tone is the form and frequency of vibration, regular vibration as opposed to the nonperiodic vibration that we call *noise;* that the complex structure of that vibration produces what we call *timbre;* that tones are seldom as simple as the form in which we visualize them; that tones not only have their spatial origin in the world around us but are slung along that unique spatial continuum that we call *pitch;* and that their final form is the result of a complex relationship between the vibrating material (string, struck object, enclosed air), actuating implement, immediate environment, transmitting medium (air, wire, water), and listener environment. The performer has a concept in his mind of what he considers to be "good" tone and tries to achieve it consistently. For the listener "good" tone is probably what we have been taught to regard as good.

The philosopher may, as most listeners do, take many of these acoustic facts for granted and find a set of more "functional" properties of tones more interesting. Paul Weiss has proposed the following set of special tonal properties, to which I have added some brief remarks.[26]

Tones are:

detachable, in that the sounds of a musical work are separate from the actual sounds of the world around us, just as the red color in a painting is detachable from our everyday experience of the color red. Sounds are also detachable from any specific location: they leave their source, they travel to the listener.

voluminous, in that tones appear to occupy both durations and spaces

insistent, in that we are compelled to shut them out if we choose not to attend to them. And when we do attend, the pattern of sounds establishes its own logic which in turn determines our pattern of expectation.

directional, in that they appear to possess ongoing movement and tendency. Even when a tone remains constant, it ultimately invites expectation that it will soon change.

self-identical, in that despite differences of loudness, timbre, duration, register, and context, a tone's basic identity can remain unchanged

interpenetrative, in that any number of tones can occupy the same duration and seem to occupy the same space. No two colors can occupy the same space and remain distinct—two tones can!

interrelatable, in that a musical work makes no sense if we consider it as a mere series of separate stimuli

Role: Music is a social art—or at least potentially social. While some philosophers argue that a musical work could, ideally, be brought to perfection in the mind, this ideal is far removed from the normal conditions under which one writes, plays, or listens to music. All the performing arts pose unique problems of *role*. To help in pointing out some of these, I reproduce a slightly amplified version of a famous chart from Vivas and Krieger's *The Problems of Aesthetics:*[27]

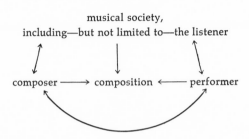

musical society,
including—but not limited to—the listener

composer ———→ composition ←——— performer

The arrows represent the particular interests or attitudes of each member of the social matrix; most obviously this skeletal diagram cannot begin to suggest the variety of peculiar concerns within musical society. To begin with, we cannot assume that society-at-large consists of a body of benevolent consumers or "culture-vultures"! Some relationships—as between performer and composer—may run the gamut from intense admiration to active hostility. Other roles in this matrix could include the philosopher, critic, teacher, student, impresario, and many others concerned with the functional application of music—priest, therapist, drill sergeant, disc jockey, and dentist. The profusion of roles presents numerous opportunities for philosophical problems and value conflicts.

The composer's attitude toward his own product will ordinarily be quite different from that of the performer or listener. The latter will regard the work as a finished product and will generally have little interest in how it came to be written. The composer, on the other hand, sees his work as the outcome and residue of a long, partly unconscious process, and the piece may lose some of its interest for him once it is completed to his satisfaction.

Many of the interesting questions involve the role of the performer and the *being* of the musical work as it passes from composer to score to performer to audience. Is the performer an interpreter or merely a faithful executor of the composer's intentions? Is he in any sense a composer too? How does improvisation—as in jazz and some ethnic musics—affect the relative standing of composer and performer? When one plays a piece, is it the same piece the composer wrote? If repeated, is it the same or different?

Musical notation is far from an exact script, and the composer's full intentions can never be transmitted to a performer by means of marks on paper. Some composers rely on an elusive concept we call *tradition,* while others—such as Gustav Mahler—struggle to specify their script by means of numerous verbal comments. The performer must rely on his training, his instincts, along with the notation, and occasionally a meeting with the composer, or even listening to another performer's recording! Composers may view their performers along a continuum: from cocomposer to necessary evil.

Much music involves ensemble performance, often under the creative vision and active direction of a conductor. Under these circumstances can we say that an orchestral musician or dancer in the corps de ballet is an artist or an artisan? Special problems such as these are inevitable when we consider how much doing an action differs from making a product, or—in the case of a composer—making a set of directions for an action.

Another set of questions might probe the aesthetic attitudes and values of the several constituencies of musical society. Should the performer's personality, charisma, mystique get in the way of the music? Is it in fact a part of the music? Should one value equally the performance and the work itself? Should or can they be separated? As Yeats wrote, "How can we know the dancer from the dance?"

It is instructive to explore various musical societies with the aid of the above model. Three come readily to mind: New York, the undisputed capital of musical activity in this hemisphere; the booming country music establishment in Nashville, Tennessee; and Hawaii's unique blend of Waikiki nightlife, an indigenous Polynesian musical culture, and midstream America.

Objectification: Music is clearly the least tangible, the most perishable of the arts. In what is called the *primitive consciousness* music is very close to man, is scarcely differentiated from speech and actions (work or dance), and can be rung from everyday objects—a bone, dish, or stick. But as civilizations have developed we have more and more sought to capture music in mental, verbal, or visual form in our insecure attempts to insure its repeatability and guard against its loss. Objectifying strategies have included thought, mnemonic aids, verbal descriptions, teaching techniques, notations, theories of music, and technology. Here are a few of the means by which music has been transformed—and sometimes reduced—into object:

> *fixed notes, pitches, time durations, and ratios*—To think of a musical tone as a single thing is the first step toward uniformity and printing-press repeatability. One musical tone is rarely ever the same as another, but screening out some of their complexity enhances our ability to remember them. Defining musical units, assigning them names, measuring them, and counting them are the initial mental acts that lead to musical knowledge.

> *bodily motions and gestures*—These serve several functions: as mnemonic aids, as accompaniment to ritual performance, as a practical means of keeping the performers together, as outward expressions of inner (rhythmic) feelings.

> *solmization syllables*—a reduction of tones to the basic set of functional scalar members: ut re mi fa sol la, or the Indian equivalent—sa ri ga ma pa dha ni[28]

> *theoretical systems*—As cultures become literate and music becomes art, theories of music arise with an array of topics, categories, genera, scales, and the like.

> *notations*—The history of musical scripts is at once a testament to human inventiveness and a demonstration of music's essential fragility. Each advance in our ability to notate music has had enormous consequences for the tradition we seek to represent; notation has been a destabilizing influence upon musical style.

> *instruments*—Instruments are designed to play the music we imagine; but our imagination can then become limited to what can be played on our instruments! It is a circular process. Because we usually know music through the mediation of instruments, we tend to think music in terms of the feel and sounds of the instruments we use and hear. This experience can impose limitations: many pianists fail to perceive the subtle intonations of a string quartet or the range of colors in the human voice.

> *recordings*—the most extraordinary step of all: music can now

be preserved in full detail on discs and tape. The potential consequences for musical aesthetics have only begun to be explored.

machines—Complex devices such as the computer and synthesizer, working at high speeds and processing huge quantities of data, can now be used not only to store music but to analyze and "compose" it.

Music could hardly have reached its present level of sophistication without such means. But it is fair to inquire how music has been influenced by the different strategies by which we have captured it. Do instruments—our tools—leave determining traces upon the musical substance and affect the ways in which a composer works with it? Has the complexity of the individual musical tone been reduced to a uniform character of type or a computer bit? And how have musical values been affected by such technical accomplishments? We will return to such questions in the final chapter.

4 Dionysus and Apollo

For all good poets, epic as well as lyric, compose their beautiful poems not by art, but because they are inspired and possessed . . . falling under the power of music and metre they are inspired and possessed. . . . For the poet is a light and winged and holy thing, and there is no invention in him until he has been inspired and is out of his senses, and reason is no longer in him. [Plato][1]

Music too, in so far as it uses audible sound, was bestowed for the sake of harmony. And harmony, which has motions akin to the revolutions of the soul within us, was given by the Muses to him who makes intelligent use of the Muses, not as an aid to irrational pleasure (as is now supposed), but as an auxiliary to the inner revolution of the soul, when it has lost its harmony, to assist in restoring it to order and concord with itself. [Plato][2]

FRENZY AND CALM, ecstasy and order, rhapsody and harmony—this chapter will explore the extraordinary ferment that we find in the musical thought of ancient Greece as a result of these opposing tendencies. It was the German philosopher Friedrich Nietzsche who chose the terms *Apollonian* and *Dionysiac* to represent what he saw as the two central impulses in Greek culture.[3] Apollo, presiding calmly over the Muses on Mt. Parnassus, symbolizes everything in Greek life and art that is orderly, moderate, proportionate, rational, comprehensible, and clear in formal structure; Dionysus, the wine god and special patron of orgies and the theater, symbolizes everything that is manic, ecstatic, disorganized, irrational, instinctive, emotional—everything that tends to submerge the individual personality in a greater whole.

The lack of source materials prevents us from pursuing the philosophy of music in earlier civilizations, so we must make a thorough exploration of the Greek corpus of musical speculation in order to build a proper base for later developments. Greek musical thought addressed a variety of important themes: the place of music in education (*paideia*), music as therapy, the effects of music upon the soul and the body (the doctrine of ethos), the sources of artistic creativity, how to judge music properly, the value of music in promoting good citizenship and furthering the best interests of the state, and the place of music among the arts. The major aesthetic issues included the concept of harmony, beauty, and the theory of art as imitation (mimesis). Plato and Aristotle, as well as other philosophers, had much to say about music. Technical theories of music were proposed by a long line of authors, ranging from the legendary Pythagoras to later writers such as Aristoxenus, Cleonides, Ptolemy, and Aristides Quintilianus. The science of music was set forth in three main divisions: harmonics (pitch), rhythmics, and metrics.

The word *mousike* is usually explained as a derivative from the collective term for the Muses, the nine daughters of Zeus and Mnemosyne (memory), who were regarded as givers of inspiration and patrons of the various arts. Calliope ("beautiful voice") is the Muse of epic poetry and is shown with tablet and stylus; Clio ("celebrate") is the Muse of history and is portrayed with a chest of books; Erato ("lovely") is the Muse of elegiac poetry and her instrument is a lyre; Euterpe ("delight"), the Muse of lyric poetry and song, has a flute; Melpomene ("choir") is the Muse of tragedy and she is shown with a tragic mask; Polyhymnia ("many songs"), the Muse of sacred poetry, has no special symbol; Terpsichore ("delight of dancing") is the Muse of choral song and the dance, and, like Erato, has a lyre; Thalia ("festivity"), the Muse of comedy, wears a comic mask; and Urania ("heavenly"), the Muse of astronomy, is shown with a staff and globe.

It is evident that music, if considered as "the art of the Muses," claimed a wider territory than it does in modern civilization. It united verse, dancing, acting, ritual and liturgy, cosmic speculation, and other branches of learning with the art of sound. Its range of expression included both the Apollonian recitation of refined lyric poetry, accompanied by the lyre, and the Dionysiac emotional intensity of the great choruses in the dramas of Aeschylus, Sophocles, and Euripides. Music was both valued and distrusted—valued for its ability to arouse, to please, to regulate the soul, and to produce good qualities in its hearers; but, at the same time, it was distrusted for its ability to overstimulate, to drug, to distract, and to lead to excessive behavior. Something of the same ambivalent attitude has persisted throughout Western civilization and is still evident today.

A few of the more important values of Greek musical society

may be mentioned briefly: the amateur musician was held in higher esteem than the professional, and the study of music was considered a part of general education. This opposition between the "high-class" amateur and "low-class" professional has survived as a subliminal attitude in later European culture, and to this day professional musicians are apt to be regarded with the faint suspicion that they are not quite respectable. The cult of the gentleman amateur was best expressed by G. K. Chesterton's famous remark, "If a thing is worth doing, it's worth doing badly!" Aristotle voiced this same attitude in the *Politics*:

> The right measure will be attained if students of music stop short of the arts which are practiced in professional contests, and do not seek to acquire those fantastic marvels of execution which are now the fashion in such contests, . . . for in this the performer practices the art, not for the sake of his own improvement, but in order to give pleasure, and that of a vulgar sort, to his hearers. For this reason the execution of such music is not the part of a freeman but of a paid performer, and the result is that the performers are vulgarized, . . .[4]

Music was generally regarded as subservient to the text, and purely instrumental music occupied a much lower social stratum than vocal music. The rhythmic patterns of poetry became the models for the rhythmic patterns of music. Plato, in the *Laws*, lashed out at contemporary poets:

> The Muses, we may be assured, would never commit the grave mistake of setting masculine language to an effeminate scale, or tune, or wedding melody, or postures worthy of free men with rhythms only fit for slaves and bondsmen, . . . but our poets go still further. They divorce rhythm and figure from melody, by giving metrical form to bare discourse, and melody and rhythm from words, by their employment of cithara and flute without vocal accompaniment, . . .[5]

Certain other old values crop up again and again in literature dealing with music: simple is better than complex, natural is better than artificial, moderation in all things, orthodoxy in music is to be sought, while innovation and novelty are to be avoided. Certainly the Greeks were not the first to express such ideas, nor were they the last. In the pseudo-Aristotelian *Problems* (5 and 40) the plaintive question is asked: "Why is it that men prefer songs they already know to songs they do not know?" But the Greek concept of creativity went further than this nostalgia.

Creativity did not mean "originality." From what we are able to determine from Greek sources, it seems clear that composition was a matter of tasteful, minor variations on and combinations of a repertoire of standard melodic/rhythmic patterns, the *nomoi* (laws). Musical orthodoxy carried a clear mandate of lawfulness. To be a good composer one had to know the theoretical system, be able to select proper material and fit it skillfully to a text, have emotional empathy for the social context of the music, and have enough technique so that all these ingredients were matched appropriately to one another. One can readily see why the following were considered the main sources for artistic creation: abstract proportion, knowledge, skill at imitation, and the supernatural.

Abstract proportion (expressed in simple number ratios) was recognized as the supreme formal principle, the theoretical scale along which an art work was to be laid out. Knowledge of these proportions, of the source, of the material, of the audience, and of the goal was likewise required of an artist. Imitation (mimesis) was the basic technique and the criterion by which a work would be judged. And certainly the most rational of the Greeks would not deny the presence of some external agency—enthusiasm, inspiration, or Plato's poetic madness—at the heart of the creative process.

The architect and sculptor could, perhaps, escape these polar tensions between Apollo and Dionysus by skillfully representing geometric shapes and proportions and the beauties of the idealized human body in stone and marble. They might remain unpossessed and deny the role of inspiration in their craft. But the musician remained in the middle, caught in the tensions between his two patrons. Perhaps the concept of harmony symbolized to him the state of equilibrium that had to be achieved, the balance that had to be found between the rational and the irrational, form and emotion.

Harmony

The Pythagoreans, whom Plato follows in many respects, call music the harmonization of opposites, the unification of disparate things, and the con-

ciliation of warring elements. . . . Music, as they say, is the basis of agreement among things in nature and of the best government in the universe.
As a rule it assumes the guise of harmony in the universe, of lawful government in a state, and of a sensible way of life in the home. It brings together and unites. [Theon of Smyrna][6]

The doctrine of harmony is a complex cluster of ideas, and we
can present only the general outlines here. *Harmonics* was the name
the Greeks gave to the science of proportioned sounds, and *harmoniai*
[pl.] was the collective term used for their musical scales. The etymol-
ogy of the word reveals a wide assortment of meanings—to fit together, adapt, reconcile, agree, administer, tune an instrument, and
even to kiss. The most general meaning is the unification of dissimilar
components into an ordered whole. Theon's testimony has hit the
mark.

This starts to sound more like science than art, and the Greek
doctrine of harmony is inescapably connected with numbers, ratios,
proportions, and acoustics. In mathematics a harmonic series is a series in which the reciprocals of the terms form an arithmetic series,
i.e., 1, 1/2, 1/3, 1/4, 1/5, 1/6 is the harmonic version of the arithmetic series 1, 2, 3, 4, 5, 6. Although an arithmetic series proceeds by
equal increments, a harmonic series involves a series of progressively
decreasing steps. One of the great coincidences of music history is
that these ratios, when applied to taut strings, produce the basic ratios of consonant intervals. Had other musical relationships been discovered and preferred, the analogy between music and numbers could
not have been so obviously drawn; or, to put it differently, if these
simple number ratios had not been applied to music, the entire course
of our music might have been drastically different.

Harmony was also a symbol of universal order, uniting all levels
of the cosmos—the four basic elements (earth, water, fire, air),
higher forms of life (man), and the structure of the universe (the
planets, sun, and moon). As Aristotle testified with respect to Pythagorean doctrines, "they supposed the elements of numbers to be the
elements of all things, and the whole heaven to be a musical scale
[*harmonian*] and a number."[7]

To this concept we owe the idea of *microcosm* and *macrocosm*:
man, the "small universe" or microcosm, contains the same complex
of elements and relationships as the greater universe itself, the macrocosm, and his nature is ruled by the same principles and propor-

"Macrocosm and Microcosm," title page from Robert Fludd,
Utriusque cosmi . . . historia, Oppenheim, 1617–1619.
Courtesy of Lilly Library, Indiana University, Bloomington, Indiana.

tions. Medieval writers diagrammed this vision of universal harmony as a human figure spread-eagled within a circle, surrounded by a series of concentric circles representing the orbits of the celestial bodies.

> The name of the bow is life, but its work is death. . . . The hidden harmony is better than the obvious. . . . People do not understand how that which is at variance with itself agrees with itself. There is a harmony in the bending back, as in the cases of the bow and the lyre. [Heraclitus][8]

In these provocative fragments the early philosopher Heraclitus expressed his view of a universe of constant change held together by the principle of harmony. I quote Edward Lippman's brilliant analysis:

> The universe is one of ceaseless change, but it contains a harmony that controls both spatial and temporal phenomena. . . . We can come to know the divine order of harmony more readily in ourselves than in the external world. . . . But things at variance really agree; unity is bestowed by harmony, or if we wish, harmony is really unity. Significantly, it is a musical instrument, the lyre, that Heraclitus uses, along with the bow, to exemplify his conception. In both, opposing forces are connected with one another and adjusted, while from a dynamic point of view, when the strings are drawn back, the restoration of harmony produces music in the one case and marksmanship in the other—parallel and really equivalent manifestations, for both overcome distance, whether with sound or arrow, to reach their target, both are outcomes of action that is at the same time harmonious and accurately directed, and both are symbols of a life correctly lived so as to achieve its goal. Even literally, whether in instrument or weapon, music and accuracy are present together, for the bow is not silent in action, and like the flight of sound, the arrow is audible in travel. The depth of the concept reaches back to the identification of musical bow and hunting bow in prehistory. In addition, although its work is death, the bow (*biós*) is life (*bíos*). . . .[9]

As the concept of a harmonious universe gradually sank down into human consciousness, the belief developed that actual music was produced by the turning of the heavenly bodies in their orbits. The heavenly harmony is inaudible to us only because, as Shakespeare wrote in *The Merchant of Venice*, our ears are clogged with "this muddy vesture of decay" (act 5, sc. 1:64). The concept of humanity in harmony with nature is not peculiar to Western thought for it has been a staple of Asian philosophy since ancient times. The distinctive feature of the Greek idea of harmony is the degree of completeness with which the concept was implemented and integrated into the whole structure of aesthetic, moral, and political thought.

Many models for the universal harmony can be found in ancient literature, but one of the best known is the "Vision of Er," from the tenth book of Plato's *Republic*. The warrior Er, reviving after his death in battle, relates his vision of a pillar of light stretching down from heaven, to which was connected the spindle of Necessity— through which a series of concentric whorls turned. The circular motion of the spindle turned in opposite direction to the seven inner circles, each turning at a different rate of speed:

> and up above on each of the rims of the circles a Siren stood, borne around in its revolution and uttering one sound, one note, and from all eight there was the concord of a single harmony. And there were three others who sat round at equal intervals, each one on her throne, the Fates, daughters of Necessity, clad in white vestments . . . Lachesis, and Clotho, and Atropos, who sang in unison with the music of the Sirens, Lachesis singing the things that were, Clotho the things that are, and Atropos the things that are to be.[10]

It is quite by design that this description of universal harmony was included in a treatise on the ideal state. For the *polis*, the city-state, required harmony in order to function properly. Harmony, to the Greeks, served as a powerful metaphor for the interdependence of all parts of the world as they knew it: the elements of nature, plants, animals, mankind, the state, the earth, and the universe formed one continuous "chain of being."[11] All levels of this complex hierarchy were ruled by the same principles, and any motion within a single member or level would—in one way or another—affect all the others. And it is worth noting that this vision coordinates the spatial and the temporal, through the presence of the three Fates who symbolize the past, present, and future.

It is easy to be critical of this picture of an ideal universe, with its implications that "things should be a certain way" and "a place for everyone, and everyone in his place." But it provided music with a powerful role within society and paved the way for its acceptance as an independent art. Perhaps less constructively, the doctrine of harmony gave the status of law to musical phenomena which might better be regarded as the result of choice. But by the early Middle Ages the doctrine of harmony was firmly in place as one of the cornerstones of *musica speculativa*. The threefold classification of music proposed by Boethius (ca. 480–524) sums it up: *musica mundana,* the music of the spheres, unheard by man; *musica humana,* the harmony that exists within man, between soul and body; and *musica instrumentalis,* the music made by man, an imperfect imitation of the higher kinds of music.[12]

Beauty

There is little agreement on what is beautiful. For some, beauty is that which gives pleasure to the senses; for others, beauty is a more abstract clarity of form; for still others, beauty is that which stands for something that is of supreme value. It is unfortunate that so many standards of beauty exist, for beauty is probably the single most important criterion for artistic value in the history of aesthetics. It is a little too easy to give up and say that "beauty lies in the eye of the beholder." To dismiss standards of judgment as wholly relative to the whim of the individual is to overlook the fact that there have been large areas of agreement on what is beautiful—such a consensus developed in Greek civilization, although spirited debate continued on various tributary issues.

The task of this section is to sort out these ideas as they appear in Greek literature. The Greeks had no monopoly on theories of beauty, but they applied themselves persistently to the concept and created an extensive body of callistic speculation. They did not address as specifically the criteria for beauty in music, so we will have to infer their positions from more general literature.

We shall also have to distinguish the positions of Plato and Aristotle. To put the distinction rather coarsely: for Plato, beauty is a quality that makes visible (audible) a representation of a higher, absolute beauty; for Aristotle, beauty is a property of appearance. Their disagreement turns on this question—is beauty a way of making apparent some set of higher qualities or does it have some objective standards of its own? Is it dependent upon some other thing, or is it self-sufficient?

When we pry into the background of important aesthetic terms, it is a good idea to remember that English words have long histories, derive from other languages, and carry an assortment of shades of meaning that contribute to the overall semantic depth of the terms we use. *Kalon* was the principal Greek word for what we now call *beauty;* it meant "well-done, pleasing, fine, physically attractive, proper, suitable, good." Immediately this opens up a variety of associated meanings.

Three important Latin words are now usually translated as "beautiful": *bellus,* a diminutive of *bonus* (good); *formosus,* literally "shapely," having beauty of form; and *pulcher,* physical beauty. Other words from Indo-European languages suggest the process of "making visible": the German adjective *schön* (beautiful), in association with the related verb *scheinen* (seem, appear, shine), represents this cluster of meanings—"making manifest, bringing to visibility, radiant, brilliant, impressive, striking." It is not hard to follow the semantics here: if beauty is a "becoming visible," the light emanating from it strikes our eyes; thus "appear," "seem," and "shine" are part of the same process of perception. This analysis suggests that beauty has often been regarded as a representation of being itself, as well as a quality or attribute of being.

Let us sort out the meanings proposed for beauty. Beauty can mean pleasing to the senses, having good form, that which is done with skill and excellent technique ("fine"), good, shining (gleaming, radiant), a manifestation of something to the senses (an epiphany, a becoming visible or audible), proper (apt, suitable), striking (something that impresses itself forcefully on the spectator), and a representation of something else that is beautiful, or good, or true in its own right.

Although Greek authors took various positions on what *to kalon* signified, they generally agreed on what its properties were: order, measure, proportion (in complex things such as a temple, statue, or ode); and unity, simplicity, regularity (in colors, shapes, and tones). A complex work of art had to be *knowable*—measured, limited, able to be grasped by the senses, *well-arranged*—its parts clearly and properly ordered, and *symmetrical*—proportionate, harmonious, with part balanced against part, forming a unified whole. Bad art resulted from disorder, a lack of definiteness, or lack of proper proportions. *Taxis* (order) was the most powerful formal concept in Greek thought and, from the time of Plato and Aristotle until the end of the Renaissance, beauty of form was held to be a good arrangement of the parts. Giving pleasure to the senses ranked far down on the list of properties that make a thing beautiful. The Greek concept of beauty emphasized not only the formalistic but the cognitive appeal of art—the perception of art was a form of knowing.

Plato considered absolute beauty as an idea, a form, which cannot be known by means of the senses—only with the mind. He described the process by which one contemplates beauty as an ascent, climbing a ladder rung-by-rung: the lowest rung is our perception of beautiful things with the senses, responding instinctively to colors, sounds, and form; our perceptions are then internalized in the mind (*nous*), the "noetic" phase of perception; finally we achieve a more general vision of the essence of absolute beauty.

To interpret: if one of the warriors in the *Iliad* sought to admire the golden shield which the armorer Hephaestus made for Achilles,[13] he would first respond to the gleaming substance and appearance of the shield itself. Next he would ponder its design in his mind, marveling at how the texture was meant to imitate the appearance of a freshly plowed field and how it might remind him of the fields at home, measuring with his eye the shield's proportions, lines, and balance. And finally he might consider the qualities of "shieldness"— more universal properties that could include the glint of morning sun on a distant battle line, how it might turn the edge of a thrusting spear, and how his body might be carried home atop it if he fell in battle.

Plato's proposal hinges upon his doctrine of *anamnesis* (recollection). According to this doctrine our souls were in direct contact with the form of pure beauty before birth, but in the shock of being born this knowledge is forgotten and can be recaptured only in the occasional moments of déjà vu and by means of a step-by-step reacquaintance with beauty. It is revealed first in physical objects, then in the mind, then in social institutions and laws, then in the principles of pure science, and finally in the ultimate vision of absolute beauty.

Beauty, for Plato, was not clearly separated from the Good, nor was it a special attribute of art. Aristotle, on the other hand, firmly connected the idea of beauty with artistic creation and brought the concept down to earth from Plato's more metaphysical plane. Aristotle's answers to the problems of beauty were based on more objectively verifiable standards—whether an object accurately represented reality, whether it pleased, and how it was put together. To follow his line of thought, we shall turn to the idea of mimesis; but first, to summarize this section, here is an important passage from Plato's *Symposium:*

> For he who would proceed aright in this matter should begin in youth to seek the company of bodily beauty; and first, if he be guided by his instructor aright, to love one beautiful body only—out of that he should create fair thoughts; and soon he will of himself perceive that the beauty of one body is akin to the beauty of another; and then if beauty of form in general is his pursuit, how foolish would he be not to recognize that the beauty in every body is one and the same! And when he perceives this he will abate his violent love of the one . . . and will become a steadfast lover of all beautiful bodies. In the next stage he will consider that the beauty of the soul is more precious than the beauty of the outward form; so that if a virtuous soul have but a little comeliness, he will be content to love and tend him, and will search out and bring to the birth thoughts which may improve the young, until he is compelled next to contemplate and see the beauty in institutions and laws, and to understand that the beauty of them all is of one family, and that personal beauty is a trifle. . . .
>
> He who has been instructed thus far in the things of love, and who has learned to see the beautiful in due order and succession, when he comes toward the end will suddenly perceive a nature of wondrous beauty (and this, Socrates, is the final cause of all our former toils)—a nature which in the first place is everlasting, knowing not birth or death, growth or decay . . . beauty absolute, separate, simple, and everlasting.[14]

Mimesis

Early Greek authors agreed that the perception of art was a cognitive process, but they did not agree on the nature of the mental activity that arises in response to a work of art. They interpreted the aesthetic experience, as Tatarkiewicz points out, in three main ways: first, art can purge and purify the mind by inducing an ecstatic experience (*katharsis*); second, it can create a fiction, an illusion, in the mind (especially in the visual arts); and finally, art can communicate by triggering an act of recognition, of discovery, when the perceiver becomes aware of similarities between the art work and its model(s) in nature.[15] The Latin equivalent for *mimesis* was *imitatio*, hence the standard English translation as "imitation." *Mimesis* was proposed as a general theory of art and became the foundation for Aristotle's aesthetic speculations. It subsequently developed into one of the most important theories of art in the history of aesthetics, although it has not received serious discussion since about 1700.

The depth of the concept and the full range of its implications for music will be apparent only after a survey of the topics in this chapter. For now my concern is with the basic position as set out by Aristotle:

> As to the origin of the poetic art as a whole, it stands to reason that two causes brought it into being, both of them rooted in human nature. Namely (1) the habit of imitating is congenital to human beings from childhood . . . and so is (2) the pleasure that all men take in works of imitation.[16]

> Again, since learning and admiring are pleasant, it follows that pleasure is given by acts of imitation, such as painting, sculpture, poetry, and by every skillful copy, even though the original be unpleasant; for one's joy is not in the thing itself; rather, there is a syllogism—"This is that," and so it comes that one learns something.[17]

Aristotle's notable omission of music from the above list of mimetic arts should not pass unremarked, but it indicates only that the concept of mimesis requires special explanation with respect to music. It is not difficult to accept the idea of a painter, sculptor, playwright, or actor imitating a landscape, a human body, or a striking personality, but what is it that music imitates—and how? The Greeks gave a variety of answers, some more convincing than others.

Mimesis is a post-Homeric word, probably deriving from acts performed during some priestly cult ritual—dancing, singing, or instrumental music; so the connection with music was an early one. Tatarkiewicz has identified four stages in the evolution of the concept in ancient Greece:[18]

1 as an expression of inner reality, through ritual actions; this type of imitation involves doing, not making. It has no application to the visual arts, nor does it seek to reproduce external reality.

2 as an imitation of the way nature functions, e.g., a spider's web (as in weaving), a swallow's nest (building), a nightingale's song (music)

3 as a copy of the appearance of things (Plato), applying to all the arts—basically a type of description

4 the creation of a work of art based on the artist's selection of general, typical, and/or essential elements of nature (Aristotle). Since Aristotle was more concerned with poetry and the theater, he probably meant human nature.

These proposals raise many questions: Does the artist imitate what is individual or what he sees as general characteristics? Does he single out the most essential element and focus upon that, or does he represent his model in a more complex and realistic way? Can there be but one model or many? Note that the artist is not obliged to invent anything; he cannot create something ex nihilo, out of nothingness. His job is to see (with his eye, with his mind), to select, and to represent skillfully in a sensuous medium. And his work will be evaluated according to Plato's formula: "[the critic must have] first, a knowledge of the nature of the original; next, a knowledge of the correctness of the copy; and thirdly, a knowledge of the excellence with which the copy is executed."[19]

The concept of music as imitation poses real problems for the philosophy of music, although—as in most widely held aesthetic theories—there is a kernel of truth that can be extracted if one penetrates deeply enough into the idea. The theory of mimesis denies independent being to music and assumes an external source or model; from this follow many other complications. And while we may agree with Aristotle that "one's joy is not in the thing [imitated]," most people will prefer to take joy in the musical phenomenon itself—not in how truthfully or skillfully it represents something else.

Various authors have gone to extremes in their efforts to justify music as an imitation—of abstract number proportions, of types of motions and physical gestures, of passions, humors, mental states,

natural and mechanical sounds, cosmic images and cosmogonies
(emergence, apocalypse, apotheosis), feelings, words, the meanings
of words, and perhaps at times even of itself! It has been a popular
theory and easy to swallow if one is prepared to overlook its difficulties. Music has extraordinary power to suggest associations, images,
perhaps even feelings—but whether this is in fact a type of imitation
rests on one's definition. To defend a mimetic theory of music requires
us to assert a likeness between model and representation, a likeness
that can be verified objectively.

Ethos

If mimesis was the artist's method, ethos signified the effects of
his work when perceived. The doctrine of ethos is easily the most
pervasive theme in Greek musical literature and was addressed re-
peatedly by most of the major philosophers. The word carries a range
of meanings: first, an accustomed place, an abode; then custom and
usage; also disposition, character—especially moral character; and,
finally, that which delineates or molds character. The doctrine of
ethos—a mixture of educational theory, psychology, and therapy—
assumes that music exerts powerful effects upon the body, the soul,
and the mind, for good or ill, immediate and residual. Developing
moral character was the first priority in Greek education, and music
—in later Greek thought—was assigned a central role in shaping
character. Many sets of correspondences were proposed (by Plato,
Aristotle, and others) between the various scales, rhythms, and character traits. In fact, as stated in Aristotle's *Politics*, the aims of music
and education were identical:[20]

> *paideia*, education in general, moral training in the specific
> *katharsis*, purgation—a term used in a special technical sense
> (see below)
> *diagoge*, intellectual knowledge
> *paidia* and *anapausis*, play and relaxation

Damon of Athens, one of Socrates' teachers, was one of the
earliest authors to suggest a specific connection between music and
the formation of human character, and his teachings formed the
basis for most of Plato's attitudes toward music. Damon's premise

is reported as follows: "Song and dance necessarily arise when the soul is in some way moved; liberal and beautiful songs and dances create a similar soul, and the reverse kind create a reverse kind of soul."[21] Aristotle was even more specific:

> Even in mere melodies there is an imitation of character, for the musical scales differ essentially from one another, and those who hear them are differently affected by each. Some of them make men sad and grave, like the so-called Mixolydian; others enfeeble the mind, . . . The same principles apply to rhythms; some have a character of rest, others of motion, and of these latter again, some have a more vulgar, others a nobler motion. . . . There seems to be in us a sort of affinity to musical scales and rhythms, which leads some philosophers to say that the soul is a tuning, others [to say] that it possesses tuning.[22]

The idea of ethos carried important political implications: since both Damon and Plato believed that music could implant all the virtues—courage, moderation, and even justice—in the human character, it is clear why Plato advocated the use of music to further state policy. He contended that music shaped the character not only of the individual citizen but of the state as a whole; music could in fact uphold or subvert the established social order, for—as Plato testifies in the *Republic*—"when the modes of music change, the fundamental laws of the state always change with them."[23]

Greek authors stressed the formative power of music upon the young, but many asserted also that each stage in life and each caste of society, freeborn or slave, had its own needs and required specific musical prescriptions. Indeed the Greeks wrote of applying music, in therapy and in education, much as one would apply a drug: theirs was an allopathic concept of medicine that prescribed ingredients chosen to counteract the symptoms displayed, aimed at restoring the patient to a balanced state of physical and emotional health. Exciting music was selected to arouse the autistic, the phlegmatic, and the feeble; soothing music to calm the irritable, the excitable, and the hyperkinetic. But for the purposes of general education, only the moderate scales and rhythms were approved—those that were thought to contain no imbalance or excess of energy or motion, only even and regular steps.

Katharsis is an important term that figures prominently in the theory of ethos and has led to much further discussion in the history of aesthetics. Aristotle used the term only once in his *Poetics*, but there it was designated as the principal human response to the tragic drama: a way of coping with the powerful feelings of pity and fear aroused by the tragic spectacle. It has been taken to mean an ecstatic experience, a draining off of excess emotion, a purifying process. The reams of scholarship that have been addressed to this concept in Aristotle's thought have helped to complicate what is really a fairly simple idea. It seems clear that catharsis involves certain phases: the arousal of strong emotion in response to stimuli, then some kind of discharge or release, and finally a return to a calmer emotional state in which one feels better and, somehow, purified. It carries also, I believe, the implication that individual emotions are swept away and replaced by a more general feeling of affect. Aristotle elaborated on the effects of catharsis in the *Politics:*

> [certain people are] affected by religious melodies; and when they come under the influence of melodies which fill the soul with religious excitement they are calmed and restored as if they had undergone a medical treatment and purging. The same sort of effect will also be produced on those who are specially subject to feelings of fear and pity, or to feelings of any kind.[24]

It is impractical to pursue the various proposals for linking specific musical formulae with specific ethical purposes—our knowledge of Greek music is too sketchy. Aristotle did divide melodies into four types, without saying what was responsible for assigning a melody to the proper category: the moderate, the enthusiastic, the sad, and the relaxed. The moderate category is obviously the most appropriate for *paideia;* and similarly, the enthusiastic, passionate type is the most likely to produce catharsis.

There is a very important, though subtle, connection in Greek musical speculation between the large topics that form the agenda for the present chapter: harmony, beauty, mimesis, and ethos. The connecting link was the parallel between musical style and human character: musical style—in terms of text, melody, scale, tempo, meter, and rhythmic patterns—was the sonorous expression of character, whether moderate and judicial, exciting and exuberant, sad and heavy, or relaxed and inert. But the process is somewhat circular: character was the inevitable result of one's exposure to a variety of musical (and other artistic) experiences. For the musician, mimesis was a matter of choosing appropriate rhythms, melodic phrases, and tempi that were in accord with the effects he sought to produce in his hearers. The composer/poet had to be able to read human nature and to represent it. He might seek to imitate his personal vision of character, of society, or the universal harmony. The finest representation (technique) of the finest object resulted in beauty, which in turn produced the finest qualities in the listener.

It is doubtful if much of this theorizing was ever implemented systematically in musical practice. Yet the idea of ethos retained much of its force for later philosophers, and the psychology of music did not advance significantly beyond the speculations of the Greeks until the present century.

Form, substance, and perception

Until this point we have been more occupied with questions of value and judgment than the grittier issues of *being* and *knowing*. For a final perspective let us examine the answers that some of the Greeks (especially Aristotle and his school) gave to three such basic questions:

1   What is the musical substance, the raw material of music?
2   How is it given form?
3   How can it be perceived?[25]

Greek authors made a clear separation between matter (*hyle*) and form (*morphe*), not unlike the distinction they drew between form and content. The general concept of form was as an activating principle which—when applied to passive, indeterminate matter— transformed it into the artistic result: a statue, temple, speech, song, or choric dance. They were fond of using sexist analogies: form was masculine, matter feminine.

The musical substance was threefold—the sounds of the voice, musical pitch, and the human body. These remain passive and formless until their activation by a form-giving principle translates them into articulate speech (poetry), melody (music), and gesture (dance). Terms such as *rhythmizomenon*, *melodoumenon*, and *hermosmenon* were coined for the rhythmic, melodic, and harmonic raw material.

All of these words are present passive participles in the nominative singular, neuter gender, derived regularly or by analogy, e.g., *rhythmizomenon* is regularly derived from the verb *rhythmizo*, "to bring into measure, rhythmicize." Thus its literal meaning is "that which is being rhythmicized"; I translate it as the "rhythmicized substance." Several such parallel terms appear in Greek technical treatises on music: *rhythmos/rhythmizomenon* (rhythm/rhythmicized substance), *melos/melodoumenon* (melody/melodized substance), *schema/schematizomenon* (form/that which is formed), *kinesis/kinoumenon* (motion/that which is moved).

Greek authors developed an extensive lexicon of formal terms, each signifying a different aspect of form: the dynamic, mobile form of music (*rhythmos*); external, visible form or shape (*schema*); form as order (*taxis*); conceptual or essential form (*eidos*); and form in general (*morphe*). This wealth of terminology testifies to the importance the Greeks attached to form in the arts: without form, substance was vague, undefined, unlimited, and therefore unknowable. Greek form tended to be geometric and modular, rather than organic. Formal units were scaled in precise increments and balanced against each other by simple numerical proportions: 1:1, 2:1, and 3:2 were those that were favored. Musical time, for the Greeks, was atomistic—a sequence of minimal time units that achieved form and continuity only when some activating formal principle was superimposed upon them.

Aristotle, in his treatise *On the Soul*, asserted that "matter is potentiality, while form is actuality."[26] The later Greek theory of perception hinged upon this opposition of potential/actual, and the role of the *aisthesis*—our faculty of sense perception—was to "actualize" the imprint of form on the mind. This is all very abstract, but the principle is clear enough: our sense organs (including the mind) are passive matter by nature, but they respond readily to the imprint of form by taking on the *likeness* of that form. Aristotle and Theophrastus were fond of the analogy of a signet ring applied to hot wax: the wax remains in a neutral, undifferentiated state until it is imprinted with the form of the ring. But the readiness with which the aesthetic sense responds to sensation cannot be attributed solely to the force of the external agent. Our minds are primed by our natural affinity for certain ratios and proportions, and also by our acquired knowledge of the forms. The perception process is mostly automatic, but it can go wrong—if the *aisthesis* is not in a balanced, receptive state or if it is under- or overstimulated.

To sum up this section briefly: music happens when the formal principles of rhythm, harmony, and melody are imposed on the neutral substances (speech, musical tone, the body), activating them into a dynamic, coordinated artistic structure. It can be perceived by one who has prior knowledge of the forms, an innate affinity for numbers and proportions, and an aesthetic sense that is in a state of good equilibrium. Perception is a noetic process—it requires knowledge and is itself a type of knowledge.

In addition to these speculations, the Greeks left an equally powerful expression of their musical beliefs and attitudes: in their myths. In the following chapter we will examine myth as an important source of "indirect testimony" and isolate certain strands of ideas, metaphors, and images of music that have left as sharp an imprint on Western thought as the direct testimony set forth in the present chapter.

5 The mythos of music

MUCH OF OUR musical ideology lies half-buried. Even in the preceding chapter, where we examined specific statements that Greek authors made about music, it was clear that their use of words revealed deeper attitudes on such things as beauty and form. These subsurface meanings contribute as much to their message as the more explicit surface meanings—what the authors consciously intended to say. In this chapter we probe an equally rich treasury of subsurface ideas, those embedded in myth.

References to music are extremely common in literature, and our response to them has become highly predictable as a result of our conditioning by the steady accumulation of myth over the last two thousand years. But our response is not always fully conscious; this complex tapestry of ideas has not been systematically examined, nor have its full implications been realized. In this chapter I propose a frame of reference for the deep stratum of musical ideas in Western cultural consciousness.

We can best deal with this "indirect testimony" by recognizing that it is all part of a gestalt—a cluster of related ideas, beliefs, and images—that has come to have thematic significance for literature. This approach, following the method Northrop Frye suggested in his *Anatomy of Criticism*, may be described as *archetypal criticism*. Its process is the analysis of the structural patterns produced in literature by myth, either explicit or implicit. Frye describes archetypes as "associative clusters . . . [that contain] a large number of specific

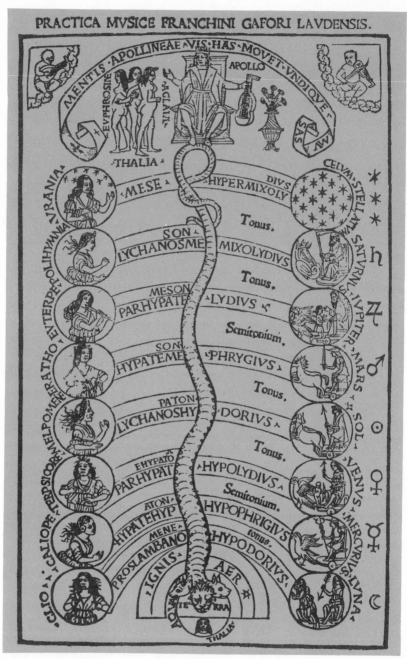

"Music of the Spheres," frontispiece from the 1496 edition
of Franchino Gafori, *Practica musicae*.

learned associations which are communicable because a large number of people in a given culture happen to be familiar with them."[1]

It is hard to get a clear picture of the myth of music as a whole. The nature of the statements varies from veiled allusion to metaphor, to symbolic reference, to explicit assertion, to conventional label. The literary reference may touch on only one or two of the myth components. And the connection between ideas may be merely by association: at times one idea seems to trigger another.

The attitude toward myth changes from time to time: in recent centuries the trend has been toward a more mechanistic interpretation of myth than was formerly the case. In nineteenth- and twentieth-century literature myth has emerged with renewed vigor as a source of ideas for the artist. Many of the themes presented in the following pages have become so deeply embedded in society's collective unconscious that their mythical origins have long since been forgotten; they survive as old sayings, clichés, personality stereotypes, and in various forms of popular literature.

Aristotle took mythos as one of his six basic categories in the *Poetics,* using the term in the sense of plot (the remaining categories are character, diction, thought, spectacle, and song).[2] Although this use of the word may seem a little narrow for our purposes, we are on solid ground in treating myths as structural or thematic patterns, no matter what the genre in which they appear.

Myth, in its wider and more familiar sense, is not as easy to define to everyone's satisfaction. Stories of gods, demons, and heroes of superhuman accomplishments fill most but not all the world's mythologies. It has become almost a truism that myth involves beginnings, crucial turning points, or endings. Myths are often associated with the cyclical rhythms of the times and seasons and the spatial structure of the orderly cosmos, and seem—according to Lévi-Strauss—to perform the same function for most societies, primitive or sophisticated.[3] But Kirk warns that "there is no one definition of myth, no Platonic form of a myth against which all actual instances can be measured."[4] The single common denominator appears to be our need to explain that which cannot be immediately understood on the basis of everyday experience.

While early authors were preoccupied with the origins and effects of music, later literature has tended to emphasize the personality of the musician, instruments, notation, and the role of music in society.

And music as myth exhibits some unique features: mythical elements attach both to the person of the musician and to his art in the abstract, unlike other traditional mythical roles such as the physician and the preacher, where the focus is clearly upon personal mystique and charisma. Also the mythos of music is built upon a curious dichotomy; it is often stated in terms of a set of antitheses, of which one or the other is dominant from time to time. By far the most significant of these antitheses is the paradoxical notion that music possesses both *power* and *transience*. Music has the power to create the universe, heal the sick, and resurrect the dead; but it is at the same time so fragile and perishable that we are in danger of losing it and grasp it mainly by means of our memory.

Location in time and space is often a feature of mythical narrative. According to Frye, a cosmic setting is essential to the operation of myth, bringing the divine, human, animal, vegetable, mineral, and (sometimes) the demonic worlds into alignment by means of some symbol of verticality, called by Frye a "point of epiphany."[5] This "symbolic presentation of the point at which the . . . apocalyptic world and the cyclical world of nature come into alignment" most commonly occurs as a tower, staircase, lighthouse, or mountaintop, or (to cite a familiar biblical example) the vision of Jacob's ladder.[6] We need but two musical examples: Orpheus' descent into the underworld to revive Eurydice and, from Polynesian mythology, the vine by which Hiku climbs down into the undersea world to rescue his wife, Kawelu.[7]

The woodcut that begins this chapter is the frontispiece from the 1496 edition of Franchino Gafori's *Practica musicae*.[8] This famous diagram of the musical cosmos is a powerful statement of the main elements in the mythos of music and contains a wealth of material for interpretation—so much that we can present only its main features. The musical scale forms the vertical at the point of epiphany, connecting the four material elements (earth, water, air, fire) with the pagan heaven of Apollo and the three Graces, shown in typical back-to-back dance with arms linked. The steps of the scale, the intervals between them, and the Greek modes are marked off along the body of the three-headed serpent Serapis. Each scale step corresponds to one of the celestial spheres, marked also by the planetary signs along the right margin, and each is presided over by one of the Muses, depicted crudely along the left margin. The animal and vegetable worlds are also represented in this cosmogram. The Latin motto at the top proclaims that "the spirit of Apollo descends into all of the Muses" including, apparently, the Muse of silence, Thalia (not the absent Muse of comedy).

Although most of the elements in Gafori's woodcut represent spatial aspects of the mythos of music, there are important associations between music and temporality in world mythology, particularly in the parallels drawn between the rhythms of the times and seasons and the recurrent cyclical patterns of musical rhythm and meter. The prevailing idea is that various types of music, scales, instruments, and the like are appropriate for the different times of day, seasons of the year, the ages of man, and other similar temporal conventions. In more abstract form, the flow of music is often seen as analogous to the passage of life, the river that runs to the sea, and the cycle of birth and rebirth. Reality imitates myth (a surprisingly common event!) in various world musical cultures in which strict rules specify the time of day at which a particular type of music may be performed.

The process by which myth is formed is rather like the way a pearl grows within an oyster—through a steady accumulation of layers around a core. The central issues of the mythos of music were already conventionalized by the beginning of the Christian era, crystallizing around the legend of Orpheus, which remains the single most explicit theme. From the seventh-century encyclopedist Isidore of Seville we assemble a compact presentation of the main ideas:

> Music is an art of modulation consisting of tone and song, called music by derivation from the Muses. . . . Unless sounds are remembered by man, they perish, for they cannot be written down. . . . Moses says that the inventor of the art of music was Tubal, who was of the race of Cain, before the flood. The Greeks say that Pythagoras found its beginnings in the sound of hammers and the striking of stretched strings. . . . For the very universe, it is said, is held together by a certain harmony of sounds, and the heavens themselves are made to revolve by the modulations of harmony. Music moves the feelings and changes the emotions. . . . Music also composes distraught minds, as may be read of David, who freed Saul from the unclean spirit by the art of melody. The very beasts also, even serpents, birds, and dolphins, music incites to listen to her melody. But every

word we speak, every pulsation of our veins, is related by musical rhythms to the powers of harmony. . . . Orpheus . . . is deemed not merely to have swayed wild beasts with this art, but to have moved rocks and forests with the modulation of his song. . . . But just as this ratio [6:8:12] appears in the universe from the revolution of the spheres, so in the microcosm it is so inexpressibly potent that the man without its perfection and deprived of harmony does not exist.[9]

These statements, scattered throughout Isidore's nine brief chapters, formed the basis for the semi-ritualistic opening chapters of medieval and Renaissance treatises on music. And in the years after 1500 there was a great flowering of musical references, especially (for reasons that remain obscure) in English literature. The number of sixteenth- and seventeenth-century English poems in praise of music is astounding, amounting to a veritable cultural explosion. But shortly after 1700 an inevitable decline set in, and the more rationalistic attitude toward myth is reflected in a literature less inclined toward cosmology and teleological interpretation. With the tradition of *musica practica* on the rise, we see a concomitant decline in the genre of *musica speculativa* and its cluster of related mythical ideas which, while hardly scientific, had been nurtured by musical scientists. The mythos of music, in a word, went underground and has rarely since emerged in explicit narrative or in other than piecemeal references. Tracing the dimensions of the myth in modern literature involves isolating the diverse strands of ideas and analyzing them on the basis of the established archetypal patterns.

The mythos of person

The legend of the Phrygian singer Orpheus provides the most familiar mythical image of the musician. The Orphic literature is so vast that it is all we can do to mention the main themes. The most familiar version of the story is told by Virgil in the fourth book of his *Georgics*. While the legend has a few features in common with many of the Near Eastern fertility myths (the *pharmakos* or sacrificial victim and the *sparagmos*, mutilation), the early versions are strikingly nontheistic. Orpheus as the singer/prophet, able to charm wild animals and uproot trees with his music, symbolizes primitive mankind's feeling of oneness with nature. Through his *katabasis*—the descent into the nether world to bring his wife Eurydice back to earth—Orpheus illustrates the transformation of the myth from a nature myth to a culture myth: the conquest of nature replaces the earlier sense of unity.

His actions bring Orpheus into contact with each of the mythical kingdoms (the divine, human, animal, vegetable, mineral, and demonic), bringing all into alignment at one point in time and in space. As the myth proceeds it focuses on Orpheus' weakness: his inability to obey Pluto's instructions not to look at Eurydice and his refusal to enjoy human company after her death, resulting in his dismemberment by a drunken mob of Thracian women. We see here a source for later views of the artist: as weak, effeminate, and/or alienated from society. The myth closes with the image of Orpheus' severed head floating downstream, still singing, and out across the Aegean to the island of Lesbos, where his singing head became an oracle and his lyre sounded without being touched. The myth has come full circle, and Orpheus is one with nature again.

Kathi Meyer-Baer has traced the interesting process by which the figure of Orpheus was split in early Christian iconography into the persons of Christ and Satan: Christ as the Good Shepherd, iconographically a direct translation of Orpheus playing to the surrounding animals, and Satan's Dance of Death, symbolizing the use of music's power for evil and as a lure to sin and death.[10] Clement of Alexandria, in his *Exhortation to the Greeks* (a second-century diatribe against the superstitions of pagan mythology), interprets Christ as a new Orpheus in a strikingly beautiful theology that has been conspicuously ignored by the Church in Rome:

> See how mighty is the new song! It has made men out of stones and men out of wild beasts. . . . it is this which composed the entire creation into melodious order, and tuned into concert the discord of the elements, that the whole universe might be in harmony with it. . . . Well, because the Word was from the first, He was and is the divine beginning of all things; but because He lately took a name . . . the Christ—I have called Him a New Song.[11]

Later Orphic references are so numerous and so varied that we can mention but a few. Rilke, in one of his *Sonnets to Orpheus*, ignores the core of the myth (the underworld descent) in favor of the beginning and ending points, contrasting order and disorder, building and destruction. Through his death, the song of Orpheus remains in lions and rocks and in trees and birds; now we, his hearers, can also be "a mouth of Nature."[12] Thomas Mann, in *Joseph and His Brothers*, has chosen to emphasize the theme of descent: Jacob, who dreamed himself to be fulfilling the mythical patterns lived by his ancestors, looked on Canaan as the land of the living and Egypt as the land of the dead; in his grief over Joseph's captivity, he visualized himself as Orpheus and an instrument of Joseph's symbolic resurrection from the Land of the Tombs.[13]

The image of the singing lyre caught the fancy of early Romantic poets who referred to the artist as an Aeolian harp:

Make me thy lyre, even as the forest is:
What if my leaves are falling like its own!
The tumult of thy mighty harmonies

Will take from both a deep, autumnal tone,
Sweet though in sadness. Be thou, Spirit fierce,
My spirit! Be thou me, impetuous one!

[Shelley, "Ode to the West Wind"]

Other musical references celebrate various givers or discoverers of music: makers of musical instruments (Jubal Cain,[14] the legendary Chinese emperor Fu Hsi), discoverers of the musical scale (Pythagoras), healers through music (King David),[15] codifiers of musical standards (the "Yellow Emperor" Huang Ti), and an array of demigods known for some particular association with music (Krishna). The symbols that represent these personages appear frequently in musical iconography: Pythagoras is shown playing upon a set of bells or listening to the sound of hammers, David appears with his harp, and Krishna with his flute.

The mythos of music also celebrates those who are preservers of music, those who are in some way responsible for making music less intangible, more permanent. Such persons have either invented systems for musical notation (Guido of Arezzo), compiled musical repertoires (St. Gregory), preserved the heritage of antiquity by means of their writing (Boethius), or have been associated with some other means of objectifying music; thus they are usually related to the theoretical branch of music. This aspect of the myth is very much operative today in the persons of the historical- and ethnomusicologist, the recording technician, and the computer programmer.

St. Gregory is often cited as the compiler of the body of Roman chant that bears his name and is depicted in medieval iconography with a dove (the Holy Spirit) perched on his shoulder, dictating the melodies into his ear. Boethius is praised for his compendious treatise, summing up the musical learning of the Greeks and written at a time when the musical science of antiquity was in danger of being irretrievably lost. For centuries his treatise represented medieval man's only contact with the Greek tradition.

In addition to his concept of the music of the spheres, Boethius seems to have been responsible for a threefold classification of musicians that was widely quoted and influential in the formation of society's attitudes. He held that he who plays an instrument ranks lowest; singers and poets deserve higher praise; but he who judges their skill rightly is superior to both.[16] From this attitude evolved the notion that the theoretical branch of music was somehow superior to the practical branch. Put more crudely, the same snide attitude toward theory and practice appears in a little Latin poem that is ascribed to Guido of Arezzo and which appears in literally hundreds of medieval music treatises:

Musicorum et cantorum magna est distantia,
Isti dicunt, illi sciunt, quae componit Musica.
Nam qui facit, quod non sapit, diffinitur bestia.

From the musician to the singer how great the distance is:
The latter says, the former *knows* what music's nature is;
For he who does, he knows not what, a beast by definition is.[17]

Guido's name is prominent among preservers of music for valid reasons. His accomplishments include the invention of the musical staff and the clef sign, the famous Guidonian "hand" (a mnemonic diagram that located the various steps of the musical scale on the finger joints), and—still more important—his system for solmization (sight-singing), which assigned syllables to the successive scale degrees. Guido based his system on a popular hymn to St. John, written by a certain Paul the Deacon, in which each line of text began a step higher:

UT quaent laxis,
REsonare fibris,   That your faithful servants
MIra gestorum,   May praise your wondrous deeds
FAmuli tuorum,   With clear voices,
SOLve polluti   Free the culprits' polluted lips,
LAbii reatum,   Saint John![18]
Sancte Joannes.

St. John, on the strength of this and other references, is sometimes invoked as one of music's patrons, but the most important saint of music is undoubtedly St. Cecilia, whose name is linked with music on the flimsiest of evidence.[19] Chaucer's account of her marriage and subsequent martyrdom cites only the organ that played during her wedding to Valerian (whom she is said to have converted to Christianity on their wedding night!):

And whyl the organs maden melodye,
To god alone in herte sang she;
"O Lord, my soul and eek my body gye
Unwemmed, lest that I confounded be."
[*Canterbury Tales*, The Second Nun's Tale]

And yet numerous Flemish and Italian Renaissance painters depicted Cecilia seated at the organ and gazing up to heaven as if for inspiration, later singing to the accompaniment of angels, playing the harp or a variety of other instruments. Her role in the myth is as patroness and protectress of musicians, and as a symbol of divine inspiration. John Dryden, in the most famous of his Cecilian odes, contrasts Orpheus and Cecilia, secular and sacred music:

Orpheus could lead the savage race;
And trees uprooted left their place,
    Sequacious of the lyre;
But bright Cecilia rais'd the wonder higher:
When to her organ vocal breath was given,
An angel heard, and straight appear'd,
    Mistaking Earth for Heaven.
["A Song for St. Cecilia's Day, 1687"]

These references to angels are more than background detail. The mythos of music features a host of surrounding figures—sirens, harpies, muses, angels—whose original connection with music is somewhat tenuous. Their basic function was as *psychopomps*, "soul-guides" assigned to lead the dead to their appointed stations in the afterlife. In early Christian art, angel musicians often accompanied the great scenes from the Bible; and in the cosmic diagrams of medieval and early Renaissance painters and sculptors, the various orders of angels (seraphim, cherubim, thrones, dominations, virtues, powers, principalities, archangels, and angels) were shown at their stations in the concentric circles of the cosmos, each presiding over one of the turning spheres and singing its characteristic tone.

The demonic world has a prominent place in the myth. The medieval Church held music in great suspicion and never succeeded in shaking off the superstition that a musician's powers came from the devil and could be used to entice the faithful to sin. Images such as the Dance of Death (vividly depicted as a dancing skeleton in Holbein's famous cycle of woodcuts), the Lorelei, and the Pied Piper of Hamlin are direct outgrowths of the popular attitude that music was a snare. The cult of the virtuoso can be shown to develop out of this interpretation of the Orphic myth: Niccolò Paganini and Franz Liszt seemed the embodiment of Orpheus to the nineteenth-century musical world, gifted with superhuman skill that surely came from the devil. Both were consummate showmen and took full advantage of this mystique, becoming exemplars for future generations of concert artists.

The most compelling portrait of the demonic in music is Thomas Mann's *Doctor Faustus*, in which his composer-protagonist Adrian Leverkühn acquires his powers from the devil—at the expense of his humanity, his health, and, ultimately, his life. Mann's descriptions of the traditional musical style, which Leverkühn rejected, and his new style (for which Mann took as his model the serial technique developed by Arnold Schoenberg) make for an interesting summary of polar attitudes toward "old" and "new" music as conditioned by centuries of myth.

Mann saw old music as a natural, organic process that was regulated by its own internal laws, a kind of alchemy that followed the principles of morphology proposed by Goethe: metamorphosis, polarity, intensification; it was a system with a rich potential for ambiguity and allusion. Traditional music, as Mann knew it, seemed a warmly human language, symbolic of feeling and expressive of emotion, appealing to the heart rather than to the intellect and always capable of suggesting the simplicity of a return to man's primordial state.

Adrian's new music, on the other hand, was described as cold, inorganic, regulated by "chilling law," at once stringently disciplined (by the twelve-tone technique) and "criminally loose" in his use of incommensurable pitches, glissandi, and barbaric inhuman sounds, amplified by electronic technology in mocking parodies of past musical styles. New music, to Mann, was symbolized by the magic square that hung over Adrian's piano, governing both the horizontal and vertical dimensions in his music by the same mathematical principles and producing unheard correspondences between the various parts. These two musics are fictions, of course, but useful fictions in that they clarify and summarize so many traditional attitudes toward old and new music. Here are the results:

old music	new music
warm	cold
natural	artificial
emotional	based on reason
inspiring	calculating
fertile	sterile
healthy	diseased
divine	demonic[20]

We will explore one further musical persona. The myth of the blind musician is one of literature's oldest themes, and visual representations date back as far as the Middle Kingdom of ancient Egypt. Many cultures have encouraged the blind to become musicians, and their usefulness as harem musicians is beyond dispute. Nor is it surprising that many blind people exhibit unusual musical ability. And yet there are overtones in the musical mystique attributed to the blind.

The blind musician is usually a folk musician, a minstrel, with practical skill rather than theoretical learning. He is of lowly birth and has had hard luck with life, but he possesses human insight denied to those with sight: he reads the heart, not the face. Arthur Schnitzler's novella *Der blinde Geronimo und sein Bruder* is a moving account of the travels of one such street musician, a story of alienation and reconciliation. In many Chinese and Japanese musics the performers have traditionally been blind, and in some other musical genres of East Asia even sighted performers play in the "blind style," with expressionless face and closed eyes. Many of the greatest French organists have been blind, noted for their skill at improvisation and trained at a school in Paris founded for that purpose. And finally, a special mystique has developed around the person of the blind jazz musician in American society.

Power

The belief that music possesses extraordinary power is probably one of the deepest layers in the mythos of music: power to suspend the laws of nature and overcome the kingdoms of heaven and hell. A sense of wonder, or sometimes of fear, accompanies most accounts of music's power. Two rather divergent illustrations of these attitudes appear in Thomas Mann's *The Magic Mountain*.

On the more rational level, the humanist Settembrini lectures Hans Castorp on the perils of music: "Music? It is the half-articulate art, the dubious, the irresponsible, the insensible. . . . That is not true clarity, it is a dreamy, inexpressive, irresponsible clarity, without consequences and therefore dangerous, because it betrays one into soft complacence. . . . For you, personally, Engineer, she is beyond all doubt dangerous."[21]

As if to fulfill Settembrini's prophecy, music causes the image of the dead Joachim (Hans's cousin) to materialize during the nightmarish seance held one evening in the sanatorium. Joachim's favorite air, Valentine's prayer from Gounod's *Faust*, is the instrument of his apparition:

The needle went on scratching in the silence, as the disc whirred round. Then Hans Castorp raised his head, and his eyes went, without searching, the right way.

There was one more person in the room than before. There in the background, where the red rays lost themselves in gloom, so that the eye scarcely reached thither, between writing-desk and screen, in the doctor's consulting chair, where in the intermission Elly had been sitting, Joachim sat. It was the Joachim of the last days, with hollow, shadowy cheeks, warrior's beard and full, curling lips.[22]

Legends of music's magical power are as old as literature: Orpheus is able to tame wild animals and uproot trees with his lyre, Amphion builds the stone walls of Thebes with his singing, Joshua destroys the walls of Jericho with trumpet blasts, and David heals Saul's mental illness with his harp. Boethius relates a story about the Greek mathematician Pythagoras who, when walking out one night, observed a young man about to set fire to his rival's house, in which a harlot was spending the night; noticing that the young man was inflamed by the music played by a nearby band of musicians, the wise man directed them to play a melody in the spondaic rhythmic mode. Lulled by the long even durations, the young man's pyromaniac passion soon abated.[23]

As these legends suggest, music and healing have been related since ancient times. Both Orpheus and Apollo were linked with the curing of disease, oracular prophecy, and purifying ritual—three different ways of focusing the healing forces of nature upon the body and the mind. Reading between the lines of the various stories, one can detect at least three therapeutic functions ascribed to music. The first one is regulation, the restoring of the soul and/or body to a state of equilibrium, arousing or soothing as needed to temper excess or deficient emotion; the second is the creation of the sensation of pleasure through movement; and the third is the inducing of an ecstatic experience (catharsis), which purges the soul of emotional conflict, expelling evil spirits.

Ancient medical tradition held that health—mental and physical—resulted from the proper blending of the four humors; when these bodily fluids were out of balance, illness resulted. Just as pharmaceutical preparations could help to restore the proper bodily equilibrium, music could in its own way influence the correct proportion of the humors and restore the desired state of mind and body. The musical therapist had to be aware of the relationship between fluid levels and the human personality, as reflected in the conventionalized doctrine of the four temperaments. Depending on the dominant humor—blood, phlegm, yellow bile, or black bile—a corresponding temperament could be predicted—sanguine, phlegmatic, choleric, or melancholic.

Complex, schematic lists of the various passions and emotional states were devised in the later Middle Ages and Renaissance, and the idea of music as regulatory agent was applied in a more mechanistic way: emotions could all be analyzed into their component passions, and a therapy could be prescribed with a specific remedy for each emotional ill. As Dryden put it in "A Song for St. Cecilia's Day, 1687," "What passion cannot Music raise and quell?"

An intriguing theme runs throughout the literature, that is, that music is able to penetrate the body. The fifteenth-century Italian Neo-Platonist philosopher Marsilio Ficino, in his commentary on Plato's *Timaeus*, provides an elaborate description:

> [Musical sound] conveys as if animated, the emotions and thoughts of the singer's or player's soul to the listeners's souls; . . . by the movement of the air [it] moves the body: by purified air it excites the aerial spirit which is the bond of body and soul: by motion it affects the senses and at the same time the soul: by meaning it works on the mind: finally, by the very movement of the subtle air it penetrates strongly: by its contemperation it flows smoothly: by the conformity of its quality it floods us with a wonderful pleasure: by its nature, both spiritual and material, it at once seizes, and claims as its own, man in his entirety.[24]

This passage bristles with ideas: music is described as a specific language that can communicate directly from performer to listener; it penetrates the body in the form of air, pressure, meaning, and movement; and its effects are felt by the body, the mind, and the soul. Ficino's account of the way in which musical sound seizes and possesses the listener has definite sexual implications. Some of this remains in popular attitudes toward the virtuoso performer: when he is described as "playing" upon his audience, it is clear that we make a subconscious equation between musical communication and the sexual experience. In fact, music has often been discussed, and its effects described, in frankly erotic language, as in the two following passages from Shakespeare: Benedict, in *Much Ado about Nothing*, remarks: "Now, divine air! Now is his soul ravished! Is it not strange that sheeps' guts should hale souls out of men's bodies?" (act 2, sc. 3:61–64). And, from *The Merchant of Venice* (one of the best sources for Shakespeare's musical imagery): "With sweetest touches pierce your mistress' ear and draw her home with music" (act 5, sc. 1:67–68).

The intensity of the musical moment is remarked by numerous authors. T. S. Eliot, in the fifth canto of "The Dry Salvages," writes of the complete identification of listener and music in the musical experience, another way of saying that music "occupies" those who perceive it deeply enough:

> For most of us, there is only the unattended
> Moment, the moment in and out of time,
> The distraction fit, lost in a shaft of sunlight,
> The wild thyme unseen, or the winter lightning
> Or the waterfall, or music heard so deeply
> That it is not heard at all, but you are the music
> While the music lasts. . . .[25]

The coupling of music and death is a natural outgrowth of the preceding themes; intense experience (musical/sexual) is interpreted as timeless, an ecstatic loss of consciousness. Death by music is no dreadful, painful death but a state of rapture, symbolized by the ancient fable of the swan song. Perhaps the most famous version is this anonymous madrigal lyric from the sixteenth century:

> The silver swan, who living had no note,
> When death approached her silent throat;
> Leaning her breast against the reedy shore,
> Thus sung her first and last and sung no more:
> Farewell, all joys; O death come close mine eyes;
> More geese than swans now live, more fools than wise.

Finally we come to the most powerful of music's gifts—the ability to overcome nature and natural law. In *The Winter's Tale* Shakespeare employs music as a symbol of resurrection: Queen Hermione has been falsely reported dead and, after an interval of sixteen years, is shown to King Leontes in the form of a statue:

> *Paulina:*
> Music, awake her: strike! [*Music.*]
> 'Tis time; descend; be stone no more: approach;
> Strike all that look upon with marvel. Come;
> I'll fill your grave up: stir; nay, come away;
> Bequeath to death your numbness, for from him
> Dear life redeems you. You perceive she stirs:
>
> [*Hermione comes down.*]

Start not; her actions shall be as holy as
You hear my spell is lawful: do not shun her
Until you see her die again, for then
You kill her double. Nay, present your hand:
When she was young you woo'd her; now in age
Is she become the suitor!

Leontes:
   [*Embracing her.*]   O! She's warm.
If this be magic, let it be an art
Lawful as eating.

[Act 5, sc. 3:99–112]

And in the ringing conclusion of his 1687 Cecilian ode, Dryden calls for the final dissolution of the universe in response to the trumpet call:

As from the power of sacred lays
   The spheres began to move,
And sung the great Creator's praise
   To all the Blest above;
So when the last and dreadful hour
This crumbling pageant shall devour,
The trumpet shall be heard on high,
The dead shall live, the living die,
And Music shall untune the sky!

After such a feat, Hermione's symbolic resurrection seems but a modest accomplishment. To sum up, the mythos of music claims on behalf of music a penetrating intensity that is not subject to natural law; it cannot be understood by means of reason, but it is a life- and health-giving agent that can be applied throughout the whole range of human experience. To possess this power is to be not less than a god.

Transience

The most striking paradox in the myth is that this incredibly powerful force is also infinitely perishable, intangible, and forever in danger of being lost. Since it cannot be touched or held in the hand, nor can it be seen, music's real existence is in the imagination and the memory. The deep mythical significance of the memory can be traced back to the role of Mnemosyne as the mother of the Muses and to the need to preserve the early repertoire of oral poetry.

Sometimes the imagined music is superior to the actual,

> Heard melodies are sweet, but those unheard
>> Are sweeter; therefore, ye soft pipes, play on;
> Not to the sensual ear, but, more endear'd,
>> Pipe to the spirit ditties of no tone:
>
> [Keats, "Ode on a Grecian Urn"]

and memory is a good substitute for the event:

> Music, when soft voices die,
> Vibrates in the memory—
> Odours, when sweet violets sicken,
> Live within the sense they quicken.
>
> Rose leaves, when the rose is dead,
> Are heaped for the belovèd's bed;
> And so thy thoughts, when thou art gone,
> Love itself shall slumber on.
>
> [Shelley]

"Where are they now?" is the refrain of a wistful lament over the inevitable passage of music from present experience to past memory. The organist Abt Vogler, in one of Robert Browning's monologues, muses sadly:

> Well, it is gone at last, the palace of music I reared;
>> Gone! and the good tears start, the praises that come too slow;
> For one is assured at first, one scarce can say that he feared,
>> That he even gave it a thought, the gone thing was to go.
>
> Never to be again! . . .

Vogler's consolation is that

> All we have willed or hoped or dreamed of good shall exist;
>> Not its semblance, but itself; no beauty, nor good, nor power
> Whose voice has gone forth, but each survives for the melodist
>> When eternity affirms the conception of an hour.
>
> [Browning, "Abt Vogler"]

And Thomas Mann sounds a similar theme when, in *Doctor Faustus*, he describes the ending of his composer/hero's masterpiece—*The Lamentation of Dr. Faustus*:

> For listen to the end, listen with me: one group of instruments after another retires, and what remains, as the work fades on the air, is the high G of a cello, the last word, the last fainting sound, slowly dying in a pianissimo-fermata. Then nothing more: silence, and night. But that tone which vibrates in the silence, which is there no longer, to which only the spirit hearkens, and which was the voice of mourning, is so no more. It changes its meaning; it abides as a light in the night.

We think about music in so many ways: is it simply perceived or remembered sound? Or is it the emotion the soul feels, the expression of an idea or a mood, the projection of a performer's personality, a metaphor for the unseen universal harmony, a language for communication? In each of these there is a sense of passage, invoked in different ways throughout Western literature. Wallace Stevens selects one such theme:

> Just as my fingers on these keys
> Make music, so the self-same sounds
> On my spirit make a music too.
>
> Music is feeling then, not sound;
> And thus it is what I feel,
> Here in this room, desiring you,
>
> Thinking of your blue-shadowed silk,
> Is music. . . .
>
> ["Peter Quince at the Clavier"]

Bishop Isidore of Seville asserted that "unless sounds are remembered by man, they perish, for they cannot be written down."[26] Musical notation plays a role in the mythos of music as one of the practical solutions to the problem of transience. John Updike, in his short story "The Music School," describes his narrator's awe of the language of musical notation and the experience of the music student:

> that unique language which freights each note with a double meaning of position and duration, a language as finicking as

Latin, as laconic as Hebrew, as surprising to the eye as Persian or Chinese. How mysterious appears that calligraphy of parallel spaces, swirling clefs, superscribed ties, subscribed decrescendos, dots and sharps and flats! How great looms the gap between the first gropings of vision and the first stammerings of percussion! Vision, timidly, becomes percussion, percussion becomes music, music becomes emotion, emotion becomes—vision. Few of us have the heart to follow this circle to its end.

Guido of Arezzo's solmization syllables have just as profound significance in older literature. They may appear as a practical means of learning music or singing a melody at sight, as symbols for the scale, as a metaphor for order and completeness (through the entire gamut from *gamma* to *ut!*), or even as a new language. The delightful music lesson scene from Shakespeare's *The Taming of the Shrew* features a clumsy parody by Hortensio, who is masquerading as a music master in order to woo Bianca:

> (Bianca reads):
> ' "Gamouth" I am, the ground of all accord,
>   "A re," to plead Hortensio's passion;
>   "B mi," Bianca, take him for thy lord,
>   "C fa ut," that loves with all affection;
>   "D sol re," one cliffe, two notes have I;
>   "E la mi," show pity or I die.'
>
> Call *you* this gamouth? Tut, I like it not.
> Old fashions please me best; I am not so nice
> To change true rules for odd inventions.
>
> [Act 3, sc. 1:71–79]

Old music is especially to be preserved! Bianca's final line has a familiar ring: traditional music is best, conservation is better than innovation, and the means of musical learning (the scale and the syllables) are upholders of tradition and had better not be tampered with. Old songs are better than new songs, simple better than complex, and the way things were is better than the way they will ever be again! Music, the custodian of the past, is invoked as its preserver. We hear from another of Shakespeare's characters, Orsino in *Twelfth Night*:

Now, good Caesario, but that piece of song,
That good and antique song we heard last night.
Methought it did relieve my passion much,
More than light airs and recollected terms
Of these most brisk and giddy-paced times.

[Act 2, sc. 4 :2–6]

Like many other myth components, the idea of the "good old song" is
a symbol of primordial time (*in illo tempore*),[27] representing an escape from the relentlessness of clock time and a return to the mythical time that we sense is both our beginning and our end.

The temporal dimension of music is a rich source of mythical
imagery. Because time is a major structural dimension in many myths,
it is not surprising that it should have thematic significance for authors who describe and marvel at music's effects. Time is not only
the neutral medium for music's unfolding, but music superimposes
its own special time over clock time. And musical time with its regular metrical rhythms is a frequent metaphor for life itself, its due seasons and even course: to keep musical time is to lead an ordered life,
in harmony with what is appropriate. When the times are "out of
joint," life has gone wrong. As Shakespeare's Richard II muses:

Music do I hear?
Ha, ha! Keep time. How sour sweet music is
When time is broke and no proportion kept!
So is it in the music of men's lives,
And here have I the daintiness of ear
To check time broke in a disordered string,
But for the concord of my state and time
Had not an ear to hear my true time broke.

[Act 5, sc. 5 :41–48]

Harmony

The concept of harmony is at once the most abstract and the
most grandiose of all musical metaphors. In the preceding chapter
we saw that the Greeks defined harmony as an equilibrium: a unity
of diverse elements, a resolution of opposing tensions, and a mutually

proportioned arrangement of the various components. These abstractions have been embodied in a number of more concrete images, some of which we have already encountered: the blending of the material elements (earth, water, air, fire) and the four properties of nature (hot, cold, moist, dry), the four humors and four temperaments, the music of the spheres, the great chain of being, macrocosm and microcosm, correspondences between these and the times and seasons, and, finally, the summation of all these ideas in the image of universal harmony, symbolized by continuous music and dance in heaven.

Nowhere have these ideas been more systematically and extravagantly expressed than in Sir John Davies's Elizabethan poem "Orchestra," a cosmic vision of a universe linked by continuous dance. Davies describes the Creation of the world, the establishment of the various hierarchic levels of animal life and human society, the seven liberal arts, and the political orders as forms of the dance, ending with a vision of Queen Elizabeth surrounded by dancing courtiers. Two stanzas will illustrate Davies's imagery:[28]

> Dancing, bright lady, then began to be
> When the first seeds whereof the world did spring,
> The fire air earth and water, did agree
> By Love's persuasion, nature's mighty king,
> To leave their first disorder'd combating
> And in a dance such measure to observe
> As all the world their motion should preserve.
>
> So music to her own sweet tunes doth trip
> With tricks of 3, 5, 8, 15, and more;
> So doth the art of numb'ring seem to skip
> From even to odd in her proportion'd score;
> So do those skills whose quick eyes do explore
> The just dimensions both of earth and heaven
> In all their rules observe a measure even.

Davies's vision of harmony as a coupling, urged on by the god of love (Eros, Amor, Cupid), and a means of sustaining the universe by motion is entirely consistent with the mainstream of harmonic imagery. His verse on music celebrates the traditional union of the four mathematical disciplines of the quadrivium (music, arithmetic, geometry, and astronomy), in harmony with one another through their use of measure, number, and proportion. The idea that harmony brings order out of chaos is responsible for the inclusion of musical imagery in many creation myths, as in (once again) Dryden's "A Song for St. Cecilia's Day, 1687":

> From harmony, from heavenly harmony,
>   This universal frame began:
> When nature underneath a heap
>   Of jarring atoms lay,
>   And could not heave her head,
> The tuneful voice was heard from high,
>   'Arise, ye more than dead!'
> Then cold, and hot, and moist, and dry,
>   In order to their stations leap,
>   And Music's power obey.
> From harmony, from heavenly harmony,
>   This universal frame began:
>   From harmony to harmony
> Through all the compass of the notes it ran,
> The diapason closing full in Man.

In "East Coker," Eliot summons up a vision of a ritualistic dance of life, a celebration of the rhythm of the seasons and the harmonious coupling of man and woman:

> On a Summer midnight, you can hear the music
> Of the weak pipe and the little drum
> And see them dancing around the bonfire
> The association of man and woman
> In daunsinge, signifying matrimonie—
> A dignified and commodiois sacrament.
> Two and two, necessarye coniunction,
> Holding eche other by the hand or the arm
> Which betokeneth concorde. . . .
>
>   . . . Keeping time,
> Keeping the rhythm in their dancing
> As in their living in the living seasons
> The time of the seasons and the constellations

The time of milking and the time of harvest
The time of the coupling of man and woman
And that of beasts.

Harmony is also a metaphor for human health, emotional and mental balance. Stringed instruments often symbolize such a balance, and the regulation of the mind, body, and soul is often compared to tuning an instrument. When, in Shakespeare's *King Lear*, Cordelia sees her insane father, she exclaims:

O you kind gods,
Cure this great breach in his abused nature!
The untun'd and jarring senses, O wind up
Of this child-changed father!

[Act 4, sc. 7:13–16]

And the beginning of Lear's madness is described in these words: "and the strings of life began to crack" (act 5, sc. 3:216–17).

Being "in tune" is also to be attuned to one's part in an ensemble; the soul must be attuned to its proper relationship with God and with mankind. John Donne, in "A Hymne to God my God, in my Sickness," wrote:

Since I am coming to that holy roome,
   Where, with thy quire of Saints for evermore,
I shall be made thy Musique; As I come
   I tune the Instrument here at the door,
   And what I must doe then, thinke here before.

Instruments

Ancient cult associations are a source for many of the symbolic meanings assigned to musical instruments in Western art and literature: the lyre and kithara were the instruments of Apollo, prototypes of later stringed instruments and signifying all the Apollonian principles—harmony, formal clarity, reason, moderation, and objectivity. The Dionysian instrument was the aulos (perversely translated as *flute* by generations of Greek scholars who ought to have known better), a double-reed instrument of piercing tone and intensity. The aulos was associated with the world of the Greek theater and signified the formless, emotional, passionate, subjective, unrestrained, irrational melodic impulse. The true ancient flute was the syrinx which, along with the panpipes, symbolized the bucolic cult of Pan. The military cult of Ares claimed as its instrument the salpinx, a type of trumpet.

Stringed instruments, especially those that are plucked rather than bowed, have come to represent harmony. The instrument consists of many notes, and its strings—not fixed in pitch—require frequent tuning. The instrument itself is viewed as extrinsic to the body, an external symbol of internal order. Leo Spitzer has pointed out the remarkable fusion of the word-stems *cor* (heart) and *chord* (string) in modern Indo-European languages, e.g., such words as *chord*, *accord*, and *concord*.[29] Many strings produce a "chord," sounding together in harmony. The representation of the world as a lute in Elizabethan imagery evoked the concept of universal harmony and its need for constant fine tuning.

Asian traditions are remarkably similar: ancient Chinese authors stressed the significance of the ch'in, the most respected of their instruments, as a symbol of harmony. Players were instructed to approach the instrument only when in harmony with themselves and nature and in a purified state of mind and body. Bell symbolism seems to parallel that of stringed instruments—probably because bells are often hung in sets of several notes, perhaps also because of the early association (in the West) with the discoveries of Pythagoras. Bells too are completely extrinsic to the body and isolated physically; their harmony comes the closest to the world harmony sounded by the heavenly spheres. In recent literature and the visual arts, the guitar appears to have replaced older string instruments and has become the primary instrument for music therapy.

The flute is the most symbolic of all musical instruments: activated by the breath of life itself, it symbolizes the direct extension of the human spirit and, by means of its phallic shape, a projection of the bodily organ. Like other classes of cultural objects, musical instruments are often assigned gender; in most world musical cultures the flute is male, whereas drums are almost invariably female. Duke Ellington's song title "A Drum Is a Woman" is neither singular nor trivial!

Because the words for *spirit* and *moving air* are the same in many ancient languages (Greek and Hebrew, to name but two), the double meaning gives special significance to the breath as the bearer of man's soul. The tones of the flute are fixed, hence such concepts as tuning, harmony, temperament, and regulation do not arise. Rather the flute—and, by extension, most wind instruments—signifies not the *many* but the *one:* the internal, the intimate, the powerful, the sexual.

Percussion symbolism is more difficult to isolate, although the themes of signal, magic, ritual, marching, and the expelling of evil spirits are obvious associations. Percussion instruments appear in such an assortment of shapes, sizes, materials, and locations that generalization becomes impossible.

Finally, we must mention the very important Elizabethan concept of the organ as another symbol of world harmony.[30] As John Donne wrote in his "Obsequies to the Lord Harrington":

> Fair soule, which wast, not onely, as all soules bee,
> Then when thou wast infused, harmony,
> But did'st continue so; and now dost beare
> A part in Gods great organ, this whole Spheare.

6   The European tradition to 1800

THIS CHAPTER PRESENTS a highly selective overview of the intellectual history of music from the beginning of the Christian era to the year 1800. In the foreground of the narrative will be the gradual accumulation of ideas about music—ideas about its origins, substance, structure, process, purpose, perception, expressive means, and other value criteria. The chapter will examine common assumptions, new proposals, the persistence of older ideas, and the way in which some of these have been reinterpreted, mutated, and eventually supplanted by more popular ideas. The background frame of reference is an equally selective account of the major schools of Western philosophy, its issues, trends, and specific proposals put forward by the main thinkers, interwoven with brief modules that detail the musical values of the successive periods of music history. If there is any unity to this long time span, it is that aesthetic speculation was not considered to be one of the major tasks of philosophy and, consequently, many of the important musical values must be inferred from the musical product, as demonstrated through the composer's praxis.

The sources are varied: some philosophers (notably Augustine) wrote specifically about music, others, about art in general, still others, about beauty in the abstract. Indeed, most of the basic issues in philosophy have important potential applications to music: virtually every contribution to epistemology, the philosophy that seeks to explain how we can obtain valid knowledge through our senses and reason, has implications for artistic perception. It is not always possible, or even illuminating, to pin down the specific source of an idea.

Ideas are frequently "in the air," and the person who first articulates a concept is, more often than not, presenting a new interpretation, application, or clarification rather than new knowledge.

For convenience I adopt here the view of historians and philosophers that the year 1600 conveniently marks the start of the "modern" world. Students of music history, like other specialists, have their own set of historical periods: to the musician "ancient" means classical antiquity and "modern" the twentieth century, with most of the active musical repertoire in between. The following periodization has become standard for music and will be adopted herein:

—the Middle Ages, defined here as the vast interregnum between the final flowering of ancient civilization and 1400, a period dominated in Western Europe by feudalism and the philosophy of the Roman Church
—the Renaissance (ca. 1400–1600), bringing the secularization of the European musical world and the spread of Netherlands techniques of imitative counterpoint throughout the Continent and Great Britain
—the Baroque (1600–1750), from the beginnings of opera in Italy to the death of J. S. Bach
—the Classical (1750–1800), the age of the great Viennese composers—Haydn, Mozart, and the young Beethoven

But in philosophy it makes considerable sense to recognize the unity and coherence of ancient thought which held together until the beginning of the modern age. This includes the contributions of the major Greek philosophers, later Hellenistic and Roman authors, the Church Fathers, the systematic synthesis of these doctrines by the Scholastics of the medieval Roman Catholic Church, and such subsequent movements as the Florentine revival of Neo-Platonism. Modern philosophy, according to this somewhat simplified but convenient view, proceeds from circa 1600 with two contemporary schools: Cartesian rationalism, named after its first major author, René Descartes (1596–1650), which was primarily a continental tradition, and empiricism, mainly a British school of thought, of which Francis Bacon (1561–1626) was the first great representative. Together the two movements dominated European philosophy until the later eighteenth century. Meanwhile, a new school of thought had arisen in Germany, German idealism, which reached its height in the writings of Immanuel Kant (1724–1804). The philosophy of art took a quantum leap with the contributions of Kant, and since his day philosophers have come more and more to include artistic speculation among their tasks.

We will pass lightly over the three main schools of thought in later antiquity—the Stoics, Epicureans, and Skeptics. But two strong dissenting voices deserve special attention, if only to remind us that the aesthetic consensus was not universal. Philodemus, a first-century B.C. author of a treatise on music (the fragments of which were found in the ruins of Herculaneum), must be regarded as a major source for Epicurean aesthetic teachings. And Sextus Empiricus, an aggressively Skeptic philosopher from the second century A.D., seemed determined to shatter most of the traditional notions about music in his polemic, *Against the Musicians*.[1]

Philodemus denied vigorously the mimetic and ethical theories of music:

> Despite the nonsense talked by some, music is not an imitative art; nor is it true what he [Diogenes the Babylonian] says that although music does not mirror characters in imitative way, it does nevertheless reveal all the aspects of character which represent magnificence and baseness, heroism and cowardice, politeness and arrogance. Music does not bring this about in any greater measure than cooking.[2]

And Sextus argued that the main value of music is as a source of pleasure and distraction: "[Music] does not repress the mental state because it possesses a moderating influence, but because its influence is distracting; consequently, when tunes of that sort have ceased to sound, the mind, as though not cured by them, reverts to its original state."[3]

Philodemus and Sextus Empiricus, like many later philosophers, had great difficulties in justifying music's existence. Their writings give clear evidence of an ambivalent attitude toward the pleasures of sense perception: the senses are capable of giving pleasure in response to external sensation, but they cannot be trusted to give true testimony. Both authors saw music as a harmless diversion, pleasant but useless; in their view music was not a rational art, nor was its perception a cognitive act. Music did not symbolize, express, or represent anything but itself. No wonder that Philodemus found music of little value in *paideia* and remarked that it was mainly suitable for "dinner parties"![4] But Sextus went still further and claimed to prove, by means of his clever verbal games, that music was essentially an illusion—like sound and time, which he also said did not exist.[5] Their contributions to the philosophy of music were basically negative, but they are useful now in assessing similar positions taken by more recent authors. Formalistic philosophies such as theirs seldom win the hearts or dent the faith of those who wish to believe in music as a vehicle of metaphysical power, but their arguments serve as an antidote to the exaggeratedly transcendental claims made on behalf of music by some of its more fuzzy-minded advocates.

One of the most influential Hellenistic treatises on the philosophy of art is the remarkable short treatise on literary style, *On the Sublime*, attributed to Cassius Longinus of Palmyra (third century A.D.). The discovery and publication of this work in the mid-sixteenth century touched off a major attempt to define the qualities that produce elevation and greatness in art and to separate the sublime from the merely beautiful. Although Longinus addressed himself only incidentally to music, his ideas have had a profound influence on the aesthetics of music. He accepted the view that the aim of art was pleasure, as an end in itself, and that the *ekstasis* (absorption or transport) of the audience was the standard of excellence in literature. Style is the shadow of the author's personality and is communicated by intensity of feeling and grandeur of expression.

Longinus specified five necessary conditions for the sublime: the first two are inborn—robust, "full-blooded" ideas and strong emotion. The other three may be acquired through training: the proper construction of figures (figures of speech and of thought), nobility of diction, and the careful arrangement of words to produce the general effect of dignity and elevation. Longinus took music as a model and referred to speech as a "rational music" that can move the mind; and he assigned rhythm an important role in producing the sense of grandeur:

Nothing is of greater service in giving grandeur to such passages than the composition of the various members. . . . If they are united into a single system and embraced moreover by the bonds of rhythm, then by being merely rounded into a single period they gain a living voice. . . . Nothing demeans an elevated passage so much as a weak and agitated rhythm, . . . For all over-rhythmical passages at once become merely pretty and cheap; the effect of the monotonous jingle is superficial and stirs no emotion.[6]

Detailing the qualities of the sublime in art became an important task for seventeenth- and eighteenth-century authors.[7] Sublimity, in their view, was linked with the feelings of awe and terror inspired by the vastness and infinite power of nature; mountains, the sea, the sky, and night were cited as typical sources of the sublime. The discussion has continued in musical aesthetics, where size, intensity, complexity, and elevated content have been asserted as criteria for greatness.[8]

The most systematic treatise on beauty in later antiquity was written by Plotinus (ca. 204–270 A.D.), the most important representative of the Neo-Platonic movement that sought to codify Plato's teachings into a coherent system. Plotinus shared Plato's view that beauty is a transcendental quality and that the response to beauty is the soul's feeling of kinship with an eternal idea, absolute Being: "The material thing becomes beautiful—by communicating in the thought that flows from the Divine."[9] The path to absolute beauty, for Plotinus as for Plato, is an ascent: from the experience of sensuous beauty, to the contemplation of intellectual and moral beauty, and finally to that beauty which is truth itself.

The musician, according to Plotinus, illustrates one of the three ways to truth, by virtue of his affinity to beauty and his innate response to measure and "shapely pattern": "This natural tendency must be made the starting point to such a man; . . . he must be led to the Beauty that manifests itself through these forms; he must be shown that what ravished him was no other than the harmony of the intellectual world and the Beauty in that sphere." And, furthermore:

The arts are not to be slighted on the ground that they create by imitation of natural objects; for, to begin with, these natural objects are themselves imitations. . . . Any skill which, beginning with the observation of the symmetry of living things, grows to the symmetry of all life, will be a portion of the Power there which observes and meditates the symmetry reigning among all beings in the Intellectual Cosmos. Thus all music—since its thought is upon melody and rhythm—must be the earthly representation of the music there is in the rhythm of the Ideal Realm.[10]

Plotinus' vision of music as the earthly image of the harmony, proportions, and motions of the eternal cosmos—when supplemented by the doctrines of Christian theology—became the standard medieval explanation. It is, at the same time, an important source for later mystical and romantic theories of music as a link between humanity and divinity, the finite and the infinite.

The Middle Ages

Our discussion of the medieval philosophy of music will feature the proposals of two major authors—St. Augustine, Bishop of Hippo (354–430), and St. Thomas Aquinas (1225–1274)—who represent the initial and terminal stages of the process by which the Catholic philosophers of the Middle Ages came to terms with Greek philosophy and brought the doctrines of Plato and Aristotle into harmony with their own beliefs. Both authors shared the traditional ambivalence of the Roman Church toward art: they distrusted it because of its addictive sensory pleasures, its emphasis upon earthly beauty, and its lingering associations with pagan culture; but at the same time they were drawn to it because of its intrinsic excellence and ability to represent eternal beauty. Augustine was well aware of this tension: "I feel that our hearts are instigated to a more fervent devotion, if the words are sung, and less moved if the words are spoken only; that all our moods have a specific quality of their own to which certain melodies in song and voice correspond. It is this secret relationship which affects us. But still I am often overpowered through the pleasure of the senses."[11]

This same ambivalence marked the official attitude of the Church toward all the culture and thought of pagan Greece and Rome; while the instinctive reaction of some of the early Church Fathers (notably Tertullian) was to condemn all the wisdom of classical civilizations, the answer of the later medieval scholars was to preserve the ancient learning and transform it into an intellectual synthesis with accepted Christian teachings.

Aesthetic speculation is one of the major streams in Augustine's thought, perhaps because many of his views on art were formed before his conversion. His writings include a lost early work, *De Pulchro et Apto* (On the Beautiful and the Fitting), a complete treatise on music (*De Musica Libri Sex*), his celebrated *Confessions*, in which many important artistic questions are discussed, and a large number of scriptural commentaries containing musical references. Augustine's aesthetic criteria are similar to those of his Greek predecessors; where he surpasses earlier authors is in the depth of his insights into psychology and the perception of art.

We may represent the framework for Augustine's aesthetic doctrines by means of the following diagram:

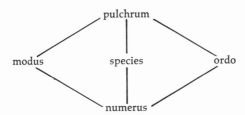

The necessary and sufficient conditions for beauty are provided in the aesthetic triad: *modus* (measure), *species* (form), *ordo* (order); and these in turn can only be reckoned on the basis of *numerus* (number). Augustine was fond of quoting the verse from The Wisdom of Solomon: "Thou hast ordered all things in number and measure and weight" (11:20). He held, with Plato and the Pythagorean tradition, that number was the fundamental principle of creation and that the being of forms could be recognized only by perceiving their numerical properties. Beauty is therefore judged by the mind. Augustine's concept of *ordo* goes far beyond the literal meaning of *taxis*, its Greek equivalent: in *The City of God*, *ordo* is defined as an arrangement of equal and unequal parts into an integrated complex in accordance with an end.[12] It is clear that the idea of *ordo* is intended to subsume such important criteria as harmony, proportion, symmetry, and perhaps even unity. The word *species* underwent a significant semantic development as an aesthetic term: its root meaning is either a *seeing* (active) or a *sight* (passive), but for Augustine its meaning was *outward appearance, visible form*. The next stage was the derivation of the adjective *speciosa*, a very popular word for *beautiful*, or—more literally—*sightly!*

Numerus is also the specific foundation for Augustine's theory and philosophy of music, as expounded in his *De Musica*. In some ways it is unfortunate that both the Greek words *arithmos* (number) and *rhythmos* (rhythm) were translated into Latin as *numerus;* much of the force of *rhythmos* is lost in this translation which blurs the distinction the Greeks were careful to draw between numbers in general and proper rhythmic proportions.[13] But Augustine cannot be faulted for lack of insight into the basic phenomena of rhythm and meter. The first five books of his treatise are addressed to the principles of musical rhythm, presenting the traditional poetic feet (iambic, trochaic, dactylic, anapestic, et al.) and specifying their correct use in the setting of Latin texts. But the sixth book, which was apparently written at a later time, is a much more profound analysis of the process by which musical rhythms are perceived, remembered, and evaluated. Here are Augustine's rhythmic categories, organized in a progression from the material/physical to the immaterial/spiritual/eternal:

> *numeri corporales,* sounding durations as produced by the voice or an instrument and the rhythms of the dance
>
> *numeri occursores,* these sounds as heard by the listener
>
> *numeri progressores,* the operation of sounds within the soul (*anima*) of the performer and the listener, causing motions of the soul
>
> *numeri recordabiles,* the sounds that we are able to reproduce, existing only in the memory and the imagination, conceived rhythms
>
> *numeri sensuales,* rhythms as perceived and evaluated (accepted or rejected) by movements of the soul
>
> *numeri iudiciales,* an a priori category implanted in the mind (*ratio*) by God and thus the highest of all the *numeri:* the rational contemplation of perfect, eternal rhythm[14]

No summary can do justice to the Augustinian theory of musical perception. Never before had anyone probed the operations of the mind with such profound insight into how it receives, processes, stores, imagines, and judges musical sensation. There are strong influences of Aristotle's theory of perception, but the entire frame of reference has been enlarged. Perception is a dialogue between *anima* and *ratio:* the sensual aspect of music speaks directly to the soul, but the judicial aspect appeals to the reason. Perception is an active search for likenesses: Augustine speaks of the soul's "straining" to conform to the sensations presented, accepting some and rejecting others. The creation of music, indeed of all the arts, is a mental act: "an active conformation (*affectio*) of the mind of the artist."[15]

Augustine defined music in this way: Musica est scientia bene modulandi.[16] We may assume that the word *scientia* is used here in its broadest sense—as knowledge; the word *modulandi* invites interpretation. It is related to a number of root meanings: to measure, regulate, limit, move, set in motion, change, model, or shape. I suggest that we may interpret it as the act of shaping a flexible, intangible substance (sound) into a form that can imprint itself upon the responsive sense and intellect. As Augustine explains: "Through this mental movement rhythm is imprinted on his faculty of mental activity, *mens*, and he achieves the active conformation, *affectio*, which is called art. . . . This rhythm is immutable and eternal, with no inequality possible in it. Therefore it must come from God."[17]

So that rhythm is best which best corresponds to ideal rhythm and motion; the perceiving mind judges on the basis of innate standards of order, unity, and proportion; and art presents form as it ought to be. And because order can be perceived only by the reason, the pleasures of order can be felt only through those senses that can perceive order—as Augustine once remarked, "One cannot smell or taste reasonably!"[18] And by means of that order, "we weave our pleasures into one."[19]

Augustine's speculations on the nature of time form another important strand of ideas that runs throughout his writings. With time, as with music, his interest was directed at the psychology of perception, which he saw as a dynamic process. In the eleventh book of the *Confessions* Augustine analyzes the interaction of music and time in the mind:

> Suppose I am about to recite a song that I know. Before I begin, my expectation is extended over the whole. But as soon as I have begun, whatever part I have plucked from the future and let fall into the past takes its station in my memory. Thus the life of my actions is divided into the memory of what I have sung and the expectation of what I am about to sing. But all the time my at-

tention is present, through which the future must pass until it has become the past. The farther I proceed, the shorter my expectation and the longer my memory, until my expectation is finally used up—at the point when my actions are completed and have passed over into memory.[20]

A final word of evaluation: Augustine is without doubt a landmark figure in the philosophy of music and possibly the keenest observer of the musical process before modern times. Certain admirable qualities stand out in his writings—a tough-minded intellectual honesty, self-knowledge, penetrating analytic skill, psychological insight, and, above all, a rare delight in music, both on a sensory and intellectual level.

The contributions of St. Thomas Aquinas to the philosophy of art are few in number but have had great influence upon later authors. His writings represent the Scholastic philosophy at its most mature stage, a unified conceptual system—a *summa*—that explained the interaction of nature and man, God and the world, action and knowledge in accordance with Christian doctrine. Although Aquinas and the earlier Schoolmen did not list aesthetic inquiry among their major tasks, they could not help but consider such questions as part of their system.

In his masterpiece, the *Summa theologica,* St. Thomas distinguishes between the beautiful and the good:

> The beautiful is the same as the good, and they differ in aspect only. For since good is what all seek, the notion of good is that which calms the desire; while the notion of the beautiful is that which calms the desire, by being seen or known. Consequently those senses chiefly regard the beautiful, which are the most cognitive, *viz.,* sight and hearing, as ministering to reason; . . . Thus it is evident that beauty adds to goodness a relation to the cognitive faculty: so that *good* means that which simply pleases the appetite; while the *beautiful* is something pleasant to apprehend.[21]

But the most famous of Aquinas's statements on aesthetics is the passage from 1.39.8 of the same work, in which he sets out the three necessary conditions for beauty: "beauty includes three conditions: integrity or perfection [*integritas sive perfectio*], since those

things which are impaired are by that very fact ugly; due proportion
or harmony [*debita proportio sive consonantia*]; and lastly, brightness, or clarity [*claritas*], whence things are called beautiful which
have a bright color."[22]

What Aquinas meant by *claritas* has been analyzed and argued
for centuries. The idea of beauty as light, radiance, clarity, or color
was not a concept original with him. It entered the formal vocabulary
of aesthetics in the writings of the fifth-century Christian Platonist,
the Pseudo-Dionysius, who held that beauty was an emanation, the
radiance of Absolute Being; his formula for beauty was *consonantia
et claritas*, harmony and radiance. The Scholastic philosophers accepted this formula but developed the idea of *lux* or *claritas* in a
number of ways: Robert Grosseteste (1175–1253) praised light as
that which makes all things visible and thus shows their beauty in
the highest degree; it is also simple, uniform, and thus in the most
perfect of all proportions. For St. Bonaventure (1221–1274) light was
more than that which displays beauty: "Light is the most beautiful,
the most pleasant, and the best among physical things."[23] Albert the
Great (1193–1280), the teacher of Aquinas, held that beauty was the
radiance of form shining through matter. And Ulrich of Strassburg
(d. 1287), a fellow student of Aquinas's, further developed this line
of thinking: "Beauty is concord [*consonantia*] and clarity [*claritate*]
as Dionysius says. But here concord is the material factor and clarity
the formal factor. Just as physical light is formally and causally the
beauty of all visible things, so intellectual light is the formal cause
of all substantial form and all material form."[24]

For a modern interpretation we turn to James Joyce's novel *A
Portrait of the Artist as a Young Man*, in which his hero, Stephen
Dedalus, analyzes St. Thomas's three conditions for beauty in language that has, as his friend Lynch jokingly remarks, "the true scholastic stink."

The connotation of the word, Stephen said, is rather vague.
Aquinas uses a term which seems to be inexact. It baffled me for
a long time. It would lead you to believe that he had in mind
symbolism or idealism, the supreme quality of beauty being a
light from some other world, the idea of which the matter is but
the shadow, the reality of which it is but the symbol. I thought
he might mean that *claritas* is the artistic discovery and repre-

sentation of the divine purpose in anything or a force of generalisation which would make the esthetic image a universal one, make it outshine its proper conditions. But that is literary talk. . . . The radiance of which he speaks is the scholastic *quidditas,* the *whatness* of a thing. This supreme quality is felt by the artist when the esthetic image is first conceived in the imagination. The mind in that mysterious instant Shelley likened beautifully to a fading coal. The instant wherein that supreme quality of beauty, the clear radiance of the esthetic image, is apprehended luminously by the mind which has been arrested by its wholeness and fascinated by its harmony is the luminous silent stasis of esthetic pleasure, . . .[25]

The significance of the term *claritas* for the later philosophy of art goes far beyond whatever Aquinas might have had in mind. The semantic breadth of the word has given rise to a number of interpretations: the light of pure Being, a making visible or audible, a quality in itself (whose properties are simplicity, uniformity, and intensity), the luminosity of form, or the defining of an aesthetic image on the senses and in the mind. The other standard medieval criteria for beauty (order, number, equality, proportion, harmony, symmetry) were quantifiable, but *claritas* signifies a quality—an intangible property not subject to precise measure. I would like to suggest that *claritas* refers to the "presentational" quality of an art work, a special luminous intensity that marks a work of real excellence. And in the case of music, the idea of *claritas* is a powerful metaphor for the phenomenon of music: a becoming audible, the radiation of complex, harmonic vibration from its source, and its definition as tonal structure and motion in the perceiving mind.

By way of summary, let us consider the relationship between medieval philosophy and medieval music. The philosophers of the Middle Ages have often been accused of living in ivory towers, indulging in amateurish speculations and mental gymnastics that were without impact on artistic praxis, and failing to grasp the real values implicit in actual works of art. To what degree were the standard medieval aesthetic criteria demonstrated in a typical musical work?

Let us review the common assumptions about art and beauty: an art work was, first of all, a symbol—a representation of some aspect of the universal and modeled upon nature, organized using ideal forms and proportions, and mathematicized into modular components. It was created for an end (knowledge, revelation, regulating the soul) and hence is useful, was made according to rule and produced in clearly defined types, idealized rather than particularized, can be interpreted on various levels of meaning, reveals form and transforms matter (without producing anything new), and is capable of giving pleasure. Its highest property is beauty, a gift of God and a transcendental quality, closely linked with the good; beauty requires the combination of harmony (order, proportion, symmetry, et al.), unity, and "clarity," has form as its essence, and may be perceived in two stages—directly, through sensory experience, and indirectly, through contemplation.

The isorhythmic motet of the twelfth and thirteenth centuries embodies these values to such a high degree that it is tempting to overstate the case.[26] This type of motet is a polyphonic composition for three or four equal voices, built on the foundation of a *cantus prius factus*—a pre-existent melody from the repertoire of Gregorian chant that serves as a structural girder for the composition. This *cantus firmus* was broken into even melodic segments, separated by rests, and sung to a rigid, repetitive rhythmic pattern in longer durations than the upper parts. The tonal structure of the whole was defined by the modality of the *cantus firmus*, the tenor (lit. holding) line; the other parts were regulated to this structural line by strict rules of interval succession and voice motion, but only loosely to each other (not unlike the social obligations of feudalism). The motet was written in consecutive layers, and the composer could not foresee the eventual outcome; each added voice became a commentary on the *cantus firmus* and the previous accretions, much like the glosses and commentaries of the medieval monastic scholars.

Most medieval motets are anonymous and were not considered as the property of individual composers—or even as individual compositions: musical materials were freely borrowed, voices were added or deleted, new pieces were built over an old *cantus* or including a complete pre-existent composition. One gets the impression that the world of medieval music was a cosmos in which each composition was potentially related to all the rest by common substance and structure. The composer was a craftsman, prizing technique more highly than talent.

The ideal sound in the motet was not a blend or fusion but a mixture in which each voice stood out clearly and separately; this was achieved by the use of more than one text (often in different languages, e.g., French and Latin), the juxtaposition of sacred and secular texts, performance by virtually any heterogeneous mix of voices and instruments, and sharply incisive rhythmic patterns. The motet was unified to a very high degree by the presence of the *cantus firmus*, the underlying melodic and rhythmic modal idioms, the phonetic content of the text, and the thought—often in very subtle ways. The music lacked a strong sense of tonal direction, because the added voices oscillate around the *cantus firmus* within the same range and using a very limited set of pitches; the result is a sense of stasis, of repetition but no motion (interpreted as "change of place"), a music more of "being" than "becoming."

The cluttered texture of the medieval motet was not organized to promote clarity of perception, nor was it suggested that the listener focus on any one of the superimposed texts; the words were not expressed in any specific way, and the work was designed to be perceived through contemplation—of structure, representation, and meaning. Its musical substance was pre-existent matter, hence no creation took place. The grouping of the material into arbitrary rhythmic and melodic units revealed the form—not of the piece but of the genre—and merely reorganized the musical substance. The source of all form was number—the imposition of pattern upon tune, time, and text.

We may ask wherein the quality of *claritas* is to be found? Perhaps in the general intensity of feeling and tension that is typical of medieval sacred music, in the overall purpose of the combined texts, or in some of the other qualitative aspects of the composition. Performing the musical work is in itself a manifestation of its substance and structure, which brings us to another basic question: What did a motet represent? A combination of thoughts, a mathematical construct, Gothic tonal architecture, a commentary on a repeated and beloved melody-cum-text, a symbol of the universal harmony, a glimpse of the divine? It could (like allegory) be interpreted variously as direct sensory experience, a moral commentary on the scripture lesson for the day, a subtle blend of Christian scripture and secular thought, a symbolic representation of feudal society and the medieval world.

We should define how one perceives by means of contemplation, which Hugh of St. Victor described as the "keen and free gazing of the soul at things scattered in time and space."[27] Contemplation was said to differ from meditation in that it dealt with evident things, whereas meditation dealt with things hidden from the mind. And Richard of St. Victor recognized three successive levels of contemplation: broadening of the mind (achieved by means of human abilities), elevation of the mind (through God's grace), and an alienation of the mind—the ultimate transfiguration of the human spirit.[28]

Most accounts of medieval music, including ours, give a distorted picture by focusing so sharply on the music and thought of the Church. No matter how the Roman Church dominated the life and works of the Middle Ages, it cannot be held responsible for all musical activity. The other important stream of music was the tradition of secular solo song, including both the songs of the noble poet/musicians (trouvères, troubadours, and minnesingers) and the vulgar songs of the lower-class professional musicians (such as the minstrels and jongleurs). Song is a constant throughout the evolution of musical style in the West, with its continuity in themes—love, joy, sorrow, dance, religious fervor, celebration of the seasons—and continuity in style. Song styles, with some obvious exceptions, tend to favor singable tunes of limited range, simple rhythmic patterns, clear text-setting, emotional expressiveness, phrase lengths that do not exceed the duration of a breath, and a relatively clear texture that exposes the vocal melody and supports it with a discreet accompaniment. More elaborate musical constructions vary with the changing fashions of the period, but solo songs maintain a remarkable similarity of structure. And in many instances throughout the history of music, the secular song is featured as one of the characteristic musical genres of its era, e.g., the Burgundian chanson of the fifteenth century, the lute ayre of Elizabethan England, and the nineteenth-century German lied.

We should add a few remarks on medieval rhythm: little is known about the proper rhythmic interpretation of early medieval music, since the notation is often imprecise and extremely difficult to decode. Until the early fourteenth century, musical rhythm was entirely dependent upon the rhythmic patterns of speech—the traditional poetic meters (iambic, trochaic, dactylic, anapestic, et al.) and the structural patterns of formal poetry. The result was what has often been called "the eternal triple meter of the Middle Ages," supported intellectually by its Trinitarian associations—God as Father,

"The Temple of Music," from Robert Fludd, *Utriusque cosmi . . . historia,*
Oppenheim, 1617–1619. This famous engraving is a graphic representation
of the components of *musica practica:* the scale, instruments, number proportions, rhythmic notation, clefs, and the proper locations of the three
types of hexachords. At the base Pythagoras observes the harmonic relationships produced by the sounds of proportioned hammers. The temple is dedicated to the patronage of Apollo, shown with his lyre. The swirls on the
tower represent the organs of hearing. Cronus with his scythe, atop an
hourglass and a clock dial, symbolizes the relationship between musical time
and clock time. Courtesy of Lilly Library, Indiana University, Bloomington,
Indiana.

Son, and Holy Spirit. Philippe de Vitry's formulation of an indigenous system of musical rhythm stands as one of the great landmarks
in music history: music thereby became independent of the principles
of prosody, developed a much wider range of patterns and durations,
established duple and triple meters as equals, and evolved a steeper
hierarchy of beats, beat divisions and subdivisions, beat groupings,
phrases, and higher architectonic levels.[29] The medieval theory of music was quite naturally concerned with rhythmic problems, especially
the new notations and their interpretation. But questions of pitch
continued to occupy most of the attention of music theorists: how to
recognize each of the eight ecclesiastical modes, guidelines for editing
a melody if it is notated incorrectly, and—most important of all—the
articulation of the set of rules governing the combination of notes into
the texture that became known as *counterpoint* (in Latin, *punctus
contra punctum* means literally "note-against-note"). It was this technique that was to bring about the great flowering of musical style in
the Renaissance.

Toward the modern world

In most views of the history of ideas, the Renaissance is seen as
a period of high artistic accomplishment but limited speculative activity; the contributions of artists outweigh by far those of philosophers
and scholars. The outstanding achievements of Renaissance aesthetics
are concerned with the visual arts and poetics. After the long and relatively static Middle Ages, the Renaissance years brought a burst of
fresh artistic energy—a period of rapid secularization, social change,
high mobility, and technological development in such fields as music
printing and instrument making. Musical style became more personal
and spread quickly from country to country, especially through the
travels of the Netherlands composers who brought their contrapuntal
skill to virtually every court in Europe. But they found the most fer-
tile soil for their craft in Italy, the spiritual home of the Renaissance,
where Flemish techniques were grafted onto a flourishing tradition of
native song and a superb repertoire of vernacular poetry; there the
Italian madrigal was developed by several generations of gifted composers into the most typical musical genre of the High Renaissance.
Musical style in the Renaissance was the product of a number of

significant changes both in technique and in values. While medieval music was confined to a relatively narrow range and written for equal voices, Renaissance composers expanded the usable musical space to approximately four octaves. It is not clear what is cause and what effect, but several related developments may be noted: the delineation of specific voice parts (cantus, altus, tenor, bassus) with individual ranges, the emergence of the bass as a foundation for the sound structure, and a dawning concept of harmony—still fairly primitive but expressed in a growing awareness of sonority and chord, occasional passages restricted to chordal motion, a less melodic bass voice that moved more by fourths and fifths than by step, and a tendency to cadence frequently on sustained chords. Two ideas came slowly to full consciousness in Renaissance theory: the gradual groupings of modal scale patterns into major and minor modes, and the recognition of the triad as a vertical entity.

A *cantus firmus* was no longer the indispensable matrix for a musical composition; its place was taken by imitative techniques that distributed the melodic activity among all the parts and treated them as equals. Musical structure became a series of "points" of imitation separated by clear cadences, and musical substance was regarded as new and unique—rather than a processing of and commentary on pre-existent material. In short, "free" composition became a possibility. The unifying element was the imitated motive, uniting all voices in a tight polyphonic web.

Many of the older medieval values were no longer operative: the medieval preference for a generalized expression of the meaning of a musical work gave way to an array of specific techniques for expressing individual words, thoughts, and emotions. The concept of a musical work or genre was no longer a collective one but a series of distinctly individual works. Musical construction was no longer a mechanistic coordination of modular patterns but a coherent flow and organic development; individual lines were given independent rhythmic structure, loosely coordinated by the *tactus* (beat) and resulting in a rich texture of cross-rhythms and accents. Other significant values of Renaissance music include the homogeneous blending of sounds, the savor of sustained vertical sonorities (chords), clearly articulated cadences at regular intervals, the careful timing of dissonance so as to provide a regular rhythm of tension and release, and a feeling of tonal motion and direction—a music of "becoming" (as opposed to the medieval view of music as eternal "being"). Renaissance music was less a symbol and more a reality, intended to be perceived and enjoyed for its own sake, appealing directly to the senses and expressive of human feeling. Beauty was an earthly property of things and existed to give pleasure to the senses. Music was valued as an autonomous art, independent of both poetry and liturgy. Instrumental music continued to be modeled upon vocal style but was beginning to evolve a number of characteristic genres: theme and variations, imitative pieces such as the ricercar (the ancestor of the fugue), and free, rhapsodic pieces such as the fantasia and toccata.

Musicians of the Renaissance became increasingly aware that they were living in the midst of exciting, innovative times. Joannes Tinctoris, the first major theorist of the Renaissance, wrote in the late fifteenth century that "at this time . . . the possibilities of our music have been so marvelously increased that there appears to be a new art, if I may so call it, . . ."[30] and again, "Further, although it seems beyond belief, there does not exist a single piece of music, not composed within the last forty years, that is regarded by the learned as worth hearing."[31]

Because this account of the history of musical aesthetics is about to take a large leap, a few reflections are in order. Few if any of the values held by ancient authors had been seriously questioned by thinkers of the Middle Ages; even the translation of the ancient Greek aesthetic principles into the Christian theology and world view seems to have been accomplished without significant distortion. New interpretations had been proposed, new emphasis had been placed upon the spectator and the act of perception, new areas of artistic activity had come under scrutiny—but the ancient system of values remained largely intact. Before the philosophy of art was to take a new direction, the world had to change: the world of medieval society, art, and thought, as well as the view of the physical universe and man's place in it. The Renaissance years brought such a change—first in the humanistic movement and in the products of practical artists, then in the natural sciences with the investigations of Copernicus, Kepler, Galileo, and Newton. The fifteenth and sixteenth centuries were years of an unprecedented outpouring of artistic activity, and their literature is dominated by practical men, not philosophers. Treatises on painting, poetics, and music were addressed to practical issues, and the leading school of Italian philosophy represented an attempt to construct yet another synthesis of the teachings of Plato and later Greek authors.

The revision in aesthetics took place over several centuries as the ancient assumptions about art and beauty were gradually replaced by newer ideas. Perhaps the most characteristic feature of "modern" aesthetics is the lack of universal assumptions. One can detect trends, fashionable new proposals, new insights, and new concerns, but no axioms, no set of propositions on which nearly everyone can agree.

As a frame of reference for the following discussion, let us consider a number of the new proposals that contradict some of the most basic assumptions of ancient and medieval aesthetic theory.

   1   Art is creativity. The artist, working primarily from his imagination, makes something that is new. Talent is necessary if he is to become a good artist; genius, if he is to become great.

   2   The being of each work of art is unique, individual, novel, and creates its own rules. An artist works in his own way and strives to achieve his own personal style.

   3   Art is not necessarily a representation of nature. It can improve upon nature, distort nature, or dispense with nature altogether—it can even be abstract.

   4   The primary purpose of art is expression, the communication of the artist's feelings through his work and to his audience. For him art fulfills a basic human need.

   5   The truth of art is not the truth of science. Art is essentially a mysterious and irrational activity. The perception of works of art is a form of knowledge but it is not knowledge of the external world.

   6   Art is diverse and not subject to any absolute canons or standards. Beauty is subjective—it is not a property of things but of our reactions to things. Our judgments are subjective and relative.

   7   Art can be a kind of play.

   8   Art exists for its own sake, not for any higher goal.

These propositions are not interdependent, nor have they ever been proposed as a set; they are surely incomplete. But they indicate some of the coming trends in the philosophy of art that were eventually to have an impact upon musical composition.

The years after 1600 were crucial ones for Western philosophy: the medieval/Renaissance world view was slowly crumbling, and the relative positions of man, mind, and music had to be redefined in the light of modern scientific discoveries. Philosophical inquiry began to focus upon the microcosmos—the individual, his mental activity, and the means by which he could obtain true knowledge. The seventeenth and eighteenth centuries are appropriately described as the Age of Reason and the Enlightenment. The ways in which the new methods and speculations infused new ideas into the philosophy of music will be the subject of the following pages.

Reason, nature, and progress were the three main themes in Enlightenment thought: the world (including the world of art) could be grasped by reason, it was based on natural principles, and history was moving in a favorable direction. The rationalist movement in philosophy is usually held to originate with the writings of René Descartes (1596–1650), and from his surname the phrase "Cartesian rationalism" was derived; Leibnitz and Spinoza are perhaps his most distinguished successors. Rationalism teaches that we can obtain valid knowledge of the world from two sources: the innate ideas and principles that we all possess and our power of reasoning. Rationalism stresses the importance of the a priori, principles that can be known to be true, independent of our experience—such as the principle of contradiction: we do not need prior experience to know, for example, that a sound cannot be both short and long at the same time. Rationalism in art tends to generalize, idealize, and favor creation by rule; as Samuel Johnson wrote in *Rasselas* (1759): "The business of a poet is to examine not the individual, but the species; to remark general properties and large appearances: he does not number the streaks of the tulip" (chap. 10). This climate of ideas proved highly favorable for the evolution of theories of music, and music theory began slowly to be transformed from a descriptive to a prescriptive discipline: although theorists continued to base their speculations on musical practice (especially the proper interpretation of the basso continuo, as will be shown below), they sought more and more to identify the principles by which music was organized and the implementation of those principles into an ideal musical system.

Descartes had relatively little to say on aesthetics, although he outlined a general theory of expression in his *Passions of the Soul* (1649). He also wrote a short treatise on music in 1618, while he was serving in the army. Although it does not deserve to be ranked among his major writings and is naïve in comparison to the more technical music treatises of his time, it still holds considerable interest for musicians. A few of his preliminary observations follow.

1   All senses are capable of experiencing pleasure.

2   For this pleasure a proportional relationship of some kind between the object and the sense itself must be present.

3   The object must be such that it does not fall on the sense in too complicated or confused a fashion.

4   An object is perceived more easily by the senses when the difference of the parts is smaller.

5   We may say that the parts of a whole object are less different when there is greater proportion between them.

6   This proportion must be arithmetic, not geometric.

7   Among the sense-objects, the most agreeable to the soul is neither that which is perceived most easily nor that which is perceived with the greatest difficulty; it is that which does not quite gratify the natural desire by which the senses are carried to the objects, yet is not so complicated that it tires the senses.

8   Finally, it must be observed that variety is in all things most pleasing.[32]

Descartes was not certain that rationalistic principles applied to the creation of art. Despite his emphasis on clear-headed intellectual method, he held that the aesthetic experience was subjective and that art was basically irrational. In a letter of March 18, 1630, to Marin Mersenne, Descartes outlined his views on the subjectivity of beauty and implied that the response to beauty is a kind of conditioned reflex.

> But neither the beautiful nor the pleasant signifies anything other than the attitude of our judgment to the object in question. And since human judgments are various, it is impossible to find any definite measure for the beautiful or the pleasant. I cannot explain this any better than I once did in my *Music*. What pleases most people can be called simply the most beautiful; but that is not anything very well defined.
>
> Secondly, that which moves some to dance, causes others to wish to cry. The reason for this is that certain images in our memories are aroused: those who once found pleasure in dancing to a particular melody, will want to do so again, when they hear it anew. And conversely, if someone has suffered while listening to the sounds of a *galliarde*, he will certainly be sad when he

hears it again. If one were to thrash a dog five or six times to the sound of a violin, when he heard that sound again, he would surely whine and run away.[33]

Descartes's methods may have been rationalistic, but his views on art are distinctly empirical and demonstrate that the application of rational principles to the organization of music requires some professional definition. It remained for one of his most distinguished successors, Jean-Philippe Rameau (1683–1764), to make such a successful application. Although Rameau was clearly one of the most significant French composers of the eighteenth century (specializing in opera and harpsichord music), his contributions to the theory of music are even of greater importance. In a series of treatises that began with the publication of his *Traité de l'harmonie* in 1722, Rameau gradually developed a comprehensive theory of harmony that was both a model of the musical thought of his era and the definitive statement of the harmonic principles governing music between 1650 and 1900.

It is no exaggeration to say that the later history of harmonic theory to the beginning of the twentieth century consisted of filling in the blanks Rameau left and footnoting some of his observations. To him we owe the recognition of the principle of inversion (of chords and of intervals), the theory of chord root, the generation of chords in imitation of the overtone series, the organization of harmonic progression according to the fundamental bass (the imaginary line formed by the successive chord roots), the V-I cadence as the model for normative harmonic progression, the tonic chord as harmonic center of the scale, the concept of IV as subdominant, the relationship between major and minor keys, the origin of seventh chords, the preparation and resolution of harmonic dissonance, and numerous other concepts that have become accepted facts of the system of tonal harmony.[34] Rameau's ideas were constantly in a state of evolution, so it is often difficult to determine his final position on a given topic, but there is scarcely an aspect of eighteenth-century musical practice that his penetrating analysis fails to illuminate.

How, specifically, do Rameau's harmonic speculations reflect the rationalistic movement in philosophy? First, he held that the rules of art were firmly based on principles of nature—acoustic facts such as the overtone series, the discovery of which was announced in 1714 by

Joseph Sauveur, and the interval ratios derived from the successive divisions of a string. He described the normative in musical harmony and claimed that tonal harmony was unconsciously molded by certain innate concepts—the tension of dissonance and the relative repose of consonance, the tendency for dissonance to resolve, the instability of chromatic tones, the stability of a simple triad with its root in the bass, the basic psychological opposition of major and minor keys, and simple rhythmic phenomena such as beat, accent, and meter. Given these "facts," all that remained was for the mind to deduce the full set of harmonic laws and confirm their existence by observing musical practice. Theorists since his time have disagreed on the question of whether music is more a product of lawful nature or whimsical art—but even the most empirical thinker cannot deny the influence of certain basic physical phenomena on the structure of tonal music.

Francis Bacon, in his *Cogitata et Visa* (1607), captured the essence of the rationalist and empiricist positions: "Empiricists are like ants, they collect and put to use; but rationalists, like spiders, spin threads out of themselves."[35] Rameau was certainly a spider, but the threads that he spun and wove were derived by sound natural instincts and attached with a skillful knowledge born of careful observation of the world. Clearly another important group of philosophers considered themselves ants and preferred not to risk speculations which experience could not validate.

According to the empirical stance, knowledge is attained only through experience—and experience in turn is obtained by the exercise of our senses and that which is discovered by means of the senses. John Locke (1632–1704) described the mind as a "blank slate" (tabula rasa) waiting to receive the imprint of experience.[36] Understandably the empiricists were reluctant to consider phenomena in terms of matter and causation; they preferred to discuss substance in terms of how it is perceived by the mind, and all doctrines of cause-and-effect were suspect. They found it safer to describe a sequence of events simply as "what comes after what."

So the method of the empiricists was, as Bacon suggested, to gather evidence, without any preconceived ideas, and draw conclusions based on the accumulation of evidence. Bacon attempted to reduce the possibilities for error in his enumeration of the famous "four idols"—mental weaknesses that are to be avoided in the search for true knowledge: "There are four classes of idols which beset men's minds. To these for the sake of distinction I have assigned names—calling the first class *Idols of the Tribe;* the second, *Idols of the Cave;* the third, *Idols of the Market-place;* the fourth, *Idols of the Theatre.*"[37]

To interpret, with examples taken from our attitudes toward new music: by "idols of the tribe" Bacon meant the common failings of mankind—such as the fear of revealing one's ignorance (the "emperor's new clothes" syndrome), which can lead to an overly facile acceptance of incompetence. His "idols of the cave" are the blind spots and peculiar quirks of each individual; mine, for example, include an instinctively negative reaction to electronic tone, which has proved a real obstacle in my efforts to appreciate electronic music. "Idols of the market-place" are, as Bertrand Russell suggests, "errors caused by the tendency of the mind to be dazzled with words, an error particularly rampant in philosophy."[38] We worship these idols when we are persuaded to reject a composer's music by the rhetoric of his critics—or when we are persuaded to accept it by means of the rhetoric in his program notes! And Bacon's "idols of the theatre" are the errors that arise when we are influenced by movements, schools of thought, systems, and the like; we fall into such an error when our judgment is colored by a composer's writing in a manner that is "in" or that adheres to a particular school of composition, e.g., total serialism or minimalism.

A long line of empirical philosophers, primarily British, addressed themselves to problems of sensory experience and artistic perception and, in the process, made important contributions to the philosophy of music. These included Thomas Hobbes (1588–1679), Locke, David Hume (1711–1776), Lord Shaftesbury (1671–1713), Joseph Addison (1672–1719), George Berkeley (1685–1753), and Edmund Burke (1729–1797). Only a few of their proposals can be mentioned here.

If the rationalist emphasis on a priori principles and sets of rules tended to idealize art (in design and proportion) and stress the typical, the normative, and the general, the empirical philosophy tended to promote the following cluster of ideas: the weakening of traditional critical standards and the validity of subjective judgments; a general attitude of skepticism toward any artistic dogmas; the importance of the individual, the specific, and the unusual in art; the idea of genius—a great person who can produce great art by defying the rules; new emphasis on the value of sensation itself and the pleasure it brings; heightened emotional content of art; and recognition of the value of creative imagination. These ideas brought a flood of new aesthetic speculations and added new dimensions to the concept of beauty that had prevailed since ancient times.

Both Hobbes and Locke stressed the role of imagination as a source of creativity and developed the very important theory of the association of ideas, the tendency for ideas to form clusters related by similarity, proximity, or some other connecting principle. In the eighteenth century, associationism was often taken to be one of the important explanations for the aesthetic response; today the principle of association seems more useful as a theory of the creative process.

In his 1757 essay, "Of the Standard of Taste," David Hume carefully analyzed the changing concept of beauty and suggested the possibility of a universal standard of taste. The idea of beauty begins to acquire new connotations: it no longer has objective status but resides in our feelings, emotions, and subjective response to the work of art: "Beauty is no quality in things themselves: it exists merely in the mind which contemplates them; and each mind perceives a different beauty. One person may even perceive deformity, where another is sensible of beauty; and every individual ought to acquiesce in his own sentiment, without pretending to regulate those of others. . . ." Nevertheless, Hume believed that this general statement deserves to be modified somewhat by our common sense:

> But though poetry can never submit to exact truth, it must be confined by rules of art, discovered to the author either by genius or observation. If some negligent or irregular writers have pleased, they have not pleased by their transgressions of rule or order, but in spite of these transgressions: they have possessed other beauties, . . . But though all the general rules of art are founded only on experience and on the observation of the common sentiments of human nature, we must not imagine that, on every occasion, the feelings of men will be conformable to these rules. Those finer emotions of the mind are of a very tender and delicate nature, and require the concurrence of many favorable circumstances to make them play with facility and exactness. . . .

So, although the judgment of beauty is ultimately subjective, it does stand on certain artistic principles, and those who have the proper refinement and training should be able to agree on the excellence of an individual work. In Hume's writing we see the emergence of a theory of criticism which every reviewer would do well to read. We conclude with Hume's description of the good critic: "Strong sense, united to delicate sentiment, improved by practice, perfected by comparison, and cleared of all prejudice, can alone entitle critics to this valuable character; and the joint verdict of such, wherever they are to be found, is the true standard of taste and beauty."[39]

We may note that beauty in the eighteenth century is seldom discussed with such formalistic concepts as proportion, order, unity, variety, or any other similar standard that can be intellectually perceived. Instead beauty is held to be that which makes a direct, immediate, and qualitative appeal to our senses, affections, and passions. In an important passage, Shaftesbury emphasizes the immediacy of our perception of beauty through some sort of "inward eye."

> Is there then . . . a natural beauty of figures? and is there not as natural a one of actions? No sooner the eye opens upon figures, the ear upon sounds, than straight the beautiful results and grace and harmony are known and acknowledged. No sooner are actions viewed, no sooner the human affections and passions discerned . . . than straight an inward eye distinguishes, and sees the fair and shapely, the amiable and admirable, apart from the deformed, the foul, the odious, or the despicable.[40]

Two of Shaftesbury's other contributions to aesthetic theory deserve mention: first, his contention that the satisfaction that art brings is a disinterested one, in which the spectator's perception is detached from his own self-interest and ego drives;[41] and second, his citation of the wild, fearsome, and irregular aspects of nature as sources for the sublime in art. Distinguishing between the sublime and the merely beautiful became a popular theme in eighteenth-century aesthetics, as in Burke's *Philosophical Enquiry into the Origin of our Ideas of the Sublime and the Beautiful* (1757). The chief qualities of the sublime were said to be terror, obscurity, difficulty, power, vastness, magnificence, and the infinite; whereas the properties of beauty include smallness, smoothness, gradual variation, delicacy, color, gracefulness, and elegance.[42] Burke explains that the sublime and the beautiful produce the same physiological effects as love and terror: the sublime triggers "an unnatural tension and certain violent emotions of the nerves," while the beautiful "acts by relaxing the solids of the whole system."[43] Whatever the merits of Burke's dubious physiology, these proposals clearly foreshadow the aesthetics of the Romantic era.

We have been following the two synchronous strands of philosophy, rationalism and empiricism, through the seventeenth and eighteenth centuries; in music, two distinct style periods ran their course during these two hundred years—the Baroque, a long period of musical development and technical accomplishment that reached its height in the first half of the eighteenth century with the works of J. S. Bach, Handel, Vivaldi, Telemann, Couperin, and an array of other gifted composers, and the Classic, a scant half-century of stylistic retrenchment and consolidation, marked by the brilliant achievements of Haydn and Mozart. As in the Renaissance, the musical products are a better guide to the prevailing values and aesthetic trends than the writings of philosophers.

Most discussions of the Baroque in art begin with an examination of the various connotations of the word: emotionalism, the subjective, exaggeration, lack of equilibrium and proportion, mannerism, illusion, monumentality, the sublime. After reading such a purple word list, one may feel slightly cheated when listening to the realities of Baroque music but only because our scale of proportions has been distorted—perhaps permanently—by the musical products of nineteenth-century romanticism. The range of expression in Baroque music is wide: from the cool, abstract polyphony of Corelli's trio sonatas to the intense drama of Bach's great Passion choruses. But, in contrast to what preceded it, the Baroque was undoubtedly a romantic age in music and began with one of the greatest stylistic upheavals in music history, unparalleled until the beginning of the twentieth century. A listing of contrasting qualities of the Renaissance and Baroque periods presents an accurate, albeit oversimplified, key to Baroque aesthetics in music and the visual arts. Renaissance art is marked by the preference for simplicity, stability, moderation, stasis, and is scaled to human proportions, whereas the Baroque stressed profusion, instability, mannerism, dynamic motion, and favored compositions that were laid out on a grandiose scale.

The beginnings of Baroque music (around 1600) were marked by a major shift in musical organization—from the linear, imitative motet style of the sixteenth century to a new vertical orientation of the musical texture, a tendency to think of music more in terms of chords than as an interweaving of separate melodic lines. The characteristic signature of Baroque music is the basso continuo, a combination of an instrumental bass line (played by a cello, bass viol, bassoon, or a number of bass instruments) and a chordal accompaniment (organ, harpsichord, or lute). Melodic activity became concentrated in the upper parts, a solo or duet of voices, violins, oboes, or other melodic instruments.

New formal principles were developed to take advantage of the possibilities inherent in the new harmonic orientation. The system of major and minor keys rapidly took hold, and by the late seventeenth century only faint traces remained of the older modal practice. Networks of major and minor keys offered new possibilities for large-scale musical form: by developing musical material through sequences of contrasting or related keys, the composer was able to achieve new dimensions in tonal structure. Musical compositions became much longer, and composers were forced to evolve new means of maintaining unity and continuity over long time spans, unaided by the structure of a text; their solutions included continuous variation (often over a bass line), rhapsodic forms such as the toccata, sequential structures such as the sonata and suite of dances, and a new formal principle based on antithesis and the conflict of solo/group—the concerto.

In both substance and structure the Baroque was an age of increasing diversification and differentiation: composers were intensely conscious of their personal idiom and of the conventionalized national styles of Italy, France, and Germany. Specific genres were developed and became distinct from one another: sacred from secular, vocal from instrumental, chamber music from orchestral style. Instrumental style finally became free of its earlier vocal models, and music began to be written in a manner idiomatic to the instruments for which it was conceived. Violin, flute, trumpet, and keyboard styles began to take full advantage of the resources of the individual instruments. One can begin to see the emergence of distinct structural functions in the composer's treatment of musical material: introductions, thematic statements, continuations, transitions, interludes, interruptions, developments, reprises, and conclusions. Music was modeled upon conventionalized figures (of speech and of thought) and was conceived as a rhetorical art.

Baroque theorists also evolved an important theory of musical meaning, the doctrine of the "affections" or *Affektenlehre,* which held that various musical figures can serve—once they have been learned—as signs of specific emotions, passions, and affections. Music was regarded as a language of emotion that could communicate specific meaning from composer, through performer, to listener.[44] But it is vital to catch the exact meaning: music was intended neither to express nor to arouse the passions—it was intended merely to signify on a more objective level that did not require subjective participation by the composer, performer, or listener.

At its worst the *Affektenlehre* took the form of a mechanistic classification of the passions, the musical figures representing them, and a highly stylized and artificial approach to the composition of music; an incompetent or unimaginative composer could approach his task as if he were translating with the aid of a dictionary. Theorists argued whether one should try to represent the changing shades of passion or try to catch the main emotional tone of a passage. Generally it was agreed that each separate musical movement should capture the dominant affection to be presented, although secondary figures (representing contributory passions) might be developed in the accompaniment or in interludes. At best, a real message could be conveyed from the composer to the competent listener; music could thus convey a blend of intrinsic musical logic and extrinsic meaning.

We may identify briefly a few additional items in the Baroque system of musical values: performance accomplishment became an important goal, and three skills in particular were highly prized—technical virtuosity, emotional delivery, and the ability to improvise. Heterogeneous instrumental colors were preferred, in contrast to the Renaissance fondness for smoothly blended, homogeneous sounds. Dramatic contrast was highly valued and embodied in such diverse contexts as the opposition between solo and tutti in the Baroque concerto and the turbulent crowd scenes from Bach's Passions. Movement, continuity, and relentless energy were the hallmarks of Baroque rhythm, implemented by a driving bass line, the rhythmic impetus provided by the brilliant instrumental figurations, goal-directed harmonic progressions, and stereotyped cadence formulae that were signaled well in advance. The great monuments of Baroque music—the orchestral concerti, Handel's oratorios, and the choral works of J. S. Bach—employed large ensembles; music thereby became a social activity for large groups and was performed increasingly in large halls for large audiences, a social milieu in which mass taste and public preferences began to have an impact upon all musical decisions. Opera was the first Baroque genre to become a commercial enterprise, but there were signs on every hand that the age of patronage was nearing its end. The aesthetics of music could not remain unaffected by such trends.

The age of the Baroque began, as we remarked, with a stylistic explosion, but the advent of the Classical period was virtually unnoticed: its beginnings may be seen in a simplification of texture (in which a more chordal texture took the place of the luxuriant counterpoint of the late Baroque), a lightening of the tone almost to frivolity and triviality (in the early phase known as the Rococo), an objective and less emotional manner that replaced the subjective pathos of the Baroque, a universal musical style in contrast to the many national styles and individual mannerisms of the Baroque, and a tendency to construct more periodic rhythmic units and a clearly articulated rhythmic flow. Classical style appears to have arisen spontaneously in several countries but reached its grand climax in Austria at the hands of Haydn, Mozart, Schubert, and Beethoven; Vienna quickly became the undisputed capital of the European musical world.

In many respects the age of Viennese Classicism invites comparison with an earlier period in music history—the age of the great Renaissance composers active around 1550 (Palestrina, Byrd, Monte, Lassus, et al.). Each group held values that contrasted sharply to those of the Baroque; each generation of composers wrote in a common language, a semiuniversal style that betrayed few national or regional mannerisms; each group worked for clarity of structure and equilibrium, and each drew fresh inspiration from simple, triadic sonorities; each group took moderation as an important aesthetic value and sought to achieve their ends with the simplest means possible. They represent two peaks of stability and high accomplishment in the history of musical style.

So solid a musical language was evolved in the half-century after 1750 that nineteenth-century composers made few substantive changes. The Romantic composers, as we will shortly see, expanded the dynamic and expressive dimensions of music and made increased use of the potential for chromaticism and ambiguity inherent in the system of tonal harmony, but theirs was a reaction more in manner and degree than in actual substance. This has led many scholars to assert that Classicism and Romanticism are two phases of the same period: a stable, objective phase followed by a more dynamic, subjective phase—a rhythm of stability and instability that seems to repeat itself in the development of European musical style.[45]

Some other important shifts away from Baroque preferences should be mentioned: Classical composers fashioned a more songlike, simpler, and more periodic melody in contrast to the convoluted, intertwining multiple melodic strands of the Baroque (especially the German Baroque); their bass line became less active and more a foundation for the successive chords. Classical composers favored multimovement genres such as the symphony, concerto, sonata, and quartet, and the idea of a musical work developed into a balanced, complementary set of movements: a powerful and intellectual first movement (always in sonata-allegro form), a lyric slow movement, a dancelike third movement, and a brilliant finale. Whereas Baroque composers restricted themselves to one "affection" per movement, the Classical composers saw value in emotional contrast and happily combined dramatic and lyric elements within the same movement. The favorite musical form of the Classical age was the sonata-allegro, a miniature drama of statement-conflict-resolution played out simultaneously on two levels—the tonal and the thematic; music thereby adopted one of the most basic structural patterns in world literature: statement-opposition-denouement. The conventionalized *tempo giusto* of the Baroque proved too confining for the new trends in melody and rhythm, and composers began to write in a wide range of musical speeds; the "terrace" dynamics and echo effects of the Baroque were likewise replaced by gradual increases and decreases in volume.

Our survey of European philosophy to 1800 concludes with the movement known as German idealism, represented by the writings of Immanuel Kant, Friedrich Schiller (1759–1805), and Georg Friedrich Wilhelm Hegel (1770–1831). The idealist philosophy provided the climate of ideas within which the aesthetic principles of Romanticism were to develop. The term *idealism* is best understood as an opposition to this triad of "isms"—naturalism, realism, and materialism; its proponents rejected both the rationalist and empiricist schools of thought. Idealist philosophy asserts the existence of some ultimate spiritual reality beyond the grasp of reason, common sense, and ordinary sense experience. This appeal to transcendental values, expressed in some of the most difficult philosophical language, marks most German philosophy of the eighteenth and nineteenth centuries. The result was a real synthesis of music and thought for perhaps the first time since the Middle Ages, a synthesis that we will explore in the following chapter.

7   The Romantic synthesis

THERE ARE TIMES in the history of art when style, values, and thought are so much in harmony with one another that a real cultural synthesis can be recognized; the nineteenth century brought such a synthesis. But this cultural climate is easier to feel than to describe, because it consists of a complex of ideas, attitudes, and only half-articulate impulses. This chapter sorts out these ideas, attitudes, and impulses as they are reflected in Romantic music, criticism, and formal philosophy.

Romantic is a slippery word. Although our immediate reaction is to link this word with the atmosphere of the nineteenth century, it is obvious that it describes a certain type of character, a basic personality type—and such personalities (e.g., Catullus, Benvenuto Cellini) can be identified throughout history! W. T. Jones defines the Romantic temperament as a set of biases toward the dynamic, the disordered, the continuous, the soft-focused, the inner, and the "this-worldly."[1] And Crane Brinton sees Romanticism as "a rejection of rationalism, and an exaltation of intuition, spirit, sensibility, imagination, faith, the unmeasurable, the infinite, the wordless . . . an escape from the . . . unlovely works that science, technology, and industry were building."[2] This set of attitudes is the direct antithesis of the Classical/rationalist temperament: Classicism is Apollonian, Romanticism Dionysian. Despite the numerous twentieth-century reactions against the spirit and works of Romanticism, its traces and influences are all around us.

Frederick Artz has summarized concisely the main themes of the Romantic movement:

> Romanticism thus represented the reaction of emotion against reason, of nature against artificiality, of simplicity against the complex, and of faith against skepticism. . . . It was not a philosophy but a sort of emotional religion, as nebulous as it was ardent. It penetrated sensitively into the psyche, into dreams and longings, into the unconscious and the mysterious, into those regions in which men sense intuitively rather than know by reasoning. The poet becomes a seer; he is wiser than he knows. His art is divinely inspired. Artists are a higher caste, not by birth, but by insight.[3]

I will here briefly mention some of the important values of Romanticism and their impact upon nineteenth-century music and musical thought:

The disordered, a reaction against the formal clarity and rationalism of the previous century. In music this led to a general "loosening" of form, less-predictable phrasing and cadencing, a blurring of outlines, and a deliberate "unhooking" of the various musical dimensions (melody, harmony, rhythm, meter) from the coordinated equilibrium that was typical of the Classical period.

The intense, a rejection of moderation and an assertion of exaggeration as an important artistic impulse. In music this led to huge climaxes, large ensembles, and expansive forms—but also to the extreme compression of emotion and musical substance into miniature forms such as the art song and the character piece for piano.

The dynamic, a tendency toward restless motion, a music more of becoming than of being that reached its apex in the prelude to Richard Wagner's *Tristan und Isolde.* The various musical consequences include an increased emphasis on the rhythmic dimension, a heightened sense of harmonic motion through chromaticism and modulation, as well as a general feeling of growth in the unfolding of the melodic line, the development of themes, and the swelling of sonority by means of long, sustained crescendi.

The inner, a tendency toward introspection and the contemplation of "essences." This characteristic expression is perhaps most evident in some of the sensitive piano pieces of Robert Schumann, speaking in the person of Eusebius, but it is also apparent in many nineteenth-century musical works in their deliberate isolation of moments of hushed poetic intensity, anticlimaxes that are as tense and powerfully expressive as the massive climaxes.

Emotion, at once a means and an end of knowledge. Reason could dissect the lifeless parts, but only emotion could discern the living whole; reason could register outward appearances, but only emotion could penetrate to the heart and spirit. By the early nineteenth century, it was generally agreed that of all the arts, music was best able to express the depths of human feelings, not in the conventionalized language of the affections but in deeper yet less definite accents. The type of communication underwent a subtle change: instead of the objective presentation of the symbol of emotion, the Romantic composer sought to purge himself of emotion through the production of his work, a kind of catharsis.

The continuous, and we may add *the infinite, the irrational,* and *the transcendental*—all antithetic to the value system of Classicism. The Romantic symphony came to embody all these values in the late nineteenth century, e.g., Gustav Mahler's monumental Eighth Symphony (the "Symphony of a Thousand") with its extreme length, huge sonic resources, sustained intensity, insistent sense of dynamic outpouring, and—in the final movement—its appropriateness to the sense of its text, the closing scene from Goethe's *Faust*. The theme of Faustian "striving" became a symbol of the musical impulse.

Color (as opposed to form), with the following musical consequences: an emphasis on the sonic value of the individual sonority, increased harmonic color by means of chromaticism and the juxtaposition of remote keys, and the expansion of the orchestra into a larger and more complex body with a greater variety of timbres.

The exotic, leading to the depiction of strange landscapes, the inclusion of ethnic elements in music, the use of national dance rhythms and melodic idioms, nationalistic themes for opera libretti, scoring for unusual instruments, and the use of exotic texts (from Persian, Indian, Chinese literature) for vocal music. Romanticism discovered, as Artz points out, "the noble savage, the virtuous Greek, the Chinese sage, and the devout medieval knight."[4]

The ambiguous or ambivalent. Obscure or double meanings are prized in nineteenth-century music: enharmonicism, especially in modulations; deceptive chord resolutions (especially playing upon the ambiguity inherent in the diminished seventh chord), elided phrases and cadences, long sustained sonorities, long passages of uncertain or unstable tonality, harmonic sequences, and melodies with ambiguous harmonic background and irrational rhythm.

The unique, emphasizing the individual work rather than the type. In music we find a variety of new titles for compositions, a highly individualistic treatment of the traditional genres (symphony, concerto, string quartet), an expanded idea content for the single composition, and the search for a personal musical style (in contrast to the more universalized style of the late eighteenth century).

The primitive. Nineteenth-century music frequently evoked the spirit of the primeval, especially the world of the forest and the sea. Music was valued for its ability to represent what the Germans call the *Ur-klang,* the age-old voice of Nature itself, communicated by the simplest of musical means—a single sustained tone or chord. The most striking example is the orchestral prelude to Richard Wagner's *Das Rheingold,* which depicts the birth of the Rhine River—a creation myth set to music and the longest (136 measures) sustained single harmony in the repertoire of tonal music.

The organic, which provided a new set of structural principles for music, although they were never asserted as such by nineteenth-century authors. Organicism holds that works of art are analogous to living things, in that they display the same natural processes and develop in accordance with the same natural principles. Goethe identified such a set of *Urphänomene* in his studies on plant morphology, subsequently taking them as the structural basis for his drama *Faust.*[5] His phenomena, with which he described the growth of what he mistakenly thought to be the *Urpflanz* (archetypal plant), were these: the seed, intensification, polarity, metamorphosis, and the supreme moment of full flowering. The errors in his botany need not detain us—what is significant is that the identical set of principles came to have structural importance for both music and literature, as in the German tradition of the *Bildungsroman* (the novel of character development), e.g., Thomas Mann's *The Magic Mountain,* in which Mann consciously applied these principles to the character development of his hero, Hans Castorp.[6]

Reality, as Goethe saw it, was basically formless; substance is constantly undergoing a process of formation and reformation. Reality must be perceived on its own terms, through its essence, not its appearance. All matter is continually passing through a series of metamorphoses in which each successive state is both a summation of its history and the seed of its future. Intensification (heat, energy, emotion, experience) provides the means by which the latent impulses in the substance are urged on through their series of metamorphoses, alternately attracted and repelled by such polarities as light and darkness, heat and cold, tension and release, reason and emotion.

It can be argued that the principle of organic growth is inherent in certain traditional musical forms—in particular the fugue and sonata-allegro; but there it is constrained by other formal impulses: the balancing of phrases and sections, the principle of reprise, the network of tonal relationships, and other formal conventions of seventeenth- and eighteenth-century musical style. But in the music of such composers as Franz Liszt and Richard Wagner, the new organic principles emerge as the ruling basis for large-scale structure: the basic substance of the composition is presented in the form of highly malleable motives, which are then amplified and intensified by various means, surrounded with new contexts, combined with other materials, subjected to various tonal and rhythmic transformations, passing on through alternate stages of stability and instability, expansion and contraction, conflict and resolution, in their drive toward the climax. Such a description most obviously fails to account for many of the formal tendencies in various musics of the nineteenth century, but the organic notion of musical structure is a significant addition to the array of traditional formal schemes and one that is fully in harmony with one of the prominent strands of Romantic thought. It is further noteworthy that the organic metaphor was applied to music history by nineteenth-century musicologists, who saw the history of the art as an evolution from "primitive" beginnings to its full flower in their own time.

At no previous time in the history of music had there been such a massive shift in musical values. My listing tends to suggest that the new aesthetic represents a unified syndrome of Romantic culture, but certainly there remained a number of unresolved tensions: between arch-Romantics and those who were temperamentally out of spirit with the movement, between (as Alfred Einstein suggests) the theatrical and the intimate, between descriptive and "absolute" music, and various other tensions within musical society.[7]

The relationship between the artist and society changed dramatically in the Romantic century in response to new conditions and new attitudes.

1   The age of patronage was coming to an end: the composer now had to please the middle class in order to be a commercial success, but without compromising his own values. The rise of public concerts brought music into the world of business.

2   The roles of the composer and performer became more specialized and, in certain instances, separated entirely. The new demands for technical accomplishment meant that many composers could no longer play their music acceptably, and the rigorous process of acquiring such a virtuoso technique made it difficult for a performer to maintain a total commitment to composition.

3   Under the influence of Romantic literature and dissatisfied with public response, many artists saw themselves as alienated from society, hypersensitive and misunderstood victims of the Philistine public; their only refuge was to withdraw into the nearest ivory tower.

4   Art began to be produced not for everyday consumption but for the special occasion and for eternity, an attitude that helped to heal the scars of public neglect. Some of the consequences for music included the production of fewer but larger works and the very real possibility that some compositions might never be performed.

5   If the artist was seen as a person of supernatural talent and hypersensitive personality, it follows that he might also be diseased! We see in Robert Schumann a notable case of the composer as schizophrenic; he spoke, in both his music and musical criticism, through his dual personalities—the exuberant Florestan and the melancholic Eusebius.

6   A popular early Romantic image was the composer as Aeolian harp: a mouth of Nature, passive yet sensitive, a lonely instrument hung in the forest with its strings stirred by the passing wind.[8]

7   A counterimage depicted the composer as Prometheus: storming the heavens, actively challenging God and Nature, a tragic and doomed figure of defiance.

8   The advent of the "art-for-art's-sake" movement had a powerful impact upon attitudes toward art: art no longer needed to be justified on any basis other than its intrinsic excellence. It need not be useful, instructive, or socially uplifting—it need only *be!*

9   And the countersuggestion—by Marx, Ruskin, and Tolstoy (among others)—suggested that the artist has a responsibility to so-

ciety at large, that he speaks to and on behalf of a constituency to whom he is heavily obligated.

The matters we have outlined on the preceding pages have had sweeping consequences for the philosophy of music: foremost among these must be reckoned the virtually complete replacement of the value system of the eighteenth century. The increased focus upon the role of the composer and the somewhat narcissistic self-preoccupation of the Romantic artist stimulated interest in the creative process, without detracting from the importance of the finished product. The ontology and epistemology of Romantic musical thought reveal some major revisions: ontologically, the classification of music into a set of clear types and genres was replaced by the idea of music as a unified, amorphous, transcendental process, manifested by a vast number of individual works, each containing its own rules. Art became a sort of superexistence, a higher category than physical reality and beyond rational knowledge. Epistemologically, music could only be known by sensation and by intuition; the heart became the organ of perception, not the mind. The assertion of transcendental values sets the philosophy of music, in a sense, beyond reach: it is a clear prelude to the aesthetics of the cop-out. Josiah Royce proposed the following as the "practical creed of Romanticism": "Trust your genius; follow your noble heart; change your doctrine whenever your heart changes, and change your heart often."[9]

As a consequence of these trends in musical style, values, and thought, criticism became more difficult—as well as more necessary. The entire social dynamics of the musical world underwent revision: the performer came to function more and more as an intermediary between composer and audience, and his role in the transmission of musical meaning came under closer scrutiny. And while the musical products of Romanticism met with a generally enthusiastic response from the new middle-class audience, the intellectual and emotional gap widened between the composer and his public, awaiting only the inevitable consequences of the accelerating evolution of musical style to arouse the irritation of a mass audience unused to such a rate of change.

Formalism was still an important presence in the nineteenth century, although its influence is more apparent in Romantic music than in Romantic letters: composers such as Mendelssohn, Saint-Saëns, Brahms, Franck, and Dvořák preferred to write within the formal constraints of Classical models—the sonata-allegro, theme and variations, rondo, scherzo and trio—although their music was infused with increased harmonic color, greater tonal variety, and set within an expanded dynamic and temporal scale. But formalism, as a philosophy, found few advocates (most notably the critic Eduard Hanslick). In the traditional antithesis of form vs. content, content (the "idea") was clearly favored; in the conflict of formal and sensuous values, the sensuous generally prevailed. The idea of art as a dialectic process and a synthesis of opposing tensions became popular with German thinkers—perhaps as a lingering resonance of the ancient Greek concept of harmony. Schiller viewed art as the synthesis of the sensuous impulse (*Stofftrieb*) and the formal impulse (*Formtrieb*), but his successors expressed more enthusiasm for the former than the latter.[10]

The relationship between the individual and society took on a new dimension with Johann Gottfried Herder's proclamation that the individual expression of the artist's work was the inevitable outcome of the collective impulses and aspirations of the people—*Das Volk*.[11] The artist, as we have seen, was held to be the spokesman for an entire nation, tradition, or race—an idea that furnished the thematic structure for Richard Wagner's *The Mastersingers of Nuremberg*.

The aesthetics of music became increasingly subjective and open to full debate; the seeds of dissension were sown and would inevitably lead to a profusion of aesthetic theories in the present century. An ominous tone has crept into these reflections, but it should not be inferred that these trends were in themselves divisive or in any way destructive. They merely portend the greater debates that lay ahead: the upheavals in musical style in the early twentieth century were accompanied by a continuing reassessment of musical values and controversies in musical thought that equaled, if they did not surpass, those that gave birth to the age of Romanticism.

The Romantic philosophers

German philosophers had a lot to say about music. In this final section I will present excerpts from several leading authors that will illustrate the progression from early German idealism to the high Romantic philosophy. Kant, in his *Critique of Judgment* (1790), writes under the influence of the eighteenth-century *Affektenlehre* and cannot be regarded as a representative of the Romantic movement; but certain ideas in the following passage suggest characteristic themes in the Romantic aesthetic—the intensity of music, its indeterminacy, and the universality of its communication by means of sensation. In comparing the various arts, Kant first asserts that poetry must occupy the highest place.

> After poetry, *if we are to deal with charm and mental movement,* I would place that art which comes nearest to the art of speech and can very naturally be united with it, viz. *the art of tone.* For although it speaks by means of mere sensations without concepts, and so does not, like poetry, leave anything over for reflection, it yet moves the mind in a greater variety of ways and more intensely, although only transitorily. It is, however, rather enjoyment than cultivation (the further play of thought that is excited by its means is merely the effect of a, as it were, mechanical association), and in the judgment of reason it has less worth than any other of the beautiful arts. Hence, like all enjoyment, it desires constant change and does not bear frequent repetition without producing weariness. Its charm, which admits of universal communication, appears to rest on this—that every expression of speech has in its context a tone appropriate to the sense. This tone indicates more or less an affection of the speaker and produces it also in the hearer, which affection excites in turn in the hearer the idea that is expressed in speech by the tone in question. Thus as modulation is, as it were, a universal language of sensations intelligible to every man, the art of tone employs it by itself alone in its full force, viz. as a language of the affections, and thus communicates universally according to the laws of association the aesthetical ideas naturally combined therewith. Now these aesthetical ideas are not concepts or determinate thoughts. Hence the form of the composition of these sensations (harmony and melody) only serves instead of the form of language, by means of their proportionate accordance, to express the aesthetical idea of a connected whole of an unspeakable wealth of thought, corresponding to a certain theme which produces the dominating affection in the piece. . . .[12]

We find a more mystical tone in the writings of G. W. F. Hegel; the following is an excerpt from his *The Philosophy of Fine Art*, which was not published until after Hegel's death in 1831:

The *second* art which continues the further realization of the romantic type and forms a distinct contrast to painting is that of *music*. Its medium, albeit still sensuous, yet proceeds into still profounder subjectivity and particularization. . . . Such an inchoate ideality of matter, which no longer appears under the form of space, but as temporal ideality, is sound or tone. We have here the sensuous set down as negated, and its abstract visibility converted into audibility. In other words sound liberates the ideal content from its fetters in the material substance. This earliest secured inwardness of matter and impregnation of it with soul-life supplies the medium for the intimacy and soul of Spirit— itself as yet indefinite—permitting, as it does, the echo and reverberation of man's emotional world through its entire range of feelings and passions. In this way music forms the centre of the romantic arts, just as sculpture represents the midway point of arrest between architecture and the arts of the romantic subjectivity. . . . Music carries within itself, like architecture, and in contrast to the emotional world simply and its inward self-seclusion, a relation of quantity conformable to the principles of the understanding and their modes of coordinated configuration.[13]

Hegel's thought is as complex as his language: he once remarked that his aim was "to teach philosophy to speak German!"[14] But this much seems clear: music is foremost among the subjective arts of Romanticism, primarily because of its unique ability to represent the ideal in sensuous, immaterial, audible form. It liberates by negating the restrictions of matter. And because music is able to express the inner life of the soul, it can represent man's entire emotional universe.

In *The World as Will and Idea* (1819), another of the great landmarks of Romantic thought, Arthur Schopenhauer saw music as a direct objectification of "the Will"—the irrational, limitless urge that moves the universe. More than any other author, Schopenhauer articulated the main themes and set the tone for Romantic German philosophy, writing with intensity and exceptional clarity:

> [Music] stands alone, quite cut off from all the other arts. In it
> we do not recognize the copy or repetition of any Idea of exis-
> tence in the world. Yet it is such a great and exceedingly noble
> art, its effect on the inmost nature of man is so powerful, and it
> is so entirely and deeply understood by him in his inmost con-
> sciousness as a perfectly universal language, the distinctness of
> which surpasses even that of the perceptible world itself, that . . .
> we must attribute to music a far more serious and deep signifi-
> cance, connected with the inmost nature of the world and our
> own self. . . .
>
> But it must never be forgotten . . . that music has no direct,
> but merely an indirect relation to [these analogies], for it never
> expresses the phenomenon, but only the inner nature, the in-
> itself of all phenomena, the will itself. It does not therefore ex-
> press this or that particular or definite joy, this or that sorrow, or
> pain, or horror, or delight, or merriment, or peace of mind; but
> joy, sorrow, pain, horror, delight, merriment, peace of mind
> *themselves*, to a certain extent in the abstract, their quintessential
> nature, without accessories, and therefore without their motives.
> Yet we completely understand them in this extracted quintes-
> sence. Hence it arises that our imagination is so easily excited by
> music, and now seeks to give form to that invisible yet actively-
> moved spirit-world which speaks to us directly. . . .[15]

English-speaking audiences are more aware of Richard Wagner's
music than his literary works, but he must be regarded as one of the
most important philosophers of the Romantic movement. He was,
moreover, one of the few philosophers in history who possessed not
only a keen mind and literary ability but the determination and musical talent that enabled him to demonstrate his philosophy in musical
practice. We present a brief excerpt from his *The Art Work of the
Future* (1850), which is characteristic of his thought:

> There is an *outer* and an *inner* man. The senses to which man
> presents himself as artistic subject are sight and hearing; to the
> eye he presents the outer man, to the ear the inner. . . . Di-
> rectly the inner man presents himself to the ear through the
> *tone of his voice. Tone* is the direct expression of feeling, as it
> has its physical seat in the heart, the starting and returning point

for the circulation of the blood. Through the sense of hearing tone penetrates from heart to heart, from feeling to feeling; . . . the art of tone divides and connects the two extreme antitheses of human art, the arts of dancing and of poetry. . . . . if dancing supplies music with its law of motion, music returns it in the form of rhythm, spiritually and sensually embodied as a measure for ennobled and intelligible movement; if poetry supplies music with its meaningful series of clear-cut words . . . , music returns this ordered series of quasi-intellectual, unfulfilled speech-sounds—indirectly representative, concentrated as image but not yet as immediate, inevitably true expression—in the form of melody, directly addressed to feeling, unerringly vindicated and fulfilled.[16]

It is time to present a dissenting viewpoint. Eduard Hanslick (1825–1904), a prominent Viennese music critic and Wagner's mortal enemy, rejected the entire complex of aesthetic principles put forward by Hegel, Schopenhauer, and Wagner, and proposed instead an aesthetic of formalism that has had a more sympathetic reception in this century than during his lifetime. Stung by Hanslick's bitter attacks, Wagner went so far as to write him into the cast of characters in his *The Mastersingers of Nuremberg*—in the unflattering person of the pedantic town clerk, Sixtus Beckmesser. Hanslick retaliated by describing Wagner's aesthetic as "formlessness exalted into a principle—the intoxicating effect of opium manifested both in vocal and instrumental music, for the worship of which a temple has been specially erected at Bayreuth."[17] These overtones of controversy have overshadowed the value of Hanslick's thoughtful position, as presented in the following excerpt from his *The Beautiful in Music* (1854):

Definite feelings and emotions are unsusceptible of being embodied in music.

Our emotions have no isolated existence in the mind and cannot, therefore, be evoked by an art which is incapable of representing the remaining series of mental states. They are, on the contrary, dependent on physiological and pathological conditions, on notions and judgments—in fact, on all the processes of human reasoning which so many conceive as antithetical to the emotions. . . .

A certain class of ideas, however, is quite susceptible of being adequately expressed by means which unquestionably belong to the sphere of music proper. This class comprises all ideas which, consistently with the organ to which they appeal, are associated with audible changes of strength, motion, and ratio: the ideas of intensity waxing and diminishing; of motion hastening and lingering; of ingeniously complex and simple progression, etc. The aesthetic expression of music may be described by terms such as graceful, gentle, violent, vigorous, elegant, fresh—all these ideas being expressible by corresponding modifications of sound. . . .

What part of the feelings, then, can music represent, if not the subject involved in them? Only their dynamic properties . . . [the element of motion] is the element which music has in common with our emotions and which, with creative power, it contrives to exhibit in an endless variety of forms and contrasts. . . . Whatever else there is in music that apparently pictures states of feeling is symbolical.[18]

Let us return to the mainstream of nineteenth-century musical thought for a few final reflections: most Romantic philosophies of music speak with an elevated rhetoric, as if to compensate for the dubious physiology and fuzzy logic that can here and there be detected. Music has clearly moved into the central position among all the arts, for perhaps the first time in history; it is described as a universal language that communicates immediately and intimately with the heart of every person. Notions of "aesthetic distance" have all but vanished from the literature; musical tone is the direct language of human feeling. And, in an important paradox, music has—because of its indefiniteness, its inability to express the specific—become the *most* definite of all the arts, that which is able to express the essential, the general, and the universal. To close, with another passage from Schopenhauer,

Music . . . gives the inmost kernel which precedes all forms, or the heart of things. . . . The unutterable depth of all music, by virtue of which it floats through our consciousness as the vision of a paradise firmly believed in yet ever so distant from us, and by which also it is so fully understood and yet so inexplicable, rests on the fact that it restores to us all the emotions of our inmost nature, but entirely without reality and far removed from their pain.[19]

8 Perception

Music is directed, not *to* the senses, but *through* the senses and *to the mind*. [Leonard B. Meyer][1]

IN THIS CHAPTER we present four of the traditional "problems" of aesthetics from the listener's point of view. Our aim is not to suggest how one ought to listen to music: the casual student of music has ready access to a large number of helpful how-to books by such eminent figures as Leonard Bernstein and Aaron Copland. Even experienced musicians can usually find something of value for themselves in these prescriptions for effective listening, but our purpose is to explore broader issues pertaining to listener attitudes, interpretation, the nature of the mental activity that accompanies the act of listening, and how one evaluates the experience.

It is obvious that there are many types of listeners, and it is equally obvious that any person's listening habits and experiences are subject to considerable variation. Listening experience is particularly difficult to describe: not only because it changes in response to different stimuli and external conditions, but also because it is such an eccentric and personal synthesis of our early musical memories, traces left by the instruments we may have studied (the "feel" of the piano keyboard under our fingers), ways in which we were taught to listen, conscious likes and dislikes, physical tensions and other responses, unconscious associations, and any number of individual quirks—colors, tastes, tactile sensations, and the like. It is harder yet to share someone else's listening experience in other than the most general way. Although most authors have held that in an ideal listening situation there should be as close a correspondence between the facts of the musical utterance (*if* they can be said to be facts) and the listener's apprehension, for many the music becomes a kind of affective back-drop, against which they project a chain of personal, highly subjective images. Listening can range from complete passivity to an intensely active process; this is clearly a matter where one must remain free to choose, but it is a good idea to be aware of the range of possibilities.

How can the philosophy of music best concern itself with the listening experience? As usual, one may make a good start by trying to separate the intertwined strands of our problem. These strands might include—but certainly are not limited to—(1) the facts of the music performed: tones, rhythms, timbres, patterns, forms, and their relationships; (2) the facts of the listener's ability to hear these frequencies, durations, and intensities; his thresholds of discrimination, his distance from the sound source, and similar limiting conditions; (3) the modes of musical listening: passive, sensuous (an immediate response to the nature of the musical surface presented), the formation of imagery, structural, technical; (4) the activities involved in listening: attention, matching, savoring, being "moved," remembering, predicting, retrodicting (reinterpreting the music one has just heard), being surprised, responding physically (with the breath, by tapping one's toes), tensing, relaxing, fusing, letting one's attention slip; (5) the values we attach to certain properties or qualities perceived in the music: climax, simplicity, lyricism, color, growth, acceleration, density, decoration, saturation; (6) the judgments we make (consciously or unconsciously), based on how a piece measures up to a set of personal or common criteria for excellence . . . and the types of statements that we make in supporting these judgments; (7) the context of the music: historical facts, the style in which a composer writes, performance practice, the composer's intention, program notes, critical commentary, the hall, the other listeners; (8) the listener's obstacles: prejudices, unfortunate prior experiences (as with one's first piano teacher), inability to concentrate, the ease with which one can be distracted, fatigue, indigestion, and the like—as well as a similar list of conditions that predispose him to a favorable response or a pleasant experience; (9) how the listener's behavior is affected by listening to music: facial expression, gesture, sweating, respiration, sexual arousal, applause, attending future concerts, practicing harder, choosing a profession. All of these strands contain potentially interesting questions and problems, some of which are more the province of the psychologist than the philosopher. Generally the present chapter is addressed to items 3, 4, 7, and 8; the subsequent chapter will consider items 5 and 6.

Modes of perception

Any exploration of the listening experience must begin by asking the question "What am I doing?" What am I thinking and feeling in response to the sounds that I hear? And this very general question includes several important subquestions:

1   To what extent does my listening involve *facts* or *learned things* such as clarinet timbre, a major triad, a reprise, sonata-allegro form, the key of E-flat major, Baroque style, recitative, a cadenza, and the like? Do I consciously put a name to them? Are there specific musical facts that are perfectly familiar but to which I cannot attach a name?

2   To what extent do I perceive separate events and under what conditions do these events fuse into larger complexes? Fusion is unquestionably one of the most vital aspects of perception—in all the arts but especially in music.

3   Do I direct my listening activity toward one of the musical dimensions—following a melody, responding to a rhythmic pattern, savoring the tonal colors, or do I register a more general impression: of the interweaving of lines, the sensuous mass of sound, the play of tonal colors and accents?

4   A question more relevant for those whose musical activity involves performance as well as listening is: Does the same type of imagery or activity arise in remembering a piece or in reading a musical score? What are the differences?

5   How does the act of *looking* (at a performer, at a score) influence my listening habits?

Edward T. Cone, in his excellent *Musical Form and Musical Performance,* contrasts two basic modes of perception: the synoptic and the mode of immediate apprehension. *Synoptic* means literally "viewed side-by-side"—no mean accomplishment in such a complex temporal art as music! Synoptic hearing is, very simply, structural hearing; it is concerned with the unity of the whole composition, its design, the way in which details fit into the whole, relationships between events separated in time, and depends heavily upon memory and expectation. To continue with Cone's words:

> The mode by which we directly perceive the sensuous medium, its primitive elements, and their closest interrelationships, is the one I wish to contrast with that of synoptic comprehension. I shall call it the mode of *immediate apprehension*. It is, I believe, what Whitehead had in mind when he wrote, "The habit of art is the habit of enjoying vivid values." . . . In part, the contrast between the two is that between experience and contemplation. Immediate apprehension is our response to a direct contact—our recognition of Whitehead's "vivid values." Synoptic comprehension is to some extent conceptual: it is our realization of the form of what we have perceived. . . . What the ordinary mind experiences is never the (space-time) continuum as a whole, but what one might call a spatio-temporal cross-section, bound together by point-to-point, moment-to-moment, area-to-area relationships. There is no guarantee that these relationships will produce a perceptible unity; the chances are that they will not. We cannot, therefore, be sure that our cross-section can be comprehended as an esthetic object—but we can still enjoy its immediacy. Let us call such a cross-section an *esthetic surface*. . . .
>
> The compositions that are ultimately the most satisfying—the only ones that, according to my usage, deserve the name of composition—are those that invite and reward both modes of perception. . . . The ideal hearing of a composition is one that enjoys both modes simultaneously, that savors each detail all the more for realizing its role in the form of the whole.[2]

This is an extremely valuable passage. Everyone who takes delight in music knows those moments of sheer sensuous pleasure when one responds immediately to the musical "surface" without thought for its role in the overall structure: it may be a single detail or a longer duration, a bright brass chord, a silky string line, crisp percussion accents, a thunderous passage for full organ. Synoptic perception grasps a musical work as object, but the mode of immediate apprehension responds to music as *process*. This is where most listening begins, and many people do not pass beyond this stage. There is no implication in this discussion that the vision of a gestalt necessarily enhances the enjoyment of a musical detail or surface—on the contrary, it may be a distraction. If what one seeks is immediate response, concentrating on the aesthetic surface is clearly the thing to do. But the perception of a musical work *as* a musical work is quite another matter, involving both direct and delayed responses, and Cone is surely correct in asserting that both are vital in the running correlation of immediate experience with the unfolding sense of total structure. Few of us are able to achieve such an ideal listening experience with any consistency, but it is a skill worth developing.

Another—and extremely popular—mode of perception has been described by Leonard B. Meyer:

> Often music arouses affect through the mediation of conscious connotation or unconscious image processes. A sight, a sound, or a fragrance evokes half-forgotten thoughts of persons, places, and experiences; stirs up dreams "mixing memory with desire"; or awakens conscious connotations of referential things. These imaginings, whether conscious or unconscious, are the stimuli to which the affective response is really made. In short, music may give rise to images and trains of thought which, because of their relation to the inner life of the particular individual, may eventually culminate in affect.[3]

We know very little about how such listening habits are acquired. People who practice the "associative" mode of listening find it difficult to retain their aural focus on the structural features of the music they hear, just as those who practice a more synoptic perception find it equally difficult to set free their train of associations. There is obviously no way to compare enjoyment levels except through testimony, a notoriously unreliable method in such subjective matters. If we accept these descriptions (or others) as true, then they hold important consequences for musical aesthetics. A critic ought to realize whether he is responding to an attractive aesthetic surface, a skillfully wrought form, a vivid evocation of mood—or an artful combination of all three—before he sits down at the typewriter. More important, a composition that places too great an emphasis on any of these properties runs the risk of underplaying the others. And for all its reported attractions, the associative mode of perception holds a very real danger—or perhaps several: the danger of letting one's experience with music degenerate into narcissism, merely using music as a stimulus to one's own thoughts and moods, a kind of mental masturbation. The more general danger lies in the separation of one's perception from its proper object, a question to which we return in the following section.

Both Roger Sessions and Paul Hindemith have stressed the active participation of the listener in the musical experience. Sessions introduces the issue in general terms.

> By the "listener," I do not mean the person who simply hears music, who is present when it is performed and who, in a general way, may either enjoy or dislike it, but who is in no sense a real participant in it. To listen implies rather a real participation, a response, a real sharing in the work of the composer and of the performer, and a greater or lesser degree of awareness of the individual and specific sense of the music performed. . . . His ideal aim is to apprehend to the fullest and most complete possible extent the musical utterance of the composer as the performer delivers it to him.[4]

Hindemith, on the other hand, provides a specific description of what he terms the listener's process of "coconstruction."

> [The listener's] activity can be described as follows. While listening to the musical structure, as it unfolds before his ears, he is mentally constructing parallel to it and simultaneously with it a mirrored image. Registering the composition's components as they reach him, he tries to match them with their corresponding parts of his mental construction. Or he merely surmises the composition's presumable course and compares it with the image of a musical structure which after a former experience he had stored away in his memory. In both cases the more closely the external musical impression approaches a perfect coincidence with his mental expectation of the composition, the greater will be his aesthetic satisfaction.[5]

This is not the place to examine Hindemith's assumption that the greater the match between event and expectation, the greater the listener satisfaction. The most predictable pieces of music are not usually reckoned among the world's great masterpieces. The crucial point for our discussion is Hindemith's vision of the inner mental music unfolding in parallel course to the sense data of the external physical music. No two listeners will coconstruct with the same degree of skill, but each listener—if he directs any of his conscious attention toward the music—will share in this mental experience, on his own level of musical accomplishment.

We have pointed out certain types of listening activities that take place within the mind: matching, fusing, predicting, remembering, registering surprise, and the like. Another common experience results when our listening circuits are overloaded with too great a profusion of sense data to be perceived separately and/or coherently: the flood of overwhelming sensation is experienced as a kind of override, a pool of irrational sensation to which perception can only respond by fusing—by interpreting the data as a more unified mass of sound, the *alogon* (the irrational). We resort to such a mode of perception under various conditions: a profusion of sense data, fatigue, distraction, or simply by a conscious act of mind; and the experience may be interpreted as either pleasant or unpleasant!

Perception takes on a new dimension when we match the performance of a concert artist against an inner image of the composition, attending to such things as quality of sound, tempo, correct intonation, playing the right notes, and other less tangible aspects of "interpretation." Technical listening is a common experience for music students and others whose concern is for the more technical side of music, but it is also a frequent activity of concert audiences, who may have the occasion to hear twenty versions of the Tschaikowsky Violin Concerto within as many years. Here we have three mental images developing simultaneously: the facts of the performance, the inner music, and the memory of the work itself—an exceedingly complex superimposition of imagery. Here once again our concern is not for the values involved but rather for the nature of the experience and the virtually automatic matching of multiple musical images in that most extraordinary of all musical instruments—the human mind.

Detachment

Distance, disinterest, and *detachment* are provocative terms that occur frequently in the literature of aesthetics. The three words have this in common: all signify some sort of separation—between the art object and the spectator, between the art object and the everyday world, or some combination of all three. One of the earliest of such proposals was Kant's famous definition of taste as "the faculty of judging of an object or a method of representing it by an *entirely disinterested* satisfaction or dissatisfaction."[6]

What Kant meant is that artistic judgment should be based, not upon the whims, prejudices, and self-attachments of the individual observer, but upon canons of judgment that should be valid for all observers. "Pleasant" is a judgment each person must make for himself; "beautiful" demands what Kant felt was a universal standard of taste. Beauty does not, in his view, lie "in the eye of the beholder" but requires a more objective assessment. We are not concerned here with whether Kant was right or wrong, merely with his use of the word *disinterested*. It does not mean a lack of concern or a casual attitude toward art; it means rather a willingness to stand back somewhat from the art object, to take a more objective view, put some emotional distance between oneself and the objects of perception, and to look beyond our own immediate and personal concerns.

The Spanish art historian Ortega y Gasset, in *The Dehumanization of Art*, provides an example:

> A work of art vanishes from sight for a beholder who seeks in it nothing but the moving fate of John and Mary or Tristan and Isolde and adjusts his vision to this. Tristan's sorrows are sorrows and can evoke compassion only in so far as they are taken as real. But an object of art is artistic only in so far as it is not real. In order to enjoy Titian's portrait of Charles the Fifth on horseback, we must forget that this is Charles the Fifth in person and see instead a portrait—that is, an image, a fiction. The portrayed person and his portrait are two entirely different things; we are interested in either one or the other. In the first case we "live" with Charles the Fifth, in the second we look at an object of art.[7]

We must realize that this ambiguous "distance factor" may be interpreted in several ways: as literal distance in space, as when we step back from a painting in order to let the individual brush strokes blend into the illusion the painter sought to convey; as distance in time, e.g., when a play is set in a past era (Orson Welles deliberately violated this convention when he produced Shakespeare's *Julius Caesar* in modern dress and set it in fascist Italy of the late 1930s). But the most important of these interpretations is the concept of "psychic distance"—an emotional detachment from the presented work of art.

Edward Bullough's famous essay on "Psychical Distance as a Factor in Art and an Aesthetic Principle" is cited in many subsequent discussions. We will return to what Bullough has to say about music, but his example of a man who attends a performance of *Othello* is worth mentioning here: if a man who is jealous of his wife spends his time during the play brooding on the similarities between Othello and himself, he is not responding to the drama in an appropriate aesthetic way; his "lack of distance" is an obstacle. As Bullough points out, were our spectator able to preserve some emotional distance, he might be able to enjoy a keener aesthetic satisfaction than one who has never been seriously afflicted with jealousy. So Bullough argues that distance should be minimal—but should not disappear.[8]

Most contributors to this aesthetic discussion see distance as measured on a sliding scale: not "distant" and "near" but "more" or "less" distant. There is no precise dividing line to cross—only the relative consciousness of the individual observer. And it is probably too much to expect a spectator to maintain the same degree of distance throughout his experience of a work of art; in reality distance tends to fluctuate for all of us—as we see a friend on stage and are alternately conscious of her as Mary and as Lady Macbeth, as we hear Isaac Stern playing a concerto and are alternately aware of him as virtuoso and him as a source of Beethoven's musical utterance.

Music, like all the other arts, requires its own interpretation of the concept of distance. Literal spatial distance is a valid point for discussion in the case of music, since all ensemble music is meant to be heard with a certain balance as foreseen by the composer. My own early experience playing trombone and seated in the back row of the orchestra directly behind the French horns gave me an entirely distorted concept of orchestral sound. The relative projective capabilities of the various instruments give music far more directional force than is generally supposed, and it will readily be agreed that a certain physical distance is necessary to obtain a gestalt of the ensemble sound. But this is more a practical than an aesthetic issue.

Bullough has this to say about distance and music:

Certain kinds of music, especially "pure" music, or "classical" or "heavy" music, appear for many people over-distanced; light, "catchy" tunes, on the contrary, easily reach that degree of decreasing Distance below which they cease to be Art and become a pure amusement. In spite of its strange abstractness which to many philosophers has made it comparable to architecture and mathematics, music possesses a sensuous, frequently sensual character: the undoubted physiological and muscular stimulus of its melodies and harmonies, no less than its rhythmic aspects, would seem to account for the occasional disappearance of Distance. To this might be added its strong tendency, especially in unmusical people, to stimulate trains of thought quite disconnected with itself, following channels of subjective inclinations—day-dreams of a more or less directly personal character.[9]

Not much is gained by arguing the relative merits of greater and lesser distance: some distance is probably vital to aesthetic experience—not too much and not too little. The unfamiliar idiom of a new twentieth-century composition can put so much distance between itself and us that aesthetic experience becomes virtually impossible; the listener who responds to the insistent rhythm of Ravel's *Bolero* by falling into a quasi-hypnotic trance reduces distance to the vanishing point.[10] The composer who hears his work butchered in a poor performance, the proud mother at her child's piano recital, the Irishman whose longings for the old country are triggered by a rendition of "Danny Boy"—all have legitimate musical concerns, but their musical experience suffers from too little distance. And similarly, the listener whose concert experience is filtered through a series of distracting factors (conversation in the hall, discomfort, ticket prices, overly technical program notes, and the conductor's seeming insistence in avoiding his favorite works) approaches the musical experience across a formidable span of distance.

Let us turn to the more general question of *detachment*. In *A Humanistic Philosophy of Music*, Edward A. Lippman writes:

Indeed the notion of detachment can justly be taken as the central characterization of traditional aesthetics. The work of art and the aesthetic experience are disinterested, purposeless, even isolated, and thus sharply distinct in nature from experience and objects in general. The contrast has without doubt been exaggerated. They are certainly distant in principle, however, from the practical purpose of the perceiver; will, desire, and practical advantage are ideally irrelevant, although there can be no doubt that they in fact impinge often upon the aesthetic realm and color the artistic experience, especially in the case of composition and performance.[11]

This is not the place to argue whether or not art (or music) is created and practiced for a purpose—moral training, ceremony, entertainment, catharsis, propaganda, narcosis, seduction, education, salvation, or the many other ends that have been proposed at one time or another. But the more our attention becomes focused upon the purpose of art, the less our chances of perceiving in an aesthetic manner.

The essential being of every musical work survives amidst a context, and it is a useful exercise to consider some of the various ways in which we detach an individual work from some or all of its context.

First, of course, we make the decision to detach the sounds of music from those of the external world, by our act of attention. Without this, there can be no separate existence of the musical work—*for us.*

Then, we detach the individual work from others of its style, genre, or milieu; we do not value *any* Beethoven quartet or Mozart aria but a particular Beethoven quartet or Mozart aria. This may seem like a trivial issue, but it is vital in the case of an art that makes frequent use of common models and multiple versions.

Next, we detach the musical work itself from the composer's activity in writing it and the performer's activity in playing it: something remains that can be remembered, contemplated, printed, recorded, studied. The experience and the activity can be re-presented or copied, but the idea of the work itself remains something separate and distinct.

Sound recording and electronic technology have tended to increase the potential for detachment and psychic distance by separating a musical work from its sound source. Lippman points out that, although sound recordings have made music more widely available and readily repeatable, their effect has been—at the same time—to increase the possibility of a casual and superficial experience.[12] It might also be argued that such an exact preservation of one version of a musical work is an unwelcome attachment, one that arbitrarily substitutes the fixed details of one interpretation—no matter how excellent—for the flexibility of the living work itself.

Various authors have proposed that the ideal musical experience (and the judgments that result) should detach a musical work from all of its context: the facts of history, geography, style, and cultural milieu; other works by the same composer, other works in the same genre, specific models and sources, the limitations of the medium, the composer's life, his intentions, or any of the other contextual features. I would like to argue against such an absolutist position.

My ideal apprehension of music would combine a grasp of the essential individuality of the single composition and an awareness of and appreciation for the numerous strands that connect the individual work to its composer, genre, style, period, and milieu. And in registering the details of a particular performance, we should probably add an awareness of the style, period, and milieu of the performance, enhancing our appreciation for both historically accurate and contemporary performances. At the same time, I prefer to preserve a degree of distance and to regard every experience of this work as something separate and distinct from any awareness of self.

It is worth noting that distance and detachment are not universally prescribed by philosophies of art. The philosophy of yoga that plays such an important role in the traditional aesthetics of India describes the aesthetic experience as the achievement of zero-distance: an intense attachment (the literal meaning of *yoga*) to the illusion of music, loss of personal identity and absorption in experience, a fusion of self and object, and the achievement of a state of transcendental bliss—*ānanda*.[13]

In summary of this section, I quote from an excellent essay by P. A. Michelis:

Aesthetic distance . . . provides a magic survey, bringing the firmament of invisible ideas close to our perception. As though art had put on us a pair of magic spectacles, our senses now endow objects of reality with another quality, another significance, making them seem to participate in an ideal existence. . . . The artist must be at the same time close to, and remote from, his experience; both detached spectator and passionate performer, unimpassioned participant of passion, a disinterested but absorbed contemplator, conceiving yet also judging his work.[14]

The phenomenal object

We return to two of the most basic questions we have posed: What is the essential being of a musical work? and How can we know it for what it is? Since Kant, the philosophy of art has tended increasingly to recognize that there is a difference between our perceptions of things and things "as they really are." To what extent can any person's knowledge of Beethoven's *Eroica* Symphony include *all* this work's essential features, while excluding all influences from the work's context and other such extraneous data acquired during its perception? Kant distinguished between objects and events as they are (*noumena*) or "things-in-themselves" and objects and events as they appear in our experience (*phenomena*).[15] I take his term *noumena* (Gk: *nous*) to mean that being that can be grasped by the mind, defined "scientifically" (to the extent that music can be so defined), invariant, containing all essential features and necessary conditions—the residue that remains independent of all perception. *Phenomena* (Gk: *phaino*) I take to mean simply "things as perceived."

This is a gross oversimplification of a complex matter, but it will do for a start. An example may help: a physical description of a painting (the "thing-in-itself") may be stated in terms of colored oil pigments brushed onto a stretched canvas surface; but the sense data, as organized in the mind of the spectator, are perceived in accordance with the illusion intended by the painter—as a landscape. The spectator's perception includes such activities as fusing certain percepts while detaching others, superimposing structure, separating the flat surface into foreground and background, interpreting, and assigning meaning. The perception of music involves quite the same set of activities, translated into the realm of the audible.

Phenomenology is a fairly recent development in philosophy, flourishing in German universities immediately before and after World War I; its chief exponents were Edmund Husserl (1859–1938), Franz Brentano, Martin Heidegger, Jean-Paul Sartre, and M. Merleau-Ponty. Husserl and his followers were primarily concerned with phenomenology as a method of inquiry and only secondarily with its implications for the psychology of perception. Phenomenology asserts that perception is/should be a process of rigorous description of our experience with sense data, based on no theories, assumptions, or presuppositions—only the a priori, that part of our knowledge which we possess independent of any experience. The new and interesting contribution that phenomenology brings to the arts is this focus upon the spectator as an active organizer of perceptions, not as a passive recipient of unchanging objects. Silliman describes its purpose as making

> the observer aware of the aesthetic object as he has perceived it, not as a fixed, immutable object passed on through several viewings, readings, or performances. It makes him aware of his own cognition, of his own role in the making of the aesthetic object. That an aesthetic object exists, has been made by a creative artist, is recognized; however, phenomenology focusses on the perceiver of the object, stressing that an observer does not separate an aesthetic object from its natural surroundings without an internal awareness and action.[16]

In short, a listener makes a reconstruction (or "coconstruction") within himself as he hears, remembers, or anticipates a piece of music. His concept of an individual work is influenced not only by his immediate sensory experience but by all the facts that inform him prior to his experience of the composition (biographical, historical, intentional, formal) and the accumulation of all his previous experience with this work. My concept of Brahms's Fourth Symphony, just as real to me as any verifiable statement of the symphony's existence, is a compound of (1) what I first learned of this work, its form, its significance as a Romantic symphony, my preliminary study of the score, my general knowledge of nineteenth-century music; (2) all my listening experiences with this work, including one particularly memorable performance by Max Rudolf and the Cincinnati Symphony and several recordings; (3) my study and teaching of this work to several theory classes, including the playing of excerpts at the piano; (4) my casual study of a facsimile edition of Brahms's autograph score, which brought some real surprises; and (5) what I am hearing now.

Obviously my version is mine alone and different from anybody else's—that may be why I prefer it slower or faster than another person. It is also different from Brahms's version (which must have been a composite of his and several conductors' versions), although I must hope that they have a lot in common. It changed radically after each of my early encounters with the work; it changes less nowadays as each new experience contributes proportionately less to the accumulation.

The phenomenological theory of perception raises profound questions for music: does any part of our knowledge of music (perhaps our concept of time) fall under the category of the a priori, or does all our knowledge derive from our experience?[17] Is it possible for even the most (or the least) practiced listener to rid himself entirely of musical presuppositions? I think not. Indeed, without some notion of music's structure and a language with which to express our understanding of it, how is it possible to describe the phenomenon, even to ourselves? And is this focus on the listener appropriate? Granting the limits of our ability to perceive, does it substitute knowledge of self for knowledge of external reality?

Monroe Beardsley has suggested six "postulates of criticism," which I have edited to make the connection with music more explicit:

1   The musical work is a perceptual object; that is, it can have presentations.

2   Presentations of the same musical work may occur at different times and to different people.

3   Two presentations of the same musical work may differ from each other.

4   The characteristics of a musical work may not be exhaustively revealed in any particular presentation of it.

5   A presentation may be truthful; that is, the characteristics of the presentation may correspond to the characteristics of the actual work.

6   A presentation may be illusory; that is, some of the characteristics of the presentation may fail to correspond to the characteristics of the musical work itself.[18]

Music, like painting, has its illusions, its "fictions," and in a sense may be said to depend upon them. Let me suggest a few: our perception of complex overtone clusters as single pitches, a phenomenon especially apparent in organ registrations using mutation stops (which add new overtones to the sound); the illusion of substantial body, by which we often come to feel that music has volume, mass, weight, energy, and occupies space; the illusion of continuity, which causes us to interpret a succession of discrete sounds as a theme or musical "line"; the illusion of tonality, which persuades us to interpret a particular tone as a referent or point of tonal focus, or a scale as an organizing matrix for the music; our perception of undulating vibrato as a steady tone; and the illusion of time passing at a certain rate—not the rate of the clock hands but the rate of a particular series of pulsations that we select from among our perceptions.

Certain of these essential illusions are acquired on the basis of minimal experience; others require some training. Certainly they must be foreseen by the composer and understood by the performer. Of all the essential listening skills, the most important one is *fusion*—the ability to perceive simultaneous tones as chords, successive tones as melodies, and successive durations and accents as rhythms. The ultimate fusion results when an entire composition is perceived as an organized gestalt.

A musical work is more than one can ever experience of it. At the same time, our version of such a work may be—for us—a richer and more complex thing than the work in itself. Musical performance is both truth and illusion, and our perception of the illusion is vital to the musical experience. One may be passively present during the performance of music, but perception is an active process that parallels and keeps a running summary of the progress of the musical work.

Meaning

A melody is a series of tones that makes sense. . . . How can tones have meaning? Words have meaning because they relate to things; sentences, because they express something about things. Pictures have meaning if they represent something; symbols, if they betoken something, indicate something. Tones do not relate to things, do not express anything about things, represent nothing, betoken nothing, indicate nothing. What is it, then, that is meaningful in tones, that allows us to distinguish sense from nonsense in successions of tones? [Victor Zuckerkandl][19]

Zuckerkandl has posed our question clearly, although his concept of musical meaning—attractive as some of us may find it—is too limited to accommodate the variety of answers that have been suggested. No other issue in the aesthetics of music has been so vigorously debated with so little progress toward reaching general agreement. The purpose of this section is to contribute to our understanding of the problem—not to propose a new theory of musical meaning or argue in favor of existing theories.[20] At the heart of the problem is a semantic issue: What do we have in mind when we use the term *meaning*? We will shortly examine a wide range of statements, but first it will be useful to consider a very general definition by Morris Cohen: "Anything acquires meaning if it is connected with, or indicates, or refers to, something beyond itself, so that its full nature points to and is revealed in that connection."[21]

Meaning then, in the broadest sense, implies some kind of connection between the intrinsic and the extrinsic, the inner and the outer: in the case of music, between the tonal events and "something else." Before considering just what this something else is and how music refers to it, we present a particularly lucid statement on the nature of musical meaning by Leonard B. Meyer. In initiating the following discussion, Meyer reminds us that meanings are not subjective observations—they are "real connections existing objectively in culture . . . not arbitrary connections imposed by the capricious mind of the particular listener."

> Meaning, then, is not in either the stimulus, or what it points to, or the observer. Rather it arises out of what both Cohen and Mead have called the "triadic" relationship between (1) an object or stimulus; (2) that to which the stimulus points—that which is its consequent; and (3) the conscious observer . . . what a musical stimulus or a series of stimuli indicate and point to are not extramusical concepts and objects but other musical events which are about to happen. That is, one musical event (be it a tone, a phrase, or a whole section) has meaning because it points to and makes us expect another musical event.[22]

Why do we concern ourselves with the question of meaning—why don't we just listen? Primarily because the word *meaning* has been flung around so loosely and in so many different senses that it is important for us to straighten out our thinking. But also because whatever music "means" (*if* it means) is vital to our interpretation and performance of music.

Archibald MacLeish's famous dictum (from his 1926 "Ars Poetica") that "a poem should not mean . . . but be" has been widely quoted and admired; but certainly he overstated the point. MacLeish's statement was intended as a reminder that meaning does not constitute the major dimension of a poem, does not represent its whole content—its rhythmic and phonetic dimensions are equally important. And surely this is true in the case of music. A musical tone or phrase may (and usually does) contain a logical tendency, but it also has value in and of itself—it not only *means* but *is*.

Beardsley points out several other ways (some of them admittedly trivial) in which music can signify or remind us of "something else":

1 A melody associated with a familiar phrase ["How dry I am"; "O say can you see"; "God save the queen"] can summon up the words themselves.
2 Functional musics: church music in "stained-glass" style, military marches, dances, college songs, and other such genres can conjure up a set of associations, even if the specific music is unfamiliar.
3 Overtly imitative or descriptive music: bird-songs, thunder, the whirring of a spinning wheel, the bleating sheep in Richard Strauss's *Don Quichote* and the explicit sexual description in Shostakovitch's *Lady Macbeth of Mzensk*.[23]

The diagram below shows something of the range of statements made in our attempts to define musical meaning, although it does not pretend to be an exhaustive list. In order to separate the different theories of meaning, it is useful to note that they can vary in verb (the connection) or in object (the "something else"). Readers are invited to select the particular combination that most accurately represents their own view.

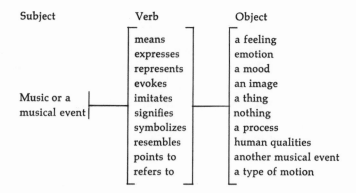

Subject	Verb	Object
	means	a feeling
	expresses	emotion
	represents	a mood
	evokes	an image
Music or a	imitates	a thing
musical event	signifies	nothing
	symbolizes	a process
	resembles	human qualities
	points to	another musical event
	refers to	a type of motion

It is ironic that discussions of the meaning of music tend to get bogged down in discussions of the meaning of words! And yet it is hard to see how this can be avoided as long as we are compelled to communicate by means of words. An elaborate analysis of the various shades of meaning in the diagram goes beyond the scope of this section, but a few comments may be useful: the verbs range from fairly simple descriptive verbs (*points to, resembles*) to verbs that stand for complex processes or that are built on elaborate assumptions (*expresses, symbolizes*). Beardsley, for example, suggests the following as a fuller explanation of the verb *express:* " 'The composer has objectified (embodied, expressed) joy in his scherzo' means '(1) he has been moved by a feeling of joy to compose the scherzo; (2) he has given the scherzo a joyful quality; and (3) the scherzo has the capacity to give him the same feeling of joy when he hears it again, and consequently to give it to other listeners, too.' "[24]

Semiotic theories of musical meaning have recently become popular. In these theories, music is said to function as a sign which may or may not be iconic of its object (a feeling, a process, motion). A green traffic light is a good example of a sign that is not iconic, but the sign for an "S" curve on a highway *is* iconic in that it resembles its object. Susanne Langer's *Feeling and Form* sets forth such a theory:

> The tonal structures we call "music" bear a close logical similarity to the forms of human feeling—forms of growth and of attenuation, flowing and stowing, conflict and resolution, speed, arrest, terrific excitement, calm, or subtle activation and dreamy lapses—not joy and sorrow perhaps, but the poignancy of either and both—the greatness and brevity and eternal passing of everything vitally felt. Such is the pattern, or logical form, of sentience; and the pattern of music is that same form worked out in pure, measured sound and silence. Music is a tonal analogue of emotive life.[25]

The various theories of musical meaning are often classified into some of the following types: referentialist, image-evocation, expressionist, signification, absolutist, formalist. I suggest that the problem is more subtle than these labels allow and that a proper theory of musical meaning can only be described by a combination of verb and object—and by means of a rigorous analysis of the words employed. I will close this chapter with a few observations.

The perception of meaning in music requires *competence* on the part of the listener; meaning embodied does not automatically result in meaning taken. Musical meanings are learned products of culture— not universal absolutes.

The composer who sets too high a standard of competence for his audience, perhaps by writing in an overly complex or unfamiliar style, must be ready to pay the price for his indulgence.

Whatever the verb employed, the object of that verb must be specifically the same for the composer and for all listeners, else communication of his meaning cannot occur.

Many listeners *take* meanings from music that have not (at least intentionally) been embedded therein by the composer.

Formalist theories are becoming increasingly popular as we discover the difficulties involved in defending any of the other theories of musical meaning. The formalist position, unfortunately, is often stated in unbecomingly negative language such as "The only proper meaning of music is music itself." It is possible, however, to state this position in positive language: music is a sensuously appealing, self-contained tonal language characterized by abstract motion, events, and dynamic process. These abstract qualities may trigger (in a listener who is so inclined) certain kinds of affect—which may even resemble at times the affect experienced by the composer and/or performer. But this affect is extrinsic to the real sense and continuity of the music. The intrinsic meaning of music is communicated in its own language: the language of tone.

Meyer has pointed out that the affective and intellectual responses to music are simply different ways of experiencing the same process.

Whether a piece of music gives rise to affective experience or to intellectual experience depends on the disposition and training of the listener. To some minds the disembodied feeling of affective experience is uncanny and unpleasant and a process of rationalization is undertaken in which the musical processes are objectified as conscious meaning. Belief also probably plays an important role in determining the character of the response. Those who have been taught to believe that musical experience is primarily emotional and who are therefore disposed to respond affectively will probably do so. Those listeners who have learned to understand music in technical terms will tend to make musical processes an object of conscious consideration.[26]

The common thread that links the four problems presented in this chapter is their significance for the epistemology of music: the listener's attempt to obtain valid knowledge (of the musical substance, of the fictions, structures, and meanings therein embodied, of self) through the experience of music. The next chapter explores those issues that lie at the core of the discipline of aesthetics, in the still more subjective realm of values, preferences, judgments, and standards.

9   Values

De gustibus non disputandum.

CAVEAT LECTOR! For if the philosophy of music is on slippery ground elsewhere, it rests on quicksand when we take up questions of value and valuation. A few preliminary observations, definitions, and cautions may be helpful. "Matters of taste are not to be
disputed" is a famous old saying that is often invoked when we agree
to disagree. It has brought comfort to many. The anonymous phrase
has a certain democratic appeal for all of us who feel (as we often
do) threatened, on the defensive, or merely uneasy when we make a
critical judgment that "This is good" or "I like it!"—two common
statements that may or may not mean the same thing. But if we fall
back upon this maxim and deny the existence of any standards, any
legitimate grounds for preferences and statements of value, we
abandon objective judgment.

The purpose of this chapter is neither to dictate taste nor to lay
down critical standards; it is rather to recognize existing values and
suggest how they may jointly influence our judgments. The chapter
does conclude with a discussion of critical strategies and a set of
guidelines, but these are proposed in terms that leave room for—and
ultimately depend upon—the perceptions and priorities of the individual listener.

By *value* I mean "worth." When we attribute value to a musical
work or a property of that work, we say that (in our judgment) it
has worth, it *ought* to be valued, because it is beautiful, pleasant,
good, or true. Such a definition is consistent with the general use of
the term *aesthetic value*, the inherent property of a work of art to
produce good or pleasing experience in those who contemplate it.

But I propose a more technical meaning for the plural *values* as used in the title and first part of the present chapter: as a set of specific predicates for music, similar to the color or textural values we recognize in the visual arts. If a painting displays a blue color value, a passage of music may be described as having a homogeneous timbre value, a staccato texture value, or the dynamic value that we call *climax*. These are unnecessarily cumbersome terms and are used here only for clarification. The assumption is that these values are qualities or properties of music that can be verified objectively and, when perceived, provide the basis for an estimate of value—in the form of a statement of recognition, perhaps also of favor (or disfavor). So a *value*, in the present sense of the word, may be either an object of interest ("I recognize it") or an object of desire ("I like it!").

It is difficult to organize the many musical values into a systematic framework, chiefly because of the unique way in which the various musical dimensions interpenetrate and correlate: the phenomenon of accent, for example, can be produced by stress, duration, choice of pitch, silence, or several other musical means, either singly or in combination. One traditional approach in aesthetics is to separate these into *sensuous* and *formal* values: we respond to sensuous values with savor, because they are primarily qualitative and invite subjective interpretation; we tend to measure the more formal values, because they are primarily quantitative and more open to objective verification. The present chapter is organized by means of the following schema:

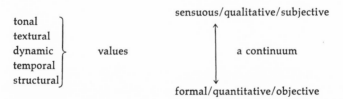

With certain values our mode of perception is set by our attitude, habit, or training: with respect to texture, the trained musical mind may untangle the contrapuntal strands of a Bach fugue and perceive structurally, while a less practiced listener is more likely to perceive the tangled web as pure tonal surface and respond sensuously. Some of the values we cite will be regional, localized in but one part of a musical work; others will be pervading or will appear intermittently.

Thus the scheme resists a neat organization from smallest part to whole. Also, we add a special category of dynamic values (e.g., climax, growth) that seems not to belong clearly in either the sensuous or the formal realm. Harmonic values are not detailed in our scheme, although some harmonic effects are subsumed under tonal and dynamic values. And finally, many of the values are expressed as an antithesis, an opposition between polar extremes (e.g., lyric as opposed to dramatic); it should be apparent that the two poles are relative, and that they too lie along a continuum, even if stated in "either/or" language.

The catalog is surely not exhaustive, and I have not attempted to give equal time to the various values. Many of these have already been mentioned in connection with the preferences of certain historical periods. The values I outline—let it be clear—are those of Western musical society as reflected in the standard concert repertoire written between 1700 and (say) 1950. Some of these must certainly be reckoned among the most basic values of human experience and, as such, may be discerned in all world musics. Chapter ten will explore how these and other values are embodied and perceived in two Asian musical cultures, but the present chapter assumes the tradition of Western civilization. The goals of this discussion are to provide a frame of reference for the values of music and to stimulate readers to explore those value complexes that most interest or appeal to them. Ultimately they may serve collectively as a basis for musical value judgments, resting upon an informed mixture of cultural consensus and personal preference.

Tonal values

Silence. It may seem contradictory to assign specific musical value to a period of silence, but the context that surrounds musical silences profoundly influences how they are perceived.[1] Rests are seldom dead spaces in music, and certain silences are invested with extraordinary amounts of tension or release of physical energy. They may be interruptive or noninterruptive, strictly measured or free, and can range from mere punctuation to significant separations between sections or movements. One of the most dramatic and tensed silences in music occurs just before the final cadence of Handel's "Hallelujah" Chorus from the *Messiah:* a sudden, unmeasured interruption of the musical flow that makes an abrupt transition to the slower pace of the last two bars. Another such climactic silence marks the downbeat of measure 280 in the first movement of Beethoven's *Eroica* Symphony, replacing the expected bass accent and somehow discharging the energies accumulated during the previous bars of intense rhythmic conflict and development.

Tone. We are seldom conscious of the subtle details of a single musical tone until our perception is directed toward some particularly exposed tone that we are able to separate from its context—in contrast to some genres of Asian music (notably the Japanese *shaku-hachi* repertoire)[2] in which attention is focused upon the manifold shadings of single tones. A musical tone, in our ordinary experience, may seem more like a piece of printer's type—an abstract unit that is readily combined into a large number of meaningful patterns, but on closer inspection tones take on sharply individual qualities. A musical tone is not so much like a piece of type as it is a character in Chinese calligraphy; directing our attention toward its details reveals properties of attack, release, fullness, breathiness, vibrato, and other subtle shadings that richly reward the effort. The number of tones that our minds process in even a brief musical experience makes it clearly impossible for us to lavish such attention on each tone we hear; we may achieve it in part while listening to single melodic lines, as in such works as Debussy's *Syrinx* or Edgard Varèse's *Density 21.5*, both for solo flute. But this intense focus on the particular tone can also get in the way of the illusion of continuity the composer sought to create. So the main value of the single tone is as a highlight, a momentary perception of beauty in isolation that is apt to strike us most forcefully at the beginning or end of a passage of music, especially when its effect is allowed to sink in.

Each of us can make catalogs of individual tones that stand out in our musical experience. Mine includes the sustained trumpet A that opens Wagner's *Rienzi* Overture, the first C-sharp of the flute solo at the beginning of Debussy's *Prelude to the Afternoon of a Faun*, the bassoon high C that begins Stravinsky's ballet *The Rite of Spring*, the final low G-sharp for bass clarinet from the same composer's *Variations*,[3] and the long-sustained pedal E-flat at the beginning of Wagner's orchestral prelude to *Das Rheingold*.[4] These are not simple percepts: in the case of the *Rienzi* trumpet tone, it is not the "trumpet-ness," nor the "A-ness," nor the swelling and fading of the tone, but the unique combination of all three. My awareness of this tone includes even the occasional bobble when the tone is not cleanly attacked by the trumpeter.

Chord. Individual sonorities, chords, often display very specific sensuous properties—sometimes in isolation, sometimes by virtue of their context. I will cite but two of music's most celebrated chords: the first, the opening chord from Stravinsky's *Symphony of Psalms*, requires no context for its recognition, due to its distinctive doubling, voicing, and scoring. The work itself is thus one of a surprisingly large number of compositions which can be recognized instantly by any person who knows the piece.[5] The more famous "Tristan" chord, in bar two of the prelude to Wagner's *Tristan und Isolde*, depends more upon its context: the intersection of two melodic motives, the tonal and rhythmic ambiguity of the first measure, and the unpredictable resolution, as well as the intervallic structure and scoring for horns and woodwinds. The value of the chord in question is a complex fusion of its ambiguity, instability, heterogeneous instrumental color, and dynamic ebb-and-flow, as well as the actual pitches.

Timbre: tone quality or "color," as produced by the configuration of the sound wave, the presence and relative intensity of the overtones, and other such acoustic facts. Timbre must be reckoned among the most important sensuous values of music, and the delight we take in the various instrumental sounds and the characteristic colors of the human voice must rank among music's major pleasures. I will suggest several subcategories for timbral value, according to the following scheme:

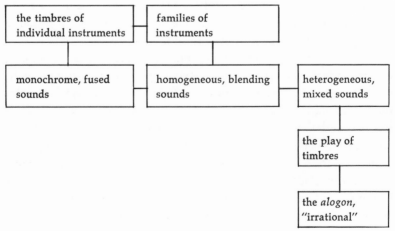

Among the distinctive individual and familial timbres, the following may be singled out: the two differing registers of the clarinet, the resonance of the open strings in the violin family, the special dark quality of the lowest string of the violin, the unusual overtone spectrum of bells, the "mellow" brass sounds of French horn and tuba in contrast to the sharper timbre of trumpets and trombones,[6] the contrast in tonal spectrum between flute and oboe,[7] the so-called chest voice of the contralto, and the brilliant "ring" of high notes in the male voice.

Combined sounds may be uniform, blending, or mixed—simultaneously and/or successively—and each, in its own way, is a source of value (unity or diversity). No voice or instrument can be scaled evenly throughout its range, but a smoothly modulated tonal scale is an ideal toward which most performers aspire. And the illusion of tonal "equality" is an important prerequisite if we are to perceive a melody in a single hue of sound. The timbres of the orchestral string instruments are remarkably similar and fuse, in works such as Witold Lutosław-ski's *Funeral Music* (for Bela Bartók), into a uniform web of monochromatic sound. The complex timbre of the full pipe organ presents a rather special case and illustrates how a rich mixture of extremely diverse sounds will also be perceived as monochrome. The juxtaposition of contrasting timbres is one of the prime values of music written for the modern orchestra: the colors of the individual instruments and their familial properties are brilliantly demonstrated in Benjamin Britten's *Young Person's Guide to the Orchestra;* the characteristic sounds of the (plucked) string, woodwind, and brass choirs of the orchestra are featured in the scherzo from Tschaikowsky's Fourth Symphony; and the second movement of Bartók's Concerto for Orchestra, entitled *Giuoco delle coppie* ("The Game of Pairs"), is organized formally in a series of duets (bassoons, oboes, clarinets, flutes, and muted trumpets), each associated with a certain musical interval. It should be noted that the standard woodwind section of an orchestra is an extremely heterogeneous collection of timbres, and similarly the woodwind quintet (flute, oboe, clarinet, bassoon, French horn) contrasts with the homogeneous timbres of a string quartet.

Heterogeneous sounds are, I believe, a source of some very special musical values. Pierre Boulez's *Le marteau sans maître* (for alto flute, vibraphone, viola, guitar, and alto voice) demonstrates a pleasingly unpredictable "play" of mixed timbres—a sensuous surface too complex to untangle into its component parts. This approaches the musical value that I like to think of as the irrational—dense masses of sound that we perceive as a single texture and volume. I can suggest four instances of the *alogon* in music: the introduction to Part Two of Stravinsky's *The Rite of Spring* begins with dark, mysterious pools of sound depicting a mood of impending sacrifice and the coming of the primeval night in pagan Russia. In the prelude to Britten's *A Midsummer Night's Dream*, the world of the fairies is evoked by means of "irrational" string glissandi, conveying the sense of the "uncanny." Gunther Schuller, in "The Twittering Machine" (from *Seven Studies on Themes of Paul Klee*), has constructed an amusing musical analogue to Klee's celebrated wind-up mechanical bird. And the episode of the herd of sheep in Richard Strauss's *Don Quixote*, which was originally criticized for being blatantly overpictorial, now takes on new significance because of the manner in which Strauss anticipates some of the trends in musical style since 1950.

These selections demonstrate an important feature of musical perception. When the level of complexity exceeds our capacity to process the individual sounds, our perception does precisely what an audio speaker does when made to perform at too high a dynamic level: it becomes overloaded and responds in an irrational manner. I suggest that these three modes of timbral perception—(1) the systematic registering of individual sounds, (2) fused perception, and (3) overloaded perception—are all potentially pleasing within certain limits set by the individual's training and preferences.

Harmonic color. The role of harmony in music is far too complex to summarize here, other than to point out several of its more structural properties: its ability to define a tonal center and suggest motion toward that goal, to support and give shape to a melodic phrase, to produce the pleasant alternation of tension and release through its properties of dissonance and consonance—all of this accomplished by the progression of chords. But certain harmonic effects may lead us to respond sensuously, especially when the harmonic dimension is unstable and shifting (as in Wagner's prelude to *Lohengrin* or the first two of Debussy's Three Nocturnes).

The affective properties of major and minor keys (i.e., major interpreted as happy, exuberant; minor interpreted as sad, pathetic) surely belong among the sensuous values of music, although their status is a matter of considerable controversy. There seems to be little question that most of us make such an equation as a routine part of our musical experience. It seems clear that these associations are learned responses that can in no way be considered among the a priori or universal values of music. Leonard Meyer argues convincingly that the affect we perceive in minor keys is the product of a cluster of related properties of the minor mode—chromaticism, ambiguity, instability, the tendency to use slower tempi than in major, and what he terms the "deviant" character of the mode (as opposed to the "normative" character of major).[8] Whatever the reasons, these affective qualities have shaped our collective musical experience for hundreds of years and cannot be dismissed lightly.

But the value we ascribe to various keys goes far beyond this simple emotional antithesis between major and minor. Ask any musician to compare the qualities of E major (four sharps) with E-flat major (three flats), and the results will be remarkably similar: keys with sharps are generally described as *bright, high,* and *intense,* while flat keys are described as *full, mellow, low,* and *bland.* And such associations are communicated unconsciously in performance through the choice of tempo, articulation, rhythmic character, and other such clues. Listeners may not be able to identify the key, but they will readily pick up the performer's signals and respond accordingly.

The process begins with the composer who (consciously or unconsciously) molds the character of his music in accordance with his concept of the key he has chosen. It is well known that Mozart consistently resorted to certain keys when he sought a specific type of expression: G minor, in his practice, meant chromatic, emotional, relatively slow, pathetic music, while C minor was more dynamic, assertive, even tempestuous. He regarded E-flat major as a key appropriate for majestic ritual, as in the symbolic rites of *The Magic Flute,* and his version of this key drew heavily on wind instruments (especially pairs of oboes, clarinets, bassoons, and French horns) in parallel thirds and sixths, chordal textures, and no more than moderate speed.[9] There are (or were, in Mozart's time) technical reasons for the "brightness" of C and D major, because these were the most convenient keys for trumpets. Certain other keys, B-flat and F major, appear to have been relatively neutral for him.

Each composer has an individual set of preferences and associations for various keys—not whims but insights that lie deeply buried in the subconscious as the result of previous musical experience, mem-

ory of specific pieces, and knowledge of what will be easy or difficult
to play on certain instruments. Beethoven's concept of the key of C
minor—as heard in the Fifth Symphony, the *Pathetique* Sonata, and
numerous other works—most obviously influenced Brahms's version
of the same key, as in the First Symphony; but Mozart's C-minor
Piano Concerto, K. 491, written when Beethoven was only sixteen
years old, reveals that Beethoven's concept was molded in part by his
prior experience. And the funeral marches from Beethoven's Op. 34
Piano Variations and the *Eroica* Symphony demonstrate that specific
musical associations can spill over from piece to piece. In this way the
music of the eighteenth and nineteenth centuries has established at
least a partial link between key and musical "character," and this
knowledge forms part of our musical tradition—a storehouse of musical meaning and virtually a "collective unconscious" that composers
learn along with their technical skills.

Textural values

By texture we mean the weave of the music, whether we con-
ceive/perceive it as an aesthetic surface or as the warp (pitch, the
vertical axis, simultaneity) and woof (time, the horizontal axis, sequence) of the musical fabric. Because the word *texture*, in common
usage, considers time as one of its two major dimensions, it is pointless
to try to avoid certain values that clearly involve the temporal in
music.

Simple/complex. The perception of music as simple or complex
must be among the most basic responses to music and one of the most
subjective. Our judgment of this as simple and that as complex is, of
course, relative to our own personal scale of values, and such judgments are verifiable only in extremely obvious instances or when we
compare greater with lesser complexity. By complex, we may mean
any or all of the following: too much information, a profusion of different types of sense data, lack of pattern or organization, ambiguity,
instability, or lack of an apparent goal. The unfamiliar is routinely
judged more complex than the familiar. We may interpret complexity
as too much data packed into a single dimension or plane (an overly
elaborate, ambiguous, rambling, or disorganized melody) or the interaction of several musical dimensions. The mind attempts instinctively

to reduce perceived complexity, either by focusing on a single strand, imposing pattern and hierarchy on the sense data, or by fusing the data into a unified "surface." But each person has his own limits past which he will not willingly go, a point past which complexity is interpreted as chaos. With these reflections in mind, it is instructive to hear Haydn's musically convincing but dated representation of "chaos" in the orchestral introduction to his oratorio *The Creation*. Many recent composers have systematically begun to explore the very complex in music in the form of "sound mass" pieces—notably Penderecki, Lutosławski, Ligeti, and Xenakis. At the other end of the simple/complex scale, curiously enough, there seems to be no limit to our relish for the simplest musical effects—other than those which, through prolonged repetition, transgress the limits of our patience.

Smooth/rough. We respond to what we perceive as a musical surface in much the same way that we react to any surface—a textile, a wall, or a marble statue. What we hear as "smooth" in music results from bound (legato), connected sounds where the inescapable transitions between tones are minimized, sometimes by means of the slide between pitches that the Italians call *portamento*, literally a carrying of the tone from one pitch to the next that implements one of music's most cherished fictions: the illusion of continuous flow. Roughness or texturing in music is the product of staccato articulation, note attacks (where some extraneous noise elements are always present), accents, rhythmic punctuation, rests that interrupt the musical flow, the juxtaposition of contrasting timbres, anything in fact that gives the illusion of discontinuity. Throughout the history of Western music, preferences for the nature of the musical surface have varied with the taste of the period: Baroque and Classical taste favored a more textured surface, but Romantic preferences were for a smoother flow of sound. In our century the pendulum has swung back again to a preference for more articulated musical textures. It is easy to cite examples: for smooth textures, a performance of Robert Schumann's *Traumerei* on the piano, the smooth prolonged vowels of an Italian aria, or Samuel Barber's *Adagio for Strings;* for rougher, sharper texture, any composition for harpsichord, the crisp staccato woodwinds in Mendelssohn's scherzo from the incidental music for *A Midsummer Night's Dream*, any pizzicato passage for strings, or the more explosive consonants heard in German and Russian song.

Thin/dense. Other textural values may be discussed more briefly.

Thin/dense refers to the number of simultaneous sounds and their relative distribution over the pitch spectrum from low to high. Musical density ranges from a solo line to textures of more than fifty parts, as in Penderecki's *Threnody for the Victims of Hiroshima,* but most musical textures are closer to the thin end of the scale. Compositions such as Thomas Tallis's motet for forty voices, *Spem in alium,* are rare. There is an important reciprocal relationship between the number of parts and the melodic activity within a single part: thinner textures leave more room for and invite melodic activity, while the thicker textures have an inhibiting effect upon the individual line. We savor both ends of the scale: the mass of a dense texture, as in Mozart's Serenade, K. 361, for thirteen wind instruments, and the lean texture of a Baroque trio sonata by Corelli or Telemann. Dense textures have often been modeled after the distribution of the overtone series, i.e., with larger intervals at the bottom and progressively smaller intervals toward the top, since close spacings in low registers are difficult to perceive with any clarity.

Economy/saturation. At first glance this antithesis appears to be a variant of the simple/complex or thin/dense scales, but I mean something along the lines of the contrasting musical styles of such composers as Gabriel Fauré (plain, severe) and Richard Strauss or Gustav Mahler (lush). Certain composers seem to have a natural affinity for lavish use of the medium: colorful orchestral effects, a wide dynamic range, a full pitch spectrum, a profusion of themes, and generally a high level of rhythmic activity; others make more conservative use of their musical resources. Mahler's Symphony No. 8 (*The Symphony of a Thousand*) and Fauré's *Requiem* stand at opposite ends of this continuum.

Orientation: toward the vertical/chordal or the horizontal/linear. In textures oriented toward the vertical (homophonic, "same-voiced"), the tones are—in a sense—dependent in that they move together in chords or are subordinated to the melodic line. In textures oriented toward the horizontal (contrapuntal), the voices demonstrate greater independence and interweave with one another. Orientation preferences are often among the most distinctive features of the style periods in music history, and a change in basic orientation is often accompanied by or may produce major changes in music's other dimensions, e.g., the beginning of the Baroque (ca. 1600) was signaled by a sudden shift in orientation from the horizontal/linear to the vertical/chordal and followed by numerous other radical developments in musical style.

Focus/interplay. By this antithesis I mean the contrast between music in which our attention is focused upon musical activity that takes place along a single plane: a melody, a progression of chords, or a prominent solo instrument; and music in which the locus of activity shifts: from the treble to the bass, from one instrument to another, in the form of a dialogue or multiple conversation that compels us to shift our attention back and forth. Typical examples of the latter include the dramatic dialogue between low and high strings at the opening of Shostakovitch's Fifth Symphony, the interplay between the two solo violins and orchestra in J. S. Bach's Concerto in D Minor (BWV 1043), or the interchange of material between solo woodwind instruments in the development section of a Mozart or Beethoven symphony.

Tangle. One of the prime musical values is the sense of tangle that results from the contrapuntal interweaving of melodies, to which we may respond at first by dividing our attention and then by interpreting the tangled strands as surface when their complexity becomes too great to permit us to follow each line simultaneously. In Bach's Brandenburg Concerto No. 2, the four solo instruments (trumpet, flute, oboe, violin) remain clearly distinct because of their heterogeneous timbres, even though wound in, over, and about each other. Other notable examples of contrapuntal interweaving include the famous passage of quintuple invertible counterpoint from the coda to the first movement of Mozart's *Jupiter* Symphony, K. 551, and the no-less complex development of the first movement of Brahms's Second Symphony.[10]

Figuration, the organization of music in patterns. Sometimes these are thematic patterns, but often they are purely decorative, geometric patterns that function much like the background patterns on wallpaper. The uses of figuration are manifold: to decorate a melodic line, to provide a pleasingly textured background or accompaniment for melodies (as in the light scales and arpeggios assigned to the soloist in a typical Mozart piano concerto), to provide rhythmic motion and continuity (as in the violin figurations of a Vivaldi concerto), to fill in the harmonic background by outlining chords (as in Bach's Prelude in C Major from Book 1 of *The Well-Tempered Clavier*), to develop musical motives by repetition and sequence, and sometimes as pure, abstract structure (as in the athematic music of Erik Satie)—the musical analogue to cubism in the visual arts.

Dynamic values

By dynamic values I mean what I think Susanne Langer had in mind when she wrote that "the tonal structures we call 'music' bear a close logical similarity to the forms of human feeling—forms of growth and of attenuation, flowing and stowing, conflict and resolution, speed, arrest, terrific excitement, calm, or subtle activation and dreamy lapses. . . ."[11] Together with the more traditional temporal/rhythmic values these "forms" represent what many believe to be the most vital aspects of music: motion, change, and process. Musicians often use the term *dynamics* in a more technical sense to signify the loudness level of music and the very important contrast and modulations between various levels of intensity, and the present usage is not inconsistent with this view; in many of the values cited below, the effect is achieved by means of a correlation between motion and intensity.

Climax, the process of building toward and arrival at a musical high point, achieved by means of some or all of the following: increase in speed, increase in loudness, compression of musical patterns and events, textural thickening, increasing frequency of musical attack points, and numerous other musical clues that signal the sense of impending climax—whether a sudden outburst or a long, gradual build-up. Western listeners have acquired a jaded palate for climaxes as a result of pieces such as Tschaikowsky's *1812 Overture* which has become a regular part of Independence Day celebrations with cannons and fireworks. The placement and relative intensity of the climaxes in a musical work is a matter of concern for composer and performer: whether planned as a set of structurally equivalent peaks or a single, monumental climax. Our expectations for climax are undoubtedly conditioned by cultural notions of time and teleology; in the Western tradition climax is more a property of endings than of beginnings (although endings are not always climactic), and there are few pieces that reach a peak early and then gradually subside.

Anticlimaxes are equally effective in music: moments of hushed intensity and concentration when maximal attention is focused upon minimal musical activity—as, for example, in those heart-stopping moments late in the final acts of Verdi's operas (often a death scene) where the melodic line seems to hover in a set of soft, rhythmically free, emotional phrases, or the canonic vocal quartet "Mir ist so wunderbar" from act 1 of Beethoven's *Fidelio*, where all dramatic action is suspended while the four characters express their respective emotions.

Climaxes and the musical paths thereto may be rational or irrational, i.e., achieved by means of the traditional structural properties of music or in a more naturalistic, dramatic way. A prime example of such a rational climax is the famous Rossini crescendo, heard in the overtures to such operas as *La gazza ladra, La Cenerentola,* and *Semiramide:* regular, periodic phrases are repeated with gradually thickening texture, increasing loudness, and the addition of more and more instruments until the peak is reached; at this point the strings play tremolo supported by rapid trombone scales that serve to prolong the climax until the final cadence. The opening storm scene from Verdi's *Otello* illustrates a more "irrational" climax that follows a realistic meteorological script: flashes of thunder and lightning, sudden intervals of calm, raging seas, cannon shots, and dramatic cries. Subsiding after a climax is more difficult to achieve; such passages are often quite abrupt, seldom spun out to any great length.

Expressive semes. There is no doubt that within a limited segment of a musical culture it is possible to implant and communicate specific forms of expressive meaning, *semes* to use Eero Tarasti's term.[12] Some of the common semes in the Western tradition would include not only the lyric and the dramatic but possibly also the tragic, epic, heroic, comic, holy, cataclysmic, the sense of apotheosis, and perhaps also such traditional personality stereotypes as the melancholic, sanguine, choleric, and phlegmatic.[13] As examples of the lyric and the dramatic, readers may compare the openings of two of Mozart's piano concertos: K. 488 in A major (lyric) and K. 491 in C minor (dramatic). Such semes may be part of universal human experience, but their meaning does not automatically communicate to a member of a foreign culture by means of music alone: while all human beings experience such things as tension, the passage of time, motion, feelings of growth and decay, orientation toward and outreach into surrounding space, the familiar rhythmic patterns and accents of speech, rhythmic repetition, ambiguity, expectation, and the like, their cultural value and relative scale of intensity will differ widely, and they will be represented in a musical tradition in ways unique to the parent culture. But within Western musical society a certain number of basic semes have become so firmly established that it is virtually impossible for even a relatively uninformed member of that society to mistake their meaning. Even when these semes appear in abstract music—a symphony or a sonata—we are able to respond appropriately because of our familiarity with the same form of expression in music with a text, a specific title, overtly programmatic music, or some other extrinsic clue to the meaning embodied in the music.

A few additional reflections: the number of such semes is limited, restricted to a few of the most basic qualities of human expression. Their signaling musical characteristics are easier to equate to actual physical responses (tension, pulse rate, blood pressure, fatigue, respiration, arousal) than to the emotions that we associate with these responses; physical behavior, and hence the associations aroused by such behavior, is triggered by analogous musical behavior. But there seems to be little possibility of formulating a set of specific musical rules that would under all conditions produce the same, accurate response. A seme is the result of a cluster of specific musical behaviors *plus* the associations evoked in members of our society: hence the feeling of the sacred in the Holy Grail scene from act 1 of Wagner's *Parsifal* is communicated by means of the slow tempo, solemn mood, and musical material that conjures up memories of religious Communion music. To an Indian devotee of Krishna, such a seme would be meaningless without explanation.

Tension/release, one of the most basic of all physiological responses. One can argue that the most important of all of music's underlying rhythms is the binary rhythm of *alternation:* between sound and silence, strong and weak, ebb and flow, systole and diastole, stability and instability, ambiguity and certainty, action and repose, strictness and freedom. Such a binary rhythm is acted out on all of music's hierarchic levels; we may be consciously aware of the larger rhythms, but the subcutaneous tensings and relaxing with which we respond to the musical surface may pass unnoticed, registered only by unconscious muscular reactions and the corresponding nerve fibers in the brain. Here once again we are dealing with the results of cultural conditioning: all people experience tension but may interpret it in different ways, respond uniquely to it, and react according to differing scales of tension. The tension that a Western listener notices in traditional styles of Japanese singing will have a different meaning for the singer and his usual audience.

Western music is a complex hierarchy of structural levels, each with its own periodicities and alternations of tension and relaxation—created by patterns of stress, duration, and pitch relationships (consonance and dissonance). Any disturbance in the predictable flow of these rhythms may be experienced as affect. Tension in music can be the result of dissonance, instability (both implying the need to resolve to consonance and/or stability), ambiguity, complexity, deviation, implication; release comes in the form of consonance, stability, certainty of reference, simplicity or recognition of structure, return to the normative, fulfillment of expectation. As examples of tension in music, I suggest the dramatic pause near the end of Richard Strauss's *Don Juan*, the build-up of dissonance just before the hushed coda to Stravinsky's *Symphony of Psalms*, the harmonic ambiguities in the slow introduction to Mozart's *Dissonant* Quartet, K. 465, the opening of the last movement of Beethoven's Ninth Symphony, and the surface-level effect of the suspension figure in the music of the Baroque.

Growth/decay: feelings of increase, momentum, maintenance of identity, extension, enlargement, assimilation, and continuity—as opposed to feelings of decrease, loss of momentum, abbreviation, discontinuity, loss of focus, dissolution. The metaphor of organic development has been frequently applied in recent aesthetic literature, viewing art (and, in particular, music) as an analogue to the life process: the evolution of a cohesive musical whole from seminal melodic substance, each stage proceeding inevitably from its former stage. Barney Childs has projected a "narrative curve" as a model of our traditional expectations for both life and music: a gradual rise to climax and quicker subsiding:[14]

As excellent examples of growth in music, I suggest the orchestral prelude to Tschaikowsky's *The Queen of Spades* or the interlude in act 3 of Alban Berg's *Wozzeck*. Examples of musical decay or dissolution are rarer but effective; a good example is the end of the slow movement of Beethoven's *Eroica* Symphony.

Athleticism. It may seem strange to insert such a category of musical value, but I suspect strongly that people respond to the sense of athletic activity and of skillful accomplishment which implies, of course, more than the ability to play twenty percent more notes than anyone else in the same span of time. Probably this response is little different from the response of a spectator at an athletic event: music and sport have much in common, particularly in the organization of their temporal dimension but also, in a more abstract way, if we equate the musical dimension of pitch with the athletic use of space— a playing field, a board, movable pieces, encounters and interactions, oppositions and outcomes, interpenetrating pieces, moves, lines and vectors. Athleticism in music may suggest the sense of winning (against odds, a stopwatch, an opponent, over seemingly insuperable technical obstacles), of competition (as in the concerto genre), or simply a sense of exercise, of healthy muscular play and rhythmic flexings (as in the Baroque violin concerto). As an example of extreme athleticism in opera, I propose the tenor aria "Ecco ridente in cielo" from Rossini's The Barber of Seville or virtually any aria for coloratura soprano.

As the counterbalance to this value, I suggest that we often attach high musical value to the feeling of transcendental simplicity, projected in such works as Beethoven's Piano Sonata in E Major, Op. 109 (the final statement of the theme in the last movement) and Aschenbach's soliloquy by the well in the final act of Benjamin Britten's Death in Venice. Music has abundant means for suggesting this vision of ideal simplicity: clear, undisturbed tonality; focus on a simple melody with only minimal accompaniment; slow, periodic, regular motion; lack of ambiguity; simple textures and pure timbres—all symbolic of a return to primordial simplicity. Such endings have become popular in nineteenth- and twentieth-century music, evoking a cluster of associations: return to the womb, the simple state before creation, reunion with the divine or with undifferentiated matter, heaven, end of all pain and tension. In general, the Western notion of ending implies an expectation of a simpler—not a more complex—state.

Ambiguity, an important value in all the arts but a special property of music. Most music is written within a system, governed by sets of probabilities, rules, preferences, and implications that generate a continuous stream of expectation in the listener, who constantly matches the actualities of the piece against the probabilities of the system as he understands it, interpreting deviation from the norm as affect.[15]

Not all musical events imply tendencies, and of those that do many of the implications are clear and unambiguous; but other musical events give rise to ambivalent or ambiguous tendencies—a sense of competing possibilities or an effect that resists interpretation. Such musical ambiguities are especially strong in the very simple and the very complex: in the very simple, the sparsity of musical clues suggests multiple references, conclusions, resolutions; in the very complex, competing possibilities cancel each other out. Composers have made skillful use of ambiguity for a number of purposes: structurally, to enhance the effect of returning tonal or metric stability; tonally, to achieve new and unexpected modulations; as a means of communicating a sense of mystery; as a device for creating tension. In Western music ambiguity is often a property of beginnings and middles but seldom (until recently) of endings. It is not possible to be more specific about ambiguity in music without becoming highly technical, but some examples may be cited: the opening of Wagner's *Parsifal* is unsurpassed as an example of almost total ambiguity within a single melodic line; and we have already mentioned the harmonic ambiguity in the slow introduction to Mozart's quartet, K. 465. In one sense, our entire processing of a musical work is a successive reinterpretation of perceived ambiguity; as a piece unfolds, its possibilities diminish until the total ambiguity of beginnings is replaced with the total certainty of its completed form.

Temporal values

Temporality in music has been one of our main themes,[16] and all musical values—apart from isolated and simultaneous sounds—involve the temporal to some degree. But our concern here is with those musical phenomena that have traditionally been identified with the dimension of time: rhythm, tempo, and motion. Each musical work establishes its own time scale (the hierarchical structure of beats, groups, phrases, rates of motion) along which the events of the work are projected (the sense of motion or stasis, normative or deviant, and so on).

Motor rhythm. Perhaps the most basic of all temporal values is the sense of regular, vigorous rhythmic activity that we hear in such works as Ravel's *Bolero* and Carl Orff's *Carmina Burana:* strongly accented repetitive patterns that cause the listeners to tap their toes, drum their fingertips, or accompany the musical pulsations with some kind of internal muscular response. Baroque composers such as Antonio Vivaldi embodied this motoric rhythmic drive in their orchestral and solo concertos and evolved the concept of *tempo giusto* (It.: "the right tempo") which was taught by tradition and found by instinct. Motor rhythm requires both repetition and recurring accent, but the two need not coincide: Stravinsky, in the second section of act 1 of *The Rite of Spring,* maintains brilliantly the sense of vigorous rhythmic drive, offset by sharply irregular rhythmic accents on offbeats. All musical values make their strongest effect by contrast, and an entire evening of military marches loses its effect after a few selections: the sense of initiating a passage of motor rhythm, or of release from such a hypnotic passage, is stronger than its continuation.

Rate: fast/slow, tempo. The temporal scale of a musical work consists of a number of interlocking rates or periodicities: the rate of pulsation, the rate of accents, the rate of the shortest regular units of surface activity (called by ethnomusicologists the "density referent"),[17] the rates of patterns, phrases, the rate at which events succeed one another along this time scale, and larger periodicities. Our daily life is similarly a hierarchy of interlocking rates: the rate of the clock's hands, the daily schedule of appointments, our biological needs and diurnal physiological cycles, pulse and respiration rates, the rate of the daily events that occur along and punctuate our time scale, and the like. We tend to interpret both our music and our lives as teleological passage through a hierarchy of time cycles, but this betrays our identity as members of Western society.

Tempo is not an absolute judgment but a ratio between some arbitrarily selected rate in the music (usually that which we identify as *the beat*) and our notion of what we mean by such terms as *fast, moderate, slow,* and various shadings along this scale. Individual judgments may vary widely: a composer may conceive his music in slow main beats, with the intervening space filled in by patterned textures of surface activity; the listener may focus upon the surface rate and interpret the music as "fast"—which, in a sense, it is! It is generally accepted that tempi are interpreted as "moderate" when they parallel the pulse rate, "fast" when they exceed this rate by a significant degree, and "slow" when they fall short of it. Tempi are usually in a state of fluctuation, seldom maintaining any rate with mechanical accuracy; increasing speed is interpreted as excitement, decreasing speed as subsiding of tension. The steady tempo of motor rhythm is perceived as constant, but the variable *tempo rubato* of a Chopin nocturne (a tempo that at times lags behind and at times forges ahead of the basic rate with artistic deviations) is also an attractive musical effect and a source of value.

Hierarchy. We remarked earlier (in chap. 3) on the hierarchical nature of the time scale in Western music. One is usually no more aware of this hierarchy than one is aware of the hierarchy of typographical levels on a map: but the longer periodicities on the larger levels of the musical hierarchy are as difficult to grasp as the word *Canada* spaced out across a map of North America, with its letters separated by names for towns, cities, and provinces. Gustav Holst's "Fantasia on the Dargason," from his Suite in F for military band, is a brilliant demonstration of music's differing architectonic levels: in listening to this work, one's attention is compelled to shift from the opening fast tune to the melody of "Greensleeves" played at a slower tempo; each of the two melodies is articulated at a different hierarchic level, the measures of the former becoming the beats of the latter.

Logogenic/melogenic, terms coined by Curt Sachs, literally mean "word-born" and "melody-born."[18] Musical time has its own intrinsic characteristics but it sometimes employs the temporal patterns of speech—as in opera recitatives and various styles of sacred chant. The time of speech is more uneven, more constant in tempo, and flatter in hierarchy than the time of music, which is more regular, features a greater variety of tempi, and a steeper hierarchy. The rate of speech is determined in part by the characteristics of the language (e.g., the pace of Italian is much faster than that of German or Russian), and the meaning conveyed in speech is lost unless the speaker adheres to the norm. To speak twice as quickly or slowly may cause the listener to miss the meaning, but music routinely employs 4 : 1 and 8 : 1 increases and decreases in tempo. The hierarchy of speech may be represented as syllable/word/sentence, but the hierarchy of even the simplest piece of music could easily be twice as steep: several levels of subdivisions/beat divisions/beats/measures/phrases/phrase-groupings. As examples of logogenic rhythm, I suggest a passage of *secco* (It.: "dry") recitative from Mozart's *Don Giovanni* or the more naturalistic speech rhythms of Vaughan Williams's *Riders to the Sea;* as an example of melogenic rhythm, any Mozart aria will do.

Free/strict, the degree of [apparent] temporal control. In the

Western tradition we consider precise timing as normative, with temporal freedom as pleasantly expressive deviation—hardly surprising in an art that features musicians playing in groups and used to accompany dancing! Practical necessity has become a source of artistic value. But, at the same time, we have come to prize the apparent spontaneity and freedom that we infer in fantasias, toccatas, preludes, cadenzas, recitatives, and the like. At times it seems as if the pieces are improvised on the spot, and we are apt to consider them more as process than as object. On a smaller scale, composers have often inserted such moments of relative freedom between stricter sections of a piece, as interludes or transitions. And even within a relatively strict section, there are numerous opportunities for freedom: subtle modifications of the tempo (some prescribed, others not), *fermate* (It.: "holds"), and other minor deviations from the steady rhythm of beats and accents. Indeed, a hallmark of many inexperienced performers is their tendency to play with distressing mechanical regularity.

But some music is really free, with only minimal control of the time flow—especially in some of the musics of Asia and in the solo repertoire. At other times the sense of freedom is an illusion: the ambiguous opening of Wagner's *Parsifal* is under complete temporal control but deliberately contrived to avoid any implication of strict metric organization. The passage from free to strict musical time has developed into an important formal archetype in world music, in the form of a slow, loosely organized piece followed by a faster, more strictly organized piece—as in the opera recitative and aria of the eighteenth century, the Baroque keyboard prelude and fugue, the slow introduction and sonata-allegro first movement of the Classical symphony, or the *ālāp* and *tānam* of India.[19] In such pieces we sense first a music of *becoming*, then of *being*.

Motion/stasis. We take for granted that music has motion, and of course it does move: sonorous bodies vibrate, sound waves move toward the listener, whose hearing apparatus and central nervous system move in response, but the illusion of motion in music is something different. The motion we identify in music is no simple concept, although it may seem so at first: it includes the ideas of continuity, the rate of regular recurrence, the identity of a theme, the apparent rate of passage through time, direction toward a future goal, our own temporal aging during a piece of music, and the difference in rate between our own changes of state and those perceived in the music. Part of the confusion stems from failure to define our terms carefully and our assumption that motion is produced by all types of change. Our simplest example of motion is *locomotion*, change of place, and music does indeed provide numerous examples of locomotion: its vibration pattern moves through space, as I have pointed out, to the listener; a theme may move from instrument to instrument or from high to low register. But these moves, although they take place within time, are primarily spatial—not temporal. Other musical events that strike us as mobile may be described as a change of state or quality, but it is again questionable whether time in such cases is anything more than the field within which such change occurs.

I suggest that what we ordinarily mean when we speak of musical motion is a kind of *vehicular* motion, similar to the progress of a railroad train along a set of tracks; the motion may be intermittent, may be at a steady or a variable rate, but we perceive a continuous musical identity moving past our field of hearing. If we accept the paradox that the vehicle is itself in a process of virtually continuous change, the analogy becomes more appropriate.[20] To complicate the matter further, the temporal scale of the entire work—although only a portion of it is revealed to our hearing at any one instant—is established and modified by the successive states of the vehicle! These reflections do not begin to suggest the complexity of the philosophical problem involved in trying to define motion in music, but they may at least serve to introduce the idea that the "flow" of music can be interpreted either as motion or stasis.

We consider motion normative in music: the logical successions of tones, chords, and phrases that generate and resolve tendencies, suggest and fulfill implications, propelling musical identities (themes, motives, gestures) at various rates and directing them toward a future goal. We can play themes backwards, reverse the order of twelve-tone rows, retrograde rhythmic patterns, and reverse the order of musical events and formal sections, but we have no model on which to base the sense of a backward flow of time. We may perhaps interpret a series of short, repetitive events as continuous passage through the same period of time—with time set side-by-side, as it were—but I think it more likely that we interpret any such departure from the traditional teleology of music as stasis: a continuous present, the mythical "eternal return,"[21] timelessness,[22] surrender of the Self in states of extended consciousness, or other models of suspended time. Examples of static music began to appear in the nineteenth century and have become more frequent since 1950: their common denominator is continuity without goal, identifiable vehicle, or articulation of structure. Clearly music that avoids thematic structure and/or the implicative properties of tonality is more likely to be perceived as stasis; thematic, tonal music remains mobile by definition. The following types of music imply such a sense of timelessness: music with extensive repetition, trance music and pieces that employ continuous sound loops, sound mass pieces, music that is nonhierarchical, music that is randomly ordered, minimalist pieces, extremely ambiguous music, extended climax, and stream-of-consciousness music with extensive use of citation and allusion to other pieces.[23] Another paradox is that too much mobility in music may cause us to lose our bearings and perceive this music as stasis. Deep within us we realize that the essence of music is vibration and that the vibration of sustained musical tones and events is analogous to the pulsating energy of a living cell; nondirected motion is interpreted as cellular oscillation—sonorous, vibrant, often pleasing, but not (in our interpretation) motion in music's traditional sense.

Conflict and *deviation.* We enjoy a certain amount of pleasant interference with the normative temporal patterns in our music. Music that subserviently follows the normal course and observes the predictable accents is seldom interesting for long, unless interest arises as a result of other dimensions of the music—attractive timbres, a compelling melody, and the like. The phenomenon we call syncopation (a displacement of the normative accents) is but one example. The establishment of temporal scale in a musical work requires the establishment of predictable, periodic accent points, similar to the inch marks along a ruler and the smaller markings that indicate the intermediate divisions. All music with any rhythmic interest deviates from this scaling to some degree: minor deviation may escape our attention, but major deviation is perceived as affect. The range of musical conflict runs from the simple interaction of two simultaneous background patterns (e.g., 2 against 3) to the complex interaction of two or more themes in a passage of symphonic development. Music may even embody the conflict between the rational and the irrational: the irrational rhythms of an African master drummer superimposed freely upon the more complex but rational rhythmic background of the ensemble.

Musical time has traditionally been a synchronized, common time, but certain recent composers (Lutosławski, Carter) have begun to explore the possibilities of nonsynchronized music and multiple time lines within the same composition. Thus musical conflict may be localized or pervasive, involving two or many components; it may suggest multiple and unrelated musical strands, or it may (in our perception) fuse together into a single, complex gestalt. To establish the time scale in any composition is to set a norm: one can deviate from the basic rate (tempo), from the overall temporal orientation (in a cadenza, recitative, or other passage in freer time), or from the scale of accents (as in syncopation). There is obviously a similar opportunity (indeed, a necessity) for deviation as a composition passes through its successive stages: from the composer's conception, through its notated form and the performer's rendition, into the listener's perception. Despite some composers' pleas for faithfully exact interpretation of their music, a certain amount of deviation is inevitable.

Structural values

The word *structure* is perhaps one of the most abused words in our language. In referring to the structure of music, we often carelessly lump together several meanings for which the Greeks had developed specialized terms, i.e., *schema*, external shape or design; *taxis*, internal pattern and arrangement; *morphe*, form as opposed to content, the most general term for form; and *eidos*, causal principle, essential form.[24] Our previous discussions have not entirely avoided aspects of structure, especially with regard to such issues as textural orientation, focus/interplay, temporal rates, and hierarchy—all exceedingly important in any consideration of the structure of music. The order in which we have dealt with the values of music and the taxonomy have been arranged in a progression from phenomena that make an immediate impact by means of sheer sensation to phenomena that require reflection and interpretation. As we have progressed from the more sensuous toward the more structural values, the emphasis has shifted from the subjective to the verifiable: the beauty, significance, and meaning of structure may be debated but its existence may not be.

Causal principle, the idea that makes a piece the way it is, the composer's vision of the whole.[25] There are many musical works so simple in structure that they consist of a single, unitary musical thought—one consistent block of music. But in more complicated works, it is surprising how few essentially different structural principles have been devised. There are, most obviously, innumerable variations on these basic principles. I suggest five specific principles that pervade the musical repertoire, described here in deliberately broad terms:

strophic, an unspecified number of more-or-less exact repetitions of a musical module, a principle deriving from the verses and stanzas of formal poetry and obviously appropriate for songs

variation, an accumulation of successive revisions (generally elaborations) of a musical module, as in a theme with variations

girder, a musical work organized around (sometimes over) a single musical line that gives support to the structure in much the same way that an encased steel rod supports a pillar of concrete; a more technical name for this principle is cantus firmus, the technique used in medieval motets and Baroque chorale preludes.

mosaic, a work put together by juxtaposing contrasting modules of music, as in the rondo and the smaller part-forms; its two primary values are contrast and reprise.

organic, a musical work that develops from some seminal substance in the manner of a living organism, featuring such properties as growth, development, ambiguity, tension, increasing complexity, climax, and perhaps also decay. This category includes such major structural types as fugue and sonata-allegro.

Several of these principles hybridize successfully, e.g., variation and girder in such forms as the ground, passacaglia, and chaconne; mosaic and organic in Beethoven's favorite type of rondo, as in the last movements of his Third Piano Concerto and Violin Concerto. The brief descriptions given above have deliberately avoided questions of tonality and tonal structure, but most obviously these forms can be given an additional dimension depending upon the degree of tonal coherence and/or contrast. Strophic forms tend to avoid tonal contrast, variation and girder forms minimize tonal contrast, while mosaic and organic forms usually employ tonal networks (of related and distant keys) and contrasts as a main part of their formal strategy.

Structural functions, the distinctive roles of the various formal components in music, each characterized by a specific formal purpose and distinctive tonal/thematic tactics or behaviors. The structural functions identified here are taken from the musical repertoire between ca. 1700 and 1950; certain, quite different, structural functions seem to be emerging in music written during the last thirty years, but it is a bit too soon to isolate them with any confidence. The function of any component of musical structure may be described in terms of its purpose (beginning, statement, transition) and its behavior—both tonal (stable, unstable) and thematic (presentation, fragmentation, recombination):

> *beginnings,* various conventionalized ways of starting a piece, with the following tactical objectives: to establish the time scale of the composition, overcome the inertia of the framing silence, give tonal focus and lay out the tonal field, forecast the scope, energy level, and accentual weight of the composition, and similar matters. Four popular strategies may be discerned: *emergence,* a kind of musical creatio ex nihilo (Beethoven's Ninth Symphony, 1); *entrainment,* drawing the listener into the musical time fabric without ceremony (Mendelssohn's Violin Concerto, 1); *assertion,* beginning the composition with a larger-than-life dramatic gesture (Strauss's *Don Juan*); and *duration,* beginning with an extended, unarticulated musical duration (Beethoven's *Egmont* Overture). Introductions and musical prefaces of various types are quite common in the music of this period and are frequently slower and looser in organization than the main section that follows.[26]

> *endings,* conventionalized ways of achieving musical closure with an appropriate sense of finality, patterned terminal units that sum up, reinforce, or disperse the tonal and rhythmic energies and tendencies accumulated during the course of the work. Typical ending strategies include *hyperbolic repetition* via hammered chords and rhythmic intensity (Beethoven's Fifth Symphony, 4); *apotheosis,* an extended, continuous coda (Stravinsky, *Symphony of Psalms*); *duration* (Mendelssohn, Overture to *A Midsummer*

Night's Dream); *dissolution into chaos* (Beethoven, *Eroica* Symphony, 2); and *return to the beginning* (Britten's *Peter Grimes*). Endings, like beginnings, tend to be rhetorical: most pieces end, but few pieces quit. Tonal reinstatement is generally a property of endings in tonal music, with but very few exceptions. It is not uncommon for a piece to be given multiple endings.

statements, thematic presentations, including also the transposition of a stated theme to another key, register, or instrument

transitions and various types of musical junctions between themes, sections, or any other structural units. There are two important types: gradual, bridging transitions that impose a sense of connection between one module and another, and interludes/episodes that serve to separate rather than to connect. Transitions are usually quite unstable in tonality, but interludes may be stable. Both types may use material from the previous or following section or may be cut from completely different material. The larger and more organic the structure, the more likely it will make use of extensive transition sections.

approaches, unstable passages that build tension and direct attention toward the beginning of a following section, implying imminent arrival at an important structural point. Approaches may feature a long chord of preparation for the forthcoming key or may bring the harmony around to the proper arrival point by means of some continuous process, such as a harmonic sequence. The characteristics of an approach include processive continuity, tension, preparation, implication, and goal direction.

prolongations, passages whose main purpose is to continue the style and sense of the previous musical section, either by extending the domain of the tonic note, chord, or key (often by means of a pedal point) or by spinning out the same musical texture, thematic substance, and rhythmic activity. It is neither a repetition nor a variation but an outgrowth of what preceded it. Prolongations are often less thematic than the sections whose effect they prolong; although often similar in manner to approaches, they are backward looking rather than forward looking.

developments, passages that fragment and analyze previously stated material, featuring tonal instability, thematic presentations in new keys, conflict and interaction, dramatic contrasts and ambiguity

combinations, passages that synthesize and combine previously stated material, either successively (forging a number of short motives into a continuous melodic line) or simultaneously (as in the reprise of Wagner's Overture to *The Mastersingers of Nuremberg*)

reprises, the return of previous material, especially near the end of a work and in the original tonality (as in the recapitulation of virtually any symphonic first movement by Haydn, Mozart, or Beethoven). The sense of recognition produced by a reprise is one of the most powerful structural values in music.

Theme. Much music is organized into clear foreground and background strata, directing attention toward a musical subject or theme that is projected against a lighter musical background or accompaniment. Thematic music may be equated with representational painting or sculpture: themes may be stated, restated, transposed, varied, developed, combined, and eventually reinstated; progressive ambiguity, loss of identity, and recovery of identity and/or context are important melodic values that occur in most works from the period under study. Athematic music is often used in introductions, episodes, conclusions, or other sections emphasizing rhythmic continuity, instability, or sheer texture. What is often taken to be athematic music is really music in which the thematic elements are obscured—either by clutter of texture, lack of clear presentation in a prominent musical line, or in contrapuntal textures where thematic activity is distributed throughout all the parts. There are, however, effective examples of truly nonthematic music that rely on repetitive patterns of surface to induce the illusion of musical stasis and present the background as subject (as in many of the piano pieces of Erik Satie).

Melody. I have deliberately avoided this controversial topic until now, preferring not to risk specifying the characteristics of what many listeners believe to be the ultimate test of a composition: whether it contains a strand of thematic continuity that (according to their preferences) is worth hanging onto. The many books that advise how to listen to music insist that the inexperienced listener attach himself to the main melodic thread, which may not be bad advice except that the listener is apt to infer that the prominence and character of a melody is the primary criterion by which a piece should be judged. For many listeners *melody* is simply equated with the values of *song* or *tune* and judged accordingly. But melodic styles change almost as often as skirt lengths, and even in the nineteenth century we can detect a variety of distinct melodic styles: an ornate, Chopinesque melodic line; a quasi-recitative with narrow ambit and speechlike rhythmic patterns; a more instrumental type of melody with wider range, leaps, scales, and idiomatic instrumental figures; and a type of line that hovers around single pitches and is distinguished more by its context and harmonic background than its tunefulness.

The main values of melody probably include the following: *exposure*, the prominence of a musical line; *shape*, the distinctive curves and contours, range, and the nature of the melodic increments (steps, leaps); *periodicity*, how a melody is articulated by regular or irregular breath pauses, caesuras, cadences, phrases, rhyme schemes, as well as the process by which it unfolds in time—the statement and development of motivic fragments, long continuous lines, and the like; *tonality*, the referential aspect of melody, its internal focus upon a central pitch and scale; and *implication*, the creation of tendencies, and the tricking or fulfilling of the listener's expectations.

Nobody can say what makes a melody "good," although overly complex and overly simplistic melodies may strike one as equally unsatisfying. Our melodic preferences, like our rhythmic preferences, are formed in early childhood and—more than any other musical values—are products of cultural conditioning. It is hard to escape the early experiences that teach us that melody "should be" lyric, songlike, mostly conjunct, clearly tonal, unambiguous, periodic, and with graceful contours. The more jagged, atonal, ambiguous, nonimplicative, motivic, instrumentally conceived melos of Schoenberg, Hindemith, Stravinsky, and Webern rewards (in many cases) the efforts of practiced students of contemporary music but faces a formidable obstacle in trying to win the hearts of the many whose musical values have been developed through exposure to simpler, more traditional melodic models.

Variation, the elaboration and/or revision (and occasionally the simplification) of previous musical substance, one of the most pervasive processes in music at all times and in all places, playing upon one of the most basic musical values—the sense of *identity*. "Identity

preserved amidst change" is perhaps the broadest definition of variation; *contrast* signifies loss of identity or the establishment of another
identity. It is clearly impossible to say at what point repetition becomes variation (when the inescapable quanta of change require interpretation as significant change), or when variation becomes contrast (when fragile identity is finally lost amidst the complexities of
change). I venture to suggest that the popularity of variation in world
music is due to its psychic symbolism: the preservation, development
of, and reinstatement of identity of the Self during the passage through
life. Variation is involved with an associated musical value: the interplay of *structure* and *decoration*. Music is an inherently decorative art,
although the amount and type of decoration varies with style and
period.

    Tonality, the referent property of music that establishes and
plays upon the allegiance of pitches to a tone of reference (the
"tonic"), a scale, and sometimes an entire network of pitch relationships. By reference I mean not only a fixed referent point but the process that determines the implicative properties of all the musical tones.
Tonality in music is easier to hear than to describe; its aural effect is
programmed into all human experience of music.

Value clusters

    Our enumeration of the preceding musical values may suggest
that they are separate phenomena that are perceived and judged one
at a time, but of course this is not the case. At times we may be aware
of a single musical process or effect that overshadows all other aspects
of a musical work, but more often the impact of a composition is the
result of an interplay of many musical qualities—sometimes reinforcing each other, sometimes contradictory. Successful works in the
many different musical genres and forms display their own distinctive
sets of values, which I will attempt to isolate in the following pages. I
propose "value clusters" for four of the major musical designs: theme
with variations, fugue, sonata-allegro, and the concerto. Certain of
these values may have much wider—perhaps even universal—application, but I would like to make clear that in this context they are values of the style period within which these forms developed and the

result of any number of personal decisions and preferences of the composers who wrote in these forms and thus created models for later composers.

Theme with variations (as in Beethoven's "Diabelli" Variations or the Piano Variations, Op. 35), one of the most popular formal plans in music history since the Renaissance and featuring these values:

> *identity preserved amidst change,* in that certain features of the theme (melody, bass, harmonic progression, phrase structure) are retained in the successive variations, in this way producing unity amidst variety
>
> *decoration,* the elaboration of the theme in ways consistent with the prevailing style and preferences
>
> *ingenuity,* in that the composer's skill in devising new variations is constantly on display and becomes one of the main goals of the piece
>
> *amplification,* in that features of the theme are subject to progressive enlargement
>
> *profusion,* delight in the abundance of new and interesting treatments in each variation of the theme. Some pieces are admired for their economy of means and tightness of organization but not variations!
>
> *cumulativeness,* in that variations are a paratactic (not a syntactic) structure and make their effect by an additive process[27]
>
> *completeness:* most successful musical works persuade us that they have achieved a certain gestalt and are really complete. In variations there is obviously no end to the possible variations one can invent, but the composer usually manages to find convincing closure—either by exhausting his audience or by some sort of summation procedure that signals imminent closure.
>
> *limited hierarchy:* the theme itself and each of its variations may be subdivided into the usual hierarchic levels (sections, phrases, measures, beats, beat divisions and subdivisions), but there is seldom any higher level other than the entire work. The structure of a theme with variations is modular; and even if the modules (variations) are not of equal length, they are, in a certain sense, perceived as equal in that their ratio of length to the landmarks

of the theme is a constant one: halfway through the theme is halfway through the theme, whether achieved in ten seconds or four minutes. There are seldom any deep structures in theme and variation works: attention is focused upon surface detail.

temporality: the time of a theme with variations is sequential, constant (for the reasons given above), cyclic (in that each variation begins anew), modular, directional, but not especially teleological—in that there is no particular goal in sight nor any particular point by which one expects to reach a goal.

tonal stasis: variations generally do not depend upon contrasting keys and key relationships for their overall structure; harmonic and textural variety are considered more important than tonal variety.

Fugue (as in any of J. S. Bach's fugues from the two books of *The Well-Tempered Clavier*), a contrapuntal keyboard genre that arose in the late Renaissance and developed into one of the most characteristic forms of the Baroque:

economy, making much out of little. Fugues are extremely thrifty, tight compositions, frequently developing the entire composition out of the distinctive intervallic/rhythmic structure of the subject.

cleverness, apparent or concealed. Writing a fugue requires dexterity in counterpoint and skill in maintaining the inexorable progress of the work. "Learned devices" such as augmentation, diminution, and inversion are often exploited.

tangle, a pleasant feeling of immersion in an ongoing process amidst the complex weave of the musical texture

identity preserved amidst change, but in a different sense than in the theme with variations: the identity in a fugue is a single musical line—the subject—surrounded by a constantly changing context. The identity of the subject is asserted intermittently, dropping out for short periods and then reappearing.

imitation between the various parts, compelling us to listen obliquely or diagonally—making a mental connection between the same musical event stated successively and overlapping in the different parts *continuity,* a sense of inevitable, perpetual motion at an even rate of speed. The temporality of a fugue is generally uniform, even relentless from beginning to end, although moments of lesser activity and lighter texture provide some relief. The motion we perceive in a fugue is the result of constant rhythmic activity distributed among the various parts and the surface-level rhythm of dissonance/consonance that helps to propel the work.

tonal interplay, in three successive stages: exposition in the main tonality, motion to and among related tonalities, and, finally, reaffirmation of the main tonality. Another type of tonal interplay—the alternation of passages of stable and unstable tonality—is heard throughout a fugue.

combination, the solution of an apparent musical puzzle by putting various thematic elements together in new combinations, occurring more and more as the piece nears its end

Sonata-allegro (as in the first movements of Mozart's Symphony in G Minor, K. 550, or Beethoven's Fourth Symphony), a complex structure developed during the Classical period at the hands of Haydn, Mozart, and others:

scenario: a dramatic cycle of establishment (exposition), conflict (development), and restoration (recapitulation), analogous to one of the pervasive structural principles in Western drama

parallel (syntactic) structure: between the exposition and recapitulation, deviating by means of various extensions, insertions, abbreviations, and different tonal tactics

differentiation of structural functions: multiple beginnings and endings, expositions differentiated from transitions, developments, arrivals, delays, and approaches

processing of musical material, especially in the development section, fragmentation and combination in various ingenious ways

predictability: the sonata-allegro structure suggests numerous possibilities for stimulating and tricking expectation, matching present event against the memory of past model.

stability and instability, a rhythm that runs throughout the work but especially in the large pattern of exposition (stability/in-stability contrasted), development (larger amounts of instability), and recapitulation (stability restored)

variable rates of motion, correlated with uneven levels of tension and alternating areas of high and low activity

connection, between intermittent or widely separated musical events. More than any of the other traditional formal plans, sonata-allegro often makes its effect by means of long-term memory, long-term anticipation, and complex syntactic processes. Consecutive events are often discontinuous but justified by high-level hierarchic structures and processes.

Concerto (as in a Handel organ concerto or any of Mozart's piano concertos), a multimovement genre that developed during the Baroque and has remained popular ever since:

the solo persona, presenting a soloist or group of soloists and projecting the performer's musical personality

interplay, between solo and group: opposition, alternation, combination, melody projected against a background, and the like

athleticism, the display of virtuoso technique, especially in brilliant solo cadenzas

figuration, the prominent use of patterns idiomatic to the solo instrument(s), producing the sense of appropriateness between medium and material

superimposition, of the above values on the structural patterns and values of other musical forms such as the sonata-allegro, rondo, theme with variations, and the smaller part-forms

multimovement designs: cycles of moderately fast and athletic first movements, slow and lyrical second movements, fast and brilliant finales

Pervading values

There are larger values that subsume many of the individual musical qualities we have identified in the preceding pages: I am thinking of the three general standards labeled by Monroe Beardsley as "General Canons" of criticism—the canons of unity, complexity, and intensity.[28] Most—if not all—of the values of music promote ultimately one of these three aims, serving thereby to unify, vary, or intensify the musical work and the listener's experience thereof. As examples of *unity*—tonality, motor rhythm, hierarchy, and the various structural principles; *complexity*—interplay, tangle, ambiguity, deviation, conflict; *intensity*—climax, growth, athleticism, certain timbral values.

One is immediately reminded of Thomas Aquinas's similar set of artistic canons (discussed in chapter 6): *perfectio, integritas*—unity, coherence, completeness; *proportio, consonantia*—by which Aquinas meant harmony, the balance achieved between dissimilar components; *claritas*—radiance, intensity.

To a medieval author, "variety" or "complexity" meant rational, proportionate complexity, not ambiguity, confusion, deviation, or any irrational artistic measure; but in all other respects we may equate these two schemes. This set of values seems not only to be timeless but even universal, not limited by any conventions of style, period, genre, medium, or culture. Unity, complexity, intensity may be achieved by various means and present in varying degree from one culture or style period to another, but their existence as objective critical standards can scarcely be disputed.

A work of art (of music), if it is to satisfy, must be coherent enough to meet the test of unity, varied enough to satisfy the canon of complexity, and colorful enough to meet the demand for intensity. Works lacking unity are chaotic and incoherent, works lacking in complexity will strike one as simplistic and boring, and works with a low level of intensity will be judged dull. It is easy to cite successful works that appear to fall short in one or another of these respects: the music of Charles Ives compels critical respect despite its frequent lack of unity; the hypnotic musics of Erik Satie and Morton Feldman display a very low level of both complexity and intensity, although it is arguable that their relatively narrow range of tonal and dynamic contrast tends to amplify whatever contrasts are present; and many lyrical miniatures of Romantic song have little intensity. One can rationalize all these "deficiencies" away, but I prefer to believe that a musical work can indeed succeed while violating virtually any aesthetic value, compensating with the sheer excellence of its ideas, content, manner, rhetoric, or structure. But such a claim does not in any way diminish the importance of these basic values as norms and critical standards to which most excellent works will conform. One cannot prescribe ideal amounts of unity, complexity, and intensity for a particular musical composition, but the unity, complexity, and intensity that the work displays may and should be cited as objective reasons for its value.

Valuation

The final section of this chapter deals with valuation and critical judgment—a process that begins with a perception, continues with a statement of preference (or lack of preference), and concludes by stating a reason for the judgment. Our verbal evaluations are often incomplete, but all three stages can easily be inferred. A typical judgment might go like this: "This music has a dramatic quality, which I find exciting; and I like it, since I enjoy excitement in a work of art."

Valuation is often built on exceedingly complicated assumptions, particularly when we try to judge a work as a whole, balancing all the qualities we perceive in the work against the personal and cultural criteria ("standards") that we hold—knowingly or unknowingly—and at the same time trying to filter out all the extraneous data and irrelevant reasons that so often crowd in upon aesthetic judgments. As I remarked earlier, this chapter is not a primer for critics; a proper investigation of musical judgments would have to include a far more extensive study of the language of criticism and the types of reasons given in support of critical judgments. These are important matters, but they carry our discussion too far afield into "applied" aesthetics. Critics generally agree that judgments ought to be as objective as possible, based on true perception of the values in an art work and made with the deepest understanding of the standards of one's cultural tradition (which includes a proper regard for the danger of applying them too rigorously). Meyer sums up our problem: "Value refers to a quality of musical experience. It is inherent neither in the musical object per se nor in the mind of the listener per se. Rather value arises as the result of a transaction, which takes place within an objective tradition, between the musical work and a listener."[29] We have attempted to isolate and organize the musical values of just such an objective tradition—musical style in Europe and America between 1700–1950. Most of these values may be subsumed under one of the three general canons of *unity, complexity,* and *intensity,* but each influences our response to music in a very specific way.

I would like to comment briefly on some judgmental clichés that are often invoked.

"Strikes an appropriate balance between . . ." (e.g., unity and variety, simplicity and complexity, ends and means, the various parts, immediate and delayed gratification). Most of us would find it hard to disagree with a judgment couched in such terms, but it misses—I think—the real reason behind the judgment. Moderation and balance have long been praised in aesthetics, but it is hard to become excited over moderation. To achieve such a balance probably means more to have avoided error than to have achieved the good. What is probably meant is that the work is neither too chaotic nor too dull, neither simplistic nor overly complex—but is this really why we like it? I think not. Such a statement can usually be supported by more specific reasons for one's favor.

"Each in its own way," another common phrase that seems at times an evasion of responsible criticism. It is certainly true that one should apply different standards at different times to different works, but to assert that everything "in its own way" is beautiful, true, or good is to misapply popular song aesthetics to philosophy. The Westerner who attempts to appreciate Asian dance, music, and theater on its own terms must indeed realize that such things as beauty, unity, variety, and intensity are implemented in culture-specific ways; in such an attempt "each in its own way" is at least an honest acknowledgment that crosscultural understanding requires learning. But to apply the phrase indiscriminately to one's own tradition is a cop-out.

"It's good, but I don't like it!" (Or, in reverse: "it may be bad, but I like it!") Individual preferences are complex, often capricious, occasionally perverse. Voltaire is reported to have said of God, "I can admire Him, but I cannot love Him"—a phrase that might describe the way one listener would react to a given composer's personality. And sometimes we are simply not up to masterpieces such as Beethoven's *Missa Solemnis* or Bach's *St. Matthew Passion,* preferring to spend our time with works that demand less from us. It is not quite as clear why we like pieces that we may know, or suspect, to be mediocre or downright bad: we tend to form relationships with particular pieces, perhaps even come to have a feeling of proprietorship or emotional investment in them, bringing to mind Touchstone's famous line in *As You Like It:* "an ill-favor'd thing . . . but mine own" (act 5, sc. 4:59). These pieces may be tinged with pleasant associations, or we may value their message or symbolic meaning, or the reason may be trivial. The only error, it seems to me, is to confuse subjective reaction with objective judgment.

"It has passed the test of time." Survival does not automatically confer excellence upon a musical work. Mediocre pieces are preserved and good pieces lost with the same frequency that the good are allowed to suffer, while the evil escape punishment! There are probably sound reasons why most musical works that have endured have endured, but the fact alone is insufficient ground for critical favor. We hear many stories of how certain works have won eventual favor despite an overwhelmingly unfavorable reception at their first performance (e.g., Bizet's opera *Carmen*), but it is undoubtedly true that other excellent works have been scrapped as a result of hostile circumstances.

"So-and-so has praised it," the medieval doctrine of *auctoritas*. Marcus Aurelius taught us how to value critical acclaim: "Whatever is in any way beautiful hath its source of beauty in itself, and is complete in itself; praise forms no part of it. So it is none the worse nor the better for being praised."[30] Criticism may and should be taken seriously, but judgments are not reasons.

"It is overwhelming." Many compositions make an intense first impression but fail to live up to this impression on subsequent hearings; and conversely many works require repeated hearings. Epictetus addressed this situation when he wrote, "Be not swept off your feet by the vividness of the impression, but say, 'Impression, wait for me a little. Let me see what you are and what you represent. Let me try you.' "[31]

"This scherzo has a demonic intensity and magically glowing colors," a type of statement that falls into what Beardsley has called the "fallacy of surreptitious emotive effect!"[32] When a critic uses colorful language as a tool of persuasion, it is a little underhanded.

Guidelines for excellence in music: a proposal

It is time to suggest how the preceding value criteria may be assembled into a workable package on which objective musical judgments can be based. The following proposed set of guidelines, with which many readers will agree only in part, is put forward as one musician's assessment of the critical standards that now exist within the cultural consensus of Western civilization. They deserve testing. The order of the guidelines does not indicate a priority ranking, since it is the total package that matters. The appeal of a particular composition may, of course, rest on other values on which there is no discernible consensus. And it is a useful and not a difficult exercise to cite individual works that have achieved excellence despite their violation of one or more of these standards. But, all things being equal (and they never are), a musical composition is more likely to deserve a rating as

excellent if—	less than excellent if—
1 it invites perception as a unified, coherent structure	it resists perception as a unified, coherent structure
2 its structure is clearly articulated and well scaled (proportionate)	its structure is obscure or disproportionate
3 it is complete and fulfilled	it is incomplete and unfulfilled
4 it is hierarchical	it is unhierarchical
5 it is focused, typically by some tonal means, so that the mind is thereby directed through the work's distinctive structure	it is unfocused
6 it is perceptibly thematic	it is athematic
7 it imparts a sense of motion, continuity, and dynamic change	it conveys a sense of stasis
8 it has a textured surface	its surface is not textured
9 it is sonically "saturated," rich in intensity and tonal color[33]	it is unsaturated
10 it avoids self-contradiction (e.g., poor text setting, clumsy	it is self-contradictory

use of the medium, pointless in-
consistencies of the musical language)

11   it strikes an appropriate   it fails to strike an appropriate
balance between   balance between

    a   unity and variety
    b   simplicity and complexity
    c   frustrating expectation and the immediate
        gratification of expectation[34]
    d   ends and means

It follows that the best performance is that which best articulates
and balances the properties of excellence. The demands for hierarchical structure, textured surface, and tonal saturation seem the most
likely to provoke argument, but I maintain that these values *are* part
of the cultural consensus, although the precise type and degree of
hierarchy, texturing, and saturation cannot be specified. The demand
for focus is perhaps the fuzziest, but it can be met in a variety of ways
and should not be equated with tonality as traditionally defined; focus
may be the result of a distinctive set of timbres, texture, or mode of
organization of the sound spectrum—or it may be a thread of continuity, a channel that preserves mental orientation amidst the unfolding structure. Perhaps the most convincing proof that these guidelines
are a valid reflection of our tradition is that avant-garde composers, in
recent years, have systematically violated each and every one. The
consensus has shown signs of crumbling since Beethoven, more rapidly since 1900. We will return to this theme in the final chapter, after
an excursus into the value systems and musical preferences of two important Asian cultures.

IO   Comparative aesthetics: India and Japan

> We worship that divine Sound, the life of consciousness in all beings and the supreme bliss, manifested in the form of the universe. By the adoration of sound, the gods Brahma, Vishnu, and Shiva are truly worshipped, for they are the embodiment of sound. [Śārṅgadeva][1]
>
> That which is unseen is flowers. [Japanese proverb]

THE PRESENT CHAPTER addresses the traditional musics and musical philosophies of India and Japan, two important and contrasting old high cultures of South and Northeast Asia. This brief introduction to comparative aesthetics will demonstrate one of our basic premises—that musical values are products of culture, not universal absolutes. The vast diversity of Asian musical thought will not be apparent from this discussion, most particularly because it excludes any consideration of the Islamic traditions of West Asia. The contrasts between various Asian schools of thought—in their views of the musical dimensions, their ontology and epistemology, their views of external nature and the internal world of the human body and mind, their psychology, genres, specific preferences, and the role of the aesthetic in human life—are as striking as the more predictable contrasts with the West. My approach will be to proceed from the external to the internal, from the phenomena of music to the underlying theoretical and philosophical concepts, from the descriptive to the prescriptive. I begin with some preliminary descriptions of typical Japanese and Indian musics, which I follow with a comparative discussion of the cultural preferences that have influenced the organization of sound, then continue with a study of certain important concepts and terms that reveal the unique values of Japanese aesthetics, and conclude with an analysis of the two most important philosophical foundations of Indian music—the theories of *rasa* (taste, flavor) and *nāda* (causal sound).

The opening quotations remind us vividly that the philosophy of art speaks many languages and that the fundamental beliefs and habits of thought are as diverse as the languages with which they are given voice. From the Western perspective, the milieu of Asian aesthetics is not only exotic but, at the same time, reminiscent of medieval Western thought with its metaphysical assumptions and transcendental values. For centuries Asian philosophers have pondered many of the great issues addressed by Western authors: the nature of beauty, the human experience of art, the being of music, how to obtain valid musical knowledge, the purpose of art, precepts for its creation, music's relationship to the other arts, the values (both sensuous and formal) embodied in the musical object, and the supporting values of the parent culture. But these issues have been approached in typically Asian ways and discussed in language arising from distinctively Asian modes of thinking and experiencing.

What can be said, in general, about the philosophy of art in the high cultures of Asia? First, that the practice of art is informed by an elaborate and ancient system of thought with traditional topics and categories and a corpus of artistic theory that represents many centuries of analysis and speculation. Asian art is prescriptive, conforming to a variety of traditional canons, models, and values. Most of the arts of Asia feature the rigorous refinement of a limited spectrum. Consciousness of the human body and its operation is a common theme in aesthetic theory. Little if any value is attached to originality, the individual, stylistic evolution, development (as progress), or the real-as-perceived; on the contrary, most Asian authors are distrustful of appearances and warn against "realistic" perception. Symbolism thus plays a major role in the creation and perception of art, and intuitive knowledge is valued above sense perception, as Ananda Coomaraswamy points out: "What the representation imitates is the idea or species of the thing, by which it is known intellectually, rather than the substance of the thing as it is perceived by the senses."[2] And, in a striking metaphor, Zeami (1363–1443) invokes a similar relationship between appearance and essence in the Nō theater of Japan: "In the art of *nō* there are skin, flesh, and bones. The skin is vision, the flesh is sound, the bones are the soul. Or, if we consider only music, then the skin is the voice, the flesh is the chant, and the bones are the breath. And in dance the skin is the appearance, the flesh is the gesture, the bones are the heart."[3]

Preliminary observations

Before proceeding, readers who lack any listening experience with the musics of Japan and India would do well to make some casual acquaintance with the wealth of Oriental music now widely available on disc and tape. Otherwise, no words will persuade them of its excellence, nor can writing convey its distinctive flavors. A personal encounter with the phenomena of sound is the only proper starting point for an understanding of Asian musical aesthetics, and the following comments will become intelligible only when it is possible to summon up vivid memories of the musical experience I attempt to describe.

Musical tone, in the Japanese tradition, is a more intricate phenomenon than in the West, so much so that it is virtually impossible to notate with any specificity. Japanese notations are even more skeletal than those of the West and leave more of the essential musical details to the traditional face-to-face instruction. A single sustained tone of the voice or flute, once we attend closely, turns out to be an astonishingly complex event with subtle shadings, thinning and thickening, tensing and relaxing, tremolo, breathiness, and slight variations of pitch and timbre. Tonal attacks and releases are similarly complex, with a variety of almost indiscernible grace notes. Western listeners will be surprised by the vocal tone, especially in the use of falsetto, the tonal slides, and what will strike them as a high degree of tension. Many Japanese vocal genres are narrative styles and are thus greatly influenced by the inflections and rhythms of spoken Japanese. The range of instruments includes flutes, sharply plucked strings (koto, biwa, shamisen), and piercing reed instruments as well as an array of drums, chimes, and other percussion instruments. The genres include solo and chamber music, as well as a variety of larger ensembles for ritual and theater musics.

The prevailing texture may best be described as *heterophonic,* often produced by the simultaneous variation of the same melodic line; this studied avoidance of simultaneity gives the illusion of multiple, superimposed tonal images. In the ensembles heterogeneous timbres are preferred, promoting clear focus and differentiation of the various sounds. Rhythmic punctuation is incisive, but ensemble beats are often deliberately offset to produce a cluster of attacks, another instance of the apparent disorder and asymmetry that is one of the highest values in the arts of Japan. Temporal control is generally precise but invites interpretation as rhythmic "freedom" because of the absence of regular pulse (in slower sections of a composition) and the large amounts of silence between events. The result is a music in which breath and gesture are important models for the rhythmic flow and in which nothingness is as much a part of the music as somethingness.

Both the pitch and time dimensions are treated as continua, in contrast to the precisely scaled grooves and striations of the Western sound spectra. Practiced listeners find themselves concentrating more on fewer sounds and on fine detail that they might previously have overlooked; their thresholds of perception and scale of reference have become more focused and more acute. But no outsider can hope to respond to this music in quite the same way that an insider can, especially in a culture so homogeneous that anthropologists have described it as a virtual "tribe." Centuries of cultural conditioning in relative isolation have produced a set of habits, instinctive responses and behaviors, preferences, and attitudes that insure the communication of musical meaning within the context of Japanese society.

Turning to the music of India, we observe first that although the nature of the musical tone is not as complex as we noted in typical Japanese practice, the organizing features of the music appear to present greater complexities. Vocal tone is the basis of all Indian music, and Indian instruments play in the same "vocal" style, i.e., sliding pitches and graceful ornaments. Abundant and varied ornamentation is a characteristic feature of all Indian music. Vocal quality in India is a more relaxed and free style of tone production with a certain nasal resonance that is imitated by many of the instruments. The most pervasive tonal feature is the constant drone, maintaining a continuous saturation of sound.

The music of India is more rhythmically active than in Japan, and athleticism is admired. The standard texture may be described simply as solo instrument or voice, drum(s), and drone. Although Indians think of their music as one-dimensional, the varied timbres of the different drumstrokes (conceived as "syllables," with properties of pitch and attack) provide a counterpoint to the main melodic line. Notations are even less specific than in Japan and are rarely used; pieces are learned from a teacher. Much of Indian music is improvised but not in the sense of "spontaneous composition." Because the techniques of improvisation have been programmed into the performer's style by his guru, the result is an indefinable mixture of habit and impulse, tradition and innovation, that the performer applies to one of a set of cherished melodic archetypes (the *rāgas*), controlled by the repetitive, cyclical rhythmic patterns known as *tāla*. One of the main aims in performance is the systematic exploration of the possibilities obtainable within the constraints of *rāga* and *tāla*.

Cultural preferences

In this section I outline more fully the contrasting cultural preferences that have shaped the traditional musics of Japan and India, with brief notes on some important issues. Certain of these preferences relate specifically to music and the other arts, others are general qualities of experience, still others are rooted in philosophy and theory. Because later sections will delve more thoroughly into Indian theories of art, this discussion will be organized around Japanese preferences, with the corresponding Indian attitude presented for purposes of contrast. A number of the contrasts are so extreme that the reader should be reminded that some important cultural similarities are bound to be overlooked.

Three important points of contrast should be made at the start: first, Japanese culture is intensely aesthetic—much more so than Indian culture. The aesthetic savor of everyday experience is a pervading feature of Japanese life; aesthetic enjoyment in India seems to be reserved for formal works of art. Second, Japanese art is focused upon nature; although natural processes are sources of value in the Indian tradition, nature as such is not. And finally, both the ends of art and the modes of perception differ: the purpose of Japanese art is aesthetic knowledge (of the essence of things), illumination, achieved by means of immediate experience and direct intuition—the way of Zen. The Hindu point of view, the basis for most Indian artistic doctrines, is that the twin goals of art are *ānanda* (bliss) and *mokṣa* (release), achieved by means of fixed, yogic concentration and absorption of self in the artistic experience. The Japanese experience of art seeks to understand and be at one with the world; perception, in Indian tradition, offers a means of release from the world of illusion.

Donald Keene, in a 1968 symposium on "Aesthetics East and West," proposed four cardinal values in Japanese art: suggestion, irregularity, simplicity, perishability.[4] Before proceeding with a longer list of specific musical preferences, let us examine each of these in turn.

Suggestion. The art work is never made explicit, never "perfected," but requires active imagination on the part of the spectator if he is to savor its allusions. Indian works of art are explicit statements that attempt to deal fully with their content. "Are we to look at cherry blossoms only in full bloom, the moon only when it is cloudless? To long for the moon while looking on the rain, to lower the blinds and be unaware of the passing of the spring—these are even more deeply moving. Branches about to blossom or gardens strewn with faded flowers are worthier of our admiration" (Kenkō).[5]

Irregularity. The famous rock-and-sand garden of Ryōanji in Kyōto deliberately avoids the regular, symmetrical, architectonic forms of design. The Japanese preference for beginnings and endings— emerging and destabilizing processes, as opposed to stabilized continuity—manifests the same impulse. Although there are many irregularities in the arts of India, equilibrium and symmetry are clearly preferred and are expressed in the "centrist" Indian consciousness and world view.

Simplicity. This preference is seen in the use of natural materials, the avoidance of decoration, dull colors, simple rough surfaces, and uncomplicated design—all combining in the studied simplicity of the tea ceremony. In contrast, profusion, vivid color, and pervading ornamentation are among the highest values in Indian art.

Perishability. The Japanese connoisseur takes delight in the knowledge that a beautiful work of art is made to be fragile and impermanent. As the poet Ton'a wrote, "It is only after the silk wrapper has frayed at top and bottom, and the mother-of-pearl has fallen from the roller, that a scroll looks beautiful."[6] Indian philosophy prefers to deny the problem: since everything is by nature illusion and impermanent, art is no more so than anything else! And perishability is not likely to be cited as a value in a country where heat, dust, monsoons, and insects have taken their toll of all the great monuments of art.

The following preferences have special relevance for music. For the sake of completeness, I include the most significant of those mentioned in the preliminary descriptions, beginning with Japan:

1   a complex, dynamic concept of musical tone, with many variables
2   constraint
3   continuity as the result of tension sustained through silence (*ma*) and held tones
4   vocal and instrumental tone valued equally
5   an unsaturated tonal field, with expressive use of silence
6   linearity and nonrepetitive patterns
7   complex tonal envelopes (beginnings and endings), sharp attacks
8   percussion as punctuation, signal, and time-marker
9   heterogeneous timbres
10   clarity of textural focus
11   a deliberate avoidance of simultaneity, a pseudo-disorganization
12   particularity—the enjoyment of the uniqueness of things, the individual sound, the hook that is a permanent fixture in every Nō theater but required for just one play in the repertoire
13   subject confronts object, a contrived distance between spectator and art object
14   improvisation is not a prominent feature
15   stasis as a source of value
16   sound valued for its own sake

These preferences can be contrasted with those of the Indian musical tradition on a point-by-point basis:

1   musical tone subject to fewer variables
2   release, symbolic of the importance attached to the breath and the role of aspiration in Indian languages
3   continuity by means of smooth streams of sound and repetitive rhythmic patterns
4   vocal tone as the model for music
5   a fully saturated tonal field
6   circularity, repetition, and recurrence
7   value attached to *anāhata* (unstruck) sounds
8   percussion prominent, used as a separate timbral dimension and frequently independent of the time-keeping function

9   *homogeneous* is too strong a word, but the range of timbres
    is narrow
10 obscurity valued above clarity
11 concurrence of sounds and confluence of patterns are valued
12 universality: Indians are Platonists and like to think in terms
    of ideal types
13 identity of subject and object, psychic fusion with the work
    of art, art as a "wrap-around" effect[7]
14 improvisation is a distinctive feature
15 motion—perhaps even "perpetual" motion—as a source of
    value
16 sound valued for what it represents

This section concludes with a brief discussion of formal archetypes in these two musics. At first glance the two cultures appear to
differ as much in their formal strategies as in their tonal preferences:
the asymmetric structure of most Japanese music seems elusive to
Western ears, while the rhythmic continuity and repetitive *tāla* patterns—especially when reinforced by the performers' gestures—mark
clearly the evolving structure of an Indian performance. In this regard,
the prevailing cyclical organization is perceived as a "chain" structure,
one module following another—an idea that violates virtually every
premise of Japanese art. But deeper similarities emerge when we examine the larger formal concepts that organize whole works.

The most basic formal archetype in the music (and theater) of
Japan is the sequence *jo* (introduction)-*ha* (scattering)-*kyū* (rush-
ing to conclusion). Arising from the structure of the Nō drama, the
pattern *jo-ha-kyū* is recognized on several levels of structure: the
work as a whole, each individual act and scene, subscenes, individual
phrases, and the single musical event. Hence it is possible for the perceptive auditor to detect a *ha* moment in a *jo* phrase in the *kyū* section
of a *ha* scene and respond appropriately. Each member of the sequence
has its own distinct properties: *jo* is communicated by constrained energy, a sense of anticipation, and relative temporal freedom; *ha*, the
consequence of *jo*, is usually signaled by greater rhythmic regularity
and continuity as well as by an increase in tempo; *kyū* is announced
by an increased density of events and a sense of denouement. Japanese writers have applied a familiar botanical metaphor to these three

aspects of form: the budding, blooming, and fading phases of a plant cycle.

Similar metaphors are common in Indian literature, with music described as an organic development from seed to pod to leaf to fruit. On another level, ideas of emergence, continuous action, and dissolution were contributed by traditional Indian cosmological speculation in which creation was seen as a continuous process with three distinct stages: the creation of forms from undifferentiated matter, presided over by Brahma; the created universe maintained in ordered motion, under the protection of Vishnu; and, finally, the dissolution of the world into its former state of primal matter, accompanied by the fiery dance of Shiva. These ideas have left their mark upon the archetypal structure of Indian music: virtually every performance begins with a slow improvisatory section, followed by a more regular, rhythmic section, and concluding with some sort of process that signals impending closure. And, in a somewhat different formulation, early Indian theorists recognized these four aspects of musical form: *sthāyī*, the static or "abiding" part; *sañcārī*, the moving part; *āhārī*, the "collecting" part; *kāpālinī*, the crowning part. It seems possible to consider these as manifestations of a single archetypal form, expressed in ways significant to each culture: a progression from gradual emergence to rhythmic process to conclusion.

The language of Japanese aesthetics

If we were to select a list of the key words in Western aesthetic theory, it would surely include the following: *beauty, unity, variety, harmony, form, color, intensity, expression, symmetry, proportion.* Although linguistic analysis can disclose hidden meanings and associations for certain of these terms (as in the case of *claritas*),[8] the word list is still a collection of relatively formalistic, abstract terms. In contrast, many of the key words in Japanese aesthetics are basically affective and are used metaphorically. Here is a brief lexicon:

yūgen, beauty, mystery, profound, remote, symbolism
shibui, astringent, in sober taste, understatement, refinement
sabi, rusty, desolate, simple, barren, old, tarnished

aware, gentle sorrow, pleasant melancholy, emotional awareness
of beauty, pathetic
miyabi, refined
en, charming

It is easy to exaggerate the significance of such a word list and
assume that Japanese aesthetic discourse is confined to qualitative,
subjective language. Such is not the case. But these are the words most
often analyzed and applied in the traditional Japanese criticism; it
should, therefore, be safe to assume that they represent important
ideals within Japanese culture.

Yūgen is a very old term in Japanese aesthetics with a long history of critical analysis. I take it to mean the quality of absolute, ideal
beauty of which the aesthetic object is merely the symbol. The realization of the presence of *yūgen* is the goal of aesthetic experience; it is,
in fact, the meaning of a work of art. Archibald MacLeish's line, "A
poem must not mean, but be" ("Ars Poetica," 1926), violates the
most basic principle of Japanese aesthetics. Japanese art is not self-
sufficient. The simplest of all the definitions of *yūgen* is the proverb
used to introduce this chapter: "That which is unseen is flowers."

Yūgen trades on the strain of ambiguity and indefiniteness that
is embodied in the Japanese language and prized in Japanese culture.
Because the language does not distinguish between singular and plural,
nor between the definite and indefinite, Bashō's famous haiku on
"crow alighting on branch" leaves it to the reader to decide whether
the author meant one or more crows. One thing is clear—explicit art
does not reveal or suggest *yūgen.* If the work of art is too perfect, too
complete in itself, it leaves no room for this quality.

One of the most famous descriptions of *yūgen* was written by
the fifteenth-century monk Shōtetsu:

Yūgen can be apprehended by the mind, but it cannot be expressed in words. Its quality may be suggested by the sight of a
thin cloud veiling the moon or by autumn mist swathing the
scarlet leaves on a mountainside. If one is asked where in these
sights lies the *yūgen,* one cannot say, and it is not surprising
that a man who fails to understand this truth is likely to prefer
the sight of a perfectly clear, cloudless sky. It is quite impossible

to explain wherein lies the interest or the remarkable nature of yūgen.[9]

As a universal canon of beauty, yūgen has its dangers. It risks overloading the art object with a heavier freight of meanings than the object can justify. It can also shift our attention away from the presentational characteristics of the art work itself. As an aesthetic value, it can probably function only within a broad consensus of agreement on aesthetic principles and a society in which the aesthetic response has been cultivated by long cultural conditioning.

Shibui and sabi combine to form the aesthetic basis for the tea ceremony:

The tea hut is extremely bare and almost devoid of color. If a flower is arranged in a vase, it is usually a single, small blossom of some quiet hue or white. The tea utensils are not of exquisite porcelain but of coarse pottery, often a dull brown or black and imperfectly formed. The kettle may be a little rusty. Yet from these objects we receive an impression not of gloominess or shabbiness but one of quiet harmony and peace, and watching the ceremony we may experience an intimation of yūgen.[10]

Sabi is almost an antiaesthetic term, a rejection of a whole spectrum of artistic values prized by other cultures. It is difficult to understand how this quality came to be valued by all segments of Japanese society: the upper classes can perhaps afford to take pleasure in the studied (and expensive) cultivation of genteel simplicity amidst faded and barren surroundings; the lower classes are fated to dwell in the midst of sabi without enjoying it, and the middle classes would appear to be a poor market. But somehow the ideal of sabi touches a responsive chord in Japanese culture and harmonizes with the other popular aesthetic qualities.

Aware is one of the oldest terms in Japanese aesthetics, and the quality of gentle sorrow that it signifies pervades Japanese literature and representational works of art, infusing them with a certain characteristic ethos. The meaning of the word has altered subtly over the years: originally an exclamation of surprised delight, a recognition of the essential quality of something, it later became tinged with the idea of sadness; in modern usage its meaning has developed into wretched or *pathetic*. It implies a sensitive awareness of the inevitabilities of life, of Kenkō's fallen cherry blossoms.

Miyabi (refined) is another term that is consistent with this cluster of values; it signifies the quiet pleasures of the connoisseur in Heian court society, isolated from the harsh facts of external reality. True, there is another side to the arts of Japan—the garish temples at Nikkō, the vulgarities of the brothel scenes in the Kabuki drama—but these contrasts emphasize all the more those qualities of understatement and refinement that are Japan's prime legacy to the world of art.

What has all this to do with music? Several points come to mind: first, that *yūgen* is suggested by the visual trappings of Japanese music, e.g., the decoration of instruments (the tassel inside the flute that not even the performer sees, the symbolic arrangement of the movable koto bridges like a flight of birds) and the ceremonial costumes, as well as by the programmatic, pictorial content of much of the musical repertoire. More important, *yūgen* is invoked by the extraordinarily open, spacious texture that surrounds the musical events with a context of silence, resisting the listener's train of expectation. In such an aesthetic of stasis, musical meaning must be sought in the reverberation and implication of the individual event and the isolated phrase, rather than in the way musical events are connected.

Shibui, in its literal meaning, may tell something about the Japanese concept of musical sound: "astringent" is an apt description of the "rough" tonal surface so highly prized in Japanese music—in the vocal production, the characteristic snap of the koto strings, the harsh plectrum stroke across the shamisen, and the heterogeneous timbres of the *gagaku* ensemble. Ideal sound in Japanese music is leaner, edgier, and more abrasive than the nineteenth-century concept of smooth, vibrant, opulent sound that was (and still is) preferred in the West, both in vocal and instrumental practice. And whereas Western performers try to maximize the "center" of the tone, Japanese practice seems to emphasize the noise elements that are present in the tonal attack. In its derived meaning ("understated refinement"), *shibui* encourages the listeners to direct concentrated attention toward the minute details of a musical sound, thereby narrowing their focus and enabling them to perceive on a finer scale.

The influence of *sabi* is reflected in the almost total absence of rhetoric in Japanese music, the economy and sparseness of the musical texture, and perhaps also the tendency of the Japanese to resist any innovation in performing the traditional repertoires, thereby encouraging their veneration as collections of old, beloved objects. And if Japanese music seems at times to approach a condition of silence rather than sound, that too is consistent with the ideal of *sabi*.

The theory of *rasa*

The musical theater has stimulated some of the major proposals in the history of aesthetics: each of the three cornerstones of ancient dramatic theory (the *Poetics* of Aristotle, Bharatas's *Nāṭyaśāstra*, and Zeami's several treatises on the Nō theater) was addressed to a type of drama in which music played a prominent role. In this section we will examine the Indian theater's main contribution to aesthetic theory—the theory of *rasa*.

Rasa (literally "sap, juice, essence") is often translated as *taste* or *flavor*, but we will let it remain untranslated in the hope of avoiding too narrow a range of meaning. It is a highly technical term in Indian aesthetics. *Rasa*, as described in Indian literature, is taken to mean a certain pervading emotional tone that suffuses the work of art and is the basis for the spectator's aesthetic experience. The poet, actor, musician, and spectator are all active participants in the creation and savor of this emotional unity, which is the goal of the performance. To equate *rasa* with "mood" is to reduce the concept to a cliché.

Indian philosophers have argued aesthetic theory more systematically than Japanese authors. The theory of *rasa* was widely debated and analyzed until its definitive formulation in the writings of the eleventh-century Kashmiri scholar, Abhinavagupta.[11] His exposition of the theory has been regarded as authoritative by most subsequent Indian authors, and it is basically his version that forms the basis for the present discussion. Like most concepts in Indian philosophy, *rasa* opens up a sea of potential complications and invites exploration in virtually endless detail by means of a vast array of Sanskrit technical terms, distinguished by fine shades of meaning. We can present only the barest outline of this complex subject and will avoid all but the most essential terms.

Just as Indian tradition recognizes six basic flavors (sweet, sour, salty, pungent, bitter, astringent—with some sixty-three subclassifications!), the theory of *rasa* identifies eight basic emotions seated deep in the subconscious, dormant but ready to be awakened by the experience of art. They are the erotic (*śṛṅgāra*), the heroic (*vīra*), the disgusting (*bībhatsa*), the furious (*raudra*), the comic (*hāsya*), the fearful (*bhayānaka*), the pathetic (*karuṇa*), the wondrous (*adbhuta*), and some authors add a ninth *rasa*—the peaceful (*śānta*).

The order is seldom the same, but most authors agree that the first four are the major *rasas* and the others dependent. Westerners are often surprised to find disgust elevated to a major emotion, but they fail to realize the depth of the concept of pollution in Indian traditional thought. Most of the plays in the repertoire fall into one of the first two *rasas*, e.g., *Śakuntalā* (the erotic) and "The Little Clay Cart" (the heroic).

Bhāva is the general Sanskrit word for *affect, emotion,* and *mental state;* it is also the basis for the following series of technical terms: *vibhāvas,* stimuli, determinants of the aesthetic experience; *anubhāvas,* responses, the resulting physical states, "mimetic" changes that occur in the spectator; *vyabhicāribhāvas,* the flickering, transient emotions that accompany the various basic states; and *sthāyibhāvas,* the permanent emotions.

Just as the theorists of the *Affektenlehre* analyzed each of the affections into its component passions,[12] Indian authors took delight in making long lists of the transient emotions and physical reactions that accompany and signify each of the basic states. These are intended as signals to the alert spectator. But the process by which *rasa* is communicated is more than a simple stimulus/response. *Rasa* is neither a mechanical cause nor an expression of emotion—it is a manifestation of the underlying emotional state by means of the dramatic presentation. It must be attained by the spectator through active reconstruction, and the emotion that he thus attains is entirely different from emotion in daily life.

Aesthetic experience, from the Indian point of view, is a process by which one gradually becomes free from limitations. The normal experience of emotion is invariably associated with consciousness of self and attachment to other persons and/or limiting conditions of our life. A theatrical experience takes us, in a special sense, "out of ourselves"; in the theater we experience emotion mediated by the persons and events on the stage, somewhat released from ordinary limitations of time and space but still attached to the characters in the drama. In the next stage, by participating in and reconstructing the pervading emotional tone of the play, we are led to an aesthetic satisfaction that is detached from the persons and events of the play, to a more distilled consciousness of an emotion that is shared by all present, regardless of their own limitations. Finally, if the process "works," the spectator achieves a certain purified and universalized emotional state (perhaps *śānta rasa*) that neutralizes the specific *rasa* of the play. Such a state of bliss and absorption is called *ānanda*—a kind of identification with the universal consciousness and a release from all limitations of self, time, space, desires, and circumstances. Although Aristotle would not have shared the metaphysical assumptions on which this theory is grounded, he would have agreed that this is a very good definition of what he called *katharsis*.

In a perceptive critique, Eliot Deutsch argues that *rasa* is neither subjective nor objective (categories that are not mutually exclusive in Indian thought) and concludes that

> the *rasa*-theory is right; for one of the factors which clearly distinguish an art-work as a structured-content from a mere collection or aggregate of elements is the manner in which a feeling-tone suffices the work and gives unity to it. And if it is the case, as Susanne K. Langer maintains, that "Art is the creation of forms symbolic of human feeling," then that feeling-tone which unifies the work must at the same time be grounded in the deepest categorical structures of feeling; it must be transpersonal and universal; it must, in short, be the *rasa*.[13]

Abhinavagupta outlined the characteristics of the ideal spectator: he must possess inborn taste, the potential to respond to *rasa*; most important of all, he must have *sahṛdayatva* (lit. the capacity to "have a common heart" with the drama), empathy; the power to visualize an aesthetic image, imagination; a certain intellectual background; the contemplative habit, the willingness to see beyond the limitations of immediate experience; suitable psycho-physical conditions, e.g., freedom from pain, desire, or personal anxiety; and the capacity to identify.[14]

Abhinavagupta identified five levels of the aesthetic experience: sense perception, imagination, recognition of emotion, universalizing,

and finally transcendental satisfaction (*ānanda*).[15] He also listed seven
impediments to the aesthetic experience and the means by which they
could be overcome in the successful performance:

Impediment	Removed by
1 inability to perceive the meaning, lack of verisimilitude	empathy and traditional associations
2 subjective limitations of time and place	stagecraft and music
3 objective limitations of time and place	stagecraft and music
4 influence of personal joys and sorrows	self-forgetfulness
5 insufficient stimulus	acting, vividness of presentation
6 subordination of the principal idea	emphasis
7 dubiousness of presentation	the total context: the situation, mimetic changes, transient emotions[16]

We pose three questions: Does the theory of *rasa* apply to Indian music apart from the theater? Has it developed into a general
theory of meaning within Indian culture? And, is it a valid description
of the universal experience of art and therefore meriting wider application? The answer to all three questions is "Yes, but . . ."

The *rasa* theory is clearly the foundation for the link between
music and emotion in later Indian thought, although the original catalog of eight (or nine) basic states has been both broadened and frag-
mented. As a general theory of musical meaning, it is almost axiom-
atic in Indian culture. The obvious connection is between *rāga* and
rasa, and many authors have argued an objective basis for the correlation of specific scale-types with specific feelings. But the linkage is
complex and tenuous.

Indian musicians agree on a number of points: A competent performance requires both musical and emotional unity. Each of the
rāgas is associated with certain emotional qualities, e.g., tender yearn-
ing or peaceful joy. *Rāgas* have also been assigned to specific times of
day and seasons of the year, a tradition that is increasingly ignored in

modern practice. Iconographic evidence is provided by the famous series of *Rāgamāla* paintings that depict the emotional content of various *rāgas*.[17] As a result, the choice of *rāga* summons up a rich cluster of associations.

Of the ancient *rasas*, *śṛṅgāra* (the erotic) was the most prominent. It was often called the *rasarāja* (the "king among *rasas*"), and some Indian authors have argued—not very convincingly—that all the remaining *rasas* may be considered aspects of *śṛṅgāra*. It is beyond dispute that *śṛṅgāra* is similarly a dominant *rasa* in modern practice, either alone or mixed with the emotional quality of *bhakti* (religious devotion). The link between the devotional and the sensual is one of the deepest bonds in Indian culture, as everyone who has visited the erotic temple sculptures at Khajuraho knows. Given the religious roots of Indian art, one wonders at the absence of *bhakti* from the original circle of the *rasas*. And according to Sambamoorthy, the present repertoire includes more compositions in *śṛṅgāra* and *bhakti rasas* than in any of the others.[18]

Vocal music in the Indian tradition is extremely specific in emotional content, which is not surprising in view of the obvious clues in any text, and it is self-evident that text and *rāga* must be well suited to one another. Indian vocal performance is saturated with emotional expression, communicated by an array of clues: text, *rāga* (including all the traditional associations), facial expression, and gesture. But instrumental performance is another matter. Although certain *rāgas* are thought to convey very specific emotional content, many others are said to demonstrate the more general quality of *rāga bhāva* ("affect"). And most improvisations end in an elevated mood of athletic exuberance where the focus appears to have shifted from the original emotional sentiment to the performance itself.

The consensus of Indian society is that musical performance *does* communicate an emotional message from performer to listener. Despite all the arguments on behalf of an objective basis for this communication, it seems clear that it is based upon learned behaviors and responses and is a product of cultural conditioning. Of the traditional theories of musical meaning (communication, expression, imitation, representation), perhaps all of them are valid in this context. Formalist theories of musical meaning violate the premises of Indian art: meaning in Indian music is referential, and what it refers to is emotion. The being of music is symbolic: the musical substance is the illusion, shadow, or reflection of the fundamental emotion. Musical knowledge is the knowledge of what the music represents. And this type of knowledge, from the Indian perspective, brings not only enjoyment—it brings liberation.

How universally valid is the idea of *rasa?* The theory itself is more important than the specific list of emotional states, which must be considered to be variable. In one sense it can be argued that most great works of art are unified by a certain consistent emotional tone, a unity of sentience, e.g., the tone of sustained epic combat that pervades *Moby Dick,* the lyrical melancholy of *Swan Lake,* the romantic fantasy of *The Tempest,* the frustrated longing of *Tristan und Isolde,* or the grotesque outrage of *Guernica.* But this is not very precise. Communication of emotion requires a competent spectator/auditor, an assortment of clues (titles, text, visual and other associations), and—in the case of music—some consensus on the musical properties that are appropriate to the desired meaning. And it is on this final point that most Western referentialist theories of musical meaning have become impaled.

The Indian theory of sound (*Nāda*)

The Indian philosophy of music is based on metaphysical assumptions, many of which are stated explicitly in the quotation that stands at the head of this chapter: sound is equated with the universal consciousness, the structure of the universe, the cosmic process of creation, and is embodied in the divine trinity of Brahma, Vishnu, and Shiva. The passage continues:

> The World-Soul, having a desire to speak, stirs the mind. The mind strikes the fire abiding in the body, and that fire strikes the wind. Then that wind abiding in the region of Brahma, rising along the upward paths, manifests the sound successively in the navel, the heart, the throat, the head, and the mouth.
> *Nāda* [sound], occupying these five positions, assumes respectively these five names—very subtle, subtle, manifested, unmanifested, and artificial. *Nāda* is so-called because the syllable NA is the synonym for the breath [*prāṇa*] and the syllable DA signifies fire; therefore *nāda* is named for the conjunction of breath and fire.[19]

Musical sound is thus a manifestation of the continuous stream of universal sound that runs deep within the human body. It is carried by the vital breath of life (prāṇa), actuated by heat energy, and shares in the metaphysical power of Vāc (Speech), addressed as a deity in the Vedic hymns. As sound emerges through the bodily channels, it strikes resonance from each of the cakras (registers, concentrations of vital air) of the body. Pure, internal sound is subtle, spiritual, undifferentiated, unmanifested, and eternal; uttered sound is gross, material, differentiated (into individual syllables, notes, and durations), manifested, and particular.

Indian philosophers recognized subtle gradations of the process by which musical sound is released: arising from the subconscious, realized as intention in the conscious mind, welling up from the inner stratum of sound, manifesting itself in the throat, formed into articulate speech by the organs of utterance (palate, tongue, lips), and emerging into the air as gross, differentiated sound. With this as background, it is easy to understand the coupling of music and articulatory phonetics in the early Indian literary genre known as śikṣā.[20] The process of musical emanation is frequently compared to the successive developmental phases of plantlife: total lack of all differentiation, the seed, the sprout, formation of leaves, differentiated types of leaves and external forms.

Imbued with this philosophy, the Indian musician regards each emission of sound—especially vocal sound—as a sacred action and as a means of entrainment with the universal sound. His opening improvisation in free time (ālāp) symbolizes the release of sound from its internal source, and his delineation of the individual pitches and registers of the rāga continues the division of his utterance into grosser units. The process of division and externalization becomes complete when the rhythm of the tāla is set in motion by the drummer. At the end of the performance, many Indian musicians consciously reverse this process, letting the sound subside into the continuous, timeless drone that has been maintained throughout the performance.

The theory of nāda demonstrates how strongly the music of a culture can be influenced by its philosophy. Most Indian philosophies are monistic, viewing matter, life, and mind as parts of a continuum, not sharply differing aspects of existence. Despite its addiction to logical categories and critical analysis, the Indian mind places the highest value on that which is continuous (rather than divided) and universal (as opposed to the individual and the particular). The flux of music represents the flux of all things, the continuous process of creation and dissolution, and the sportive play (*līlā*) of forms that we interpret as external reality. But all of this is illusion (*māyā*). By tapping the inner source of pure sound and fixed absorption in the musical process, both performer and listener can escape their attachments to material things and attain the condition of *mokṣa*—liberation.

The result of the musical experience is eloquently described in the *Vijñānabhairava Tantra:* "To the yogin whose spirit attains a unified state in the uniform bliss engendered by the delectation of objects like music, there occurs an absorption and anchoring of the mind in that bliss. Where there is a continuous and long flow of sounds from stringed instruments, one becomes freed of other objects of cognition and becomes merged in that ultimate and verily of the form of that Supreme Being [Brahman]."[21]

The theory also reminds us of the importance of the human body as a model for music in Asian cultures. In the absence of precise notations and other external objectifications of music and conditioned by the traditional philosophies, the musical culture of India measures both pitches and durations by and on the body: hand motions accompany the various beats and express the structure and energies of the different *tālas;* other gestures are used to signify the pitches and tonal accents of Samavedic chant; the breath serves as a model for the musical phrase and a source of tension, as well as the primary vehicle for musical sound. From the perspective of Asia, musical sound is not something external, as when one sits down at a piano and activates a sound-producing mechanism. It is something internal to be brought forth, a process to which one can become attuned—ultimately it is an identification.

We view the philosophy of music in Asian cultures with more than a casual curiosity for the exotic. For many years principles of Asian aesthetics have been infiltrating Western thought and culture, so much so that few if any contemporary composers can claim to have remained unaffected. Traditional Asian categories of thought resist direct translation into Western language and experience; and even the most perceptive Western musicians encounter cultural barriers beyond which they cannot pass. But any account of musical thought in the twentieth century must consider, as one of its strands, the developing synthesis of Eastern and Western thought and its long-range implications for music. We will return to this issue in the final chapter.

II   Clotho and Atropos

> And there were three others who sat round at equal intervals, each one on her throne, the Fates, daughters of Necessity, clad in white vestments . . . Lachesis, and Clotho, and Atropos, who sang in unison with the music of the Sirens, Lachesis singing the things that were, Clotho the things that are, and Atropos the things that are to be. [Plato][1]

MOST OF OUR INQUIRY has fallen within the jurisdiction of Lachesis; it is time to explore the domains of Clotho and Atropos. In Greek mythology Clotho (the spinner) unwinds the linen thread of life from her spindle, under the guidance of Lachesis (the measurer), while Atropos ("she who cannot be averted") prepares to sever the thread.[2] The myth of the Three Fates (the *Moerae*), like most myths, is rooted in a profound understanding: as the present unfolds, we measure it by the past, yet in the certain knowledge that the future will bring inevitable, unpredictable change and discontinuity. And so it is with music.

This chapter is about New Music and its implications for philosophy. By *New Music* I mean simply that which is new in music, a broader and more useful category than the labels *experimental* or *avant-garde* imply. New Music is, as it has always been, an incitement to heated debate and partisanship. But no good purpose would be served by rehearsing the familiar adversary positions viv-à-vis "old" and "new" music. For this one does not need philosophy.

The present chapter is an exploration of three main themes: the individual and the individual's role within musical society, musical material, and its organization. We begin with more conservative, humanistic issues (these have received considerable attention from philosophers) and proceed to more technical matters and radical positions (these are represented by testimony from composers). It seems appropriate to question the authority with which a composer speaks, since we often look to his utterances for guidance in assessing his works.

A composer is unquestionably able to supply privileged information about his own music, particularly the manner in which it came to be. On the other hand, composers have no greater immunity than we to "idol" worship and have often fallen victim to the urge to pronounce cryptic interpretations and utter prophesies. Their testimony cannot be dismissed lightly, but neither should it be regarded as oracular.

It is a little too soon to evaluate the contributions of formal philosophy with regard to New Music. Philosophers practice the admirable habit of arguing from principles, and the principles underlying the musical trends in this century are still gradually emerging from the tangle of technical descriptions, theories, critical rhetoric, aesthetic speculations, and "in"-group jargon. They are in need of clearer definition. As usual, the best course is to try and sort out the various strands of ideas, isolate the important issues, and pose the relevant questions as sharply as possible.

There are many and obvious reasons for the confused state of musical thought—the virtually complete overturn of the set of musical values held in the nineteenth century, the sweeping social and political changes of this century, the rise and subsequent splintering of the mass market for music, commercialism, the development of advanced technologies, the information explosion, and a climate favorable to experiment. An important new stream of thought reflects the development of the social sciences as scholarly disciplines, resulting in studies that apply to music the principles and methods of psychology, sociology, political science, semiotics, and structural linguistics. All of these contain potentially productive approaches to music, but no more so to New Music than to music of the past.

Two present conditions provide the inescapable context for any musical inquiry—the ever-accelerating development of the musical language and the lack of any consensus on musical values.

The individual and society

When Plato argued, in *The Republic* (and especially in book three), that the primary function of music was to train the citizen to become an ideal member of society, he could scarcely have foreseen the full consequences of his proposal. The idea itself was widely accepted in the civilizations of antiquity: the sages of ancient China prescribed ritual music as the symbolic reinforcement of the harmony that embraced society, its rulers, and the world of external nature.[3] The promotion of music as an instrument of state policy has been and remains one of the major issues in the philosophy of music, raising important questions of authority, free will, and meaning. This practice, which has generally prevailed in "controlled" societies and institutions, has provoked a vigorous debate, although the positions have often been argued in terms that Plato would have found highly unpalatable.

The politicizing of music in the twentieth century is usually explained as a reaction against the "art-for-art's-sake" movement popular in the previous century, a movement whose main premise was that the artist's only obligation was to art itself. The counterargument, in its simplest form, is that the purpose of art is to reflect, affirm, and promote the highest ideals of society; art that is remote or divorced from the society that nurtured it degenerates into mere *formalism*, the Soviet code word for bad art. The impact of Marxist-Leninist doctrines upon music in the Soviet Union provides the clearest examples of this philosophy at work, although one could with equal justification cite the status of music during Hitler's Third Reich, the musical consequences of Maoist teachings in modern China, and the reaction of Roman Catholic church music to some of the papal pronouncements earlier in this century.

There is a certain traditional ambivalence in the Soviet attitude toward music and the other arts. Philosophers have often viewed music with a mixture of admiration and suspicion, praising music's ability to promote the general well-being of society, yet fearful that its sensual properties may seduce the citizens from their responsibilities. As Lenin himself once remarked: "I can't listen to music too often. It affects your nerves, makes you want to say stupid things and stroke the heads of people who could create such beauty while living in this vile hell."[4]

Well before the 1917 October Revolution, G. V. Plekhanov was preaching Marxist aesthetics to an increasingly receptive audience, and the great internal debates of the twenties and thirties established the principle of Socialist Realism as the main aesthetic pillar of Soviet thought, applied first to literature and the visual arts but soon extended to music. In the *Statute of the Union of Soviet Writers* Andrei Zhdanov, Stalin's chief spokesman in artistic matters, set forth the basic definition: "Socialist Realism is the fundamental method of Soviet literature and criticism: it demands of the artist a true, historically concrete representation of reality in its revolutionary development. Further it ought to contribute to the ideological transformation and education of the workers in the spirit of socialism."[5]

Realism is easy to implement in the representational arts of literature and painting, less so in the abstract art of music. But a brilliant solution was at hand: the provocative theory of intonation as formulated by the composer and critic Boris Asafiev (1884–1949). There have been other attempts to attribute the means of musical expression to the intonations inherent in the language of a people (particularly those embedded in the folksong repertoires) but none as profound and systematic as Asafiev's:

> Soviet realism demands that Soviet composers write music based on musical intonations, that is, intoned meanings which are supposed to be the carriers of the ideological significance of Russian nationalism and of Soviet reality. . . . Musical recollections, impressions, and fragments become interwoven with life experiences, feelings, and aspirations, penetrating the artistic life and traditions of peoples. . . . The background of great compositions is a world of music as an activity of public consciousness: musical interjections, rhythmic intonations, popular motivic fragments, harmonic turns, and extracts of musical impressions of an epoch.[6]

Marxist thought stresses that art is inherently and essentially an instrument for education and progressive social change. The artist has an ideological responsibility to society—to reflect that which is good, to help transform that which is bad, to educate and inspire the audiences in ways consistent with the highest aims of society. Curiously enough, one of the most eloquent defenses of the Soviet position was written by Joseph Goebbels, Hitler's minister of propaganda:[7]

> Art must not only be good; it must be conditioned by the needs of the people—or, to put it better, only an art which springs from the integral soul of the people can in the end be good and have meaning for the people for whom it was created. Art, in an

absolute sense, as liberal democracy knows it, has no right to exist. Any attempt to further such an art could, in the end, cause the people to lose their inner relationship to art and the artist to isolate himself from the moving forces of his time, shut away in the airless chambers of "art for art's sake." Art must be good, but beyond that, conscious of its responsibility, competent, close to the people, and combative in spirit.

Similar references to the militant role of art in the class struggle are characteristic features of "boilerplate" Soviet aesthetic rhetoric: "Society's views on art indicate to art what its place in the life of the people is and determine what its subject matter should be. Receding reactionary social forces demand of art 'pure' beauty and abstract dreams. On the other hand, new, ascending social forces, in their development, regard art as a participant in the earthly struggle. . . ."[8]

Both Prokofiev and Shostakovitch encountered harsh criticism during the thirties and forties, and both eventually recanted the errors into which "formalism" had led them. There is a strong tendency toward "guilt and repentance" in the Russian character which renders such artistic confessions more believable. Here are excerpts from a statement by Dmitri Shostakovitch in support of the 10 February 1948 Resolution of the Central Committee of the All-Union Communist Party:

> As we look back on the road traversed by our art, it becomes quite clear to us that every time that the Party corrects errors of a creative artist and points out the deviations in his work, or else severely condemns a certain tendency in Soviet art, it invariably brings beneficial results for Soviet art and for individual artists. . . . The absence, in my works, of the interpretation of folk art, that great spirit by which our people lives, has been with utmost clarity and definiteness pointed out by the Central Committee of the All-Union Communist Party. . . . Work—arduous, creative, joyous work on new compositions which will find their way to the heart of the Soviet people, which will be understandable to the people, loved by them, and which will be organically connected with the people's art, developed and enriched by the great traditions of Russian classicism—this will be a fitting response. . . .[9]

The future course of Soviet music was outlined in the set of guidelines adopted by the Second International Congress of Composers and Musicologists, meeting in Prague in May 1948:

> A successful solution of the crisis in contemporary music seems to be possible under the following conditions:
>
> (1)   If composers renounce in their art the tendencies of extreme subjectivism; then their music would express great, new, and progressive ideas and aspirations of the popular masses and progressive ideals of contemporary life.
>
> (2)   If creative artists turn decisively towards national culture of their lands and become its true defenders against the cosmopolitan tendencies of contemporary life, for true internationalism in music is attained only on the basis of the strengthening of national culture.
>
> (3)   If the attention of composers is directed first of all towards musical forms that are most concrete in their contents, particularly operas, oratorios, cantatas, songs, mass choruses, etc.
>
> (4)   If composers and music critics become active and practical workers in the musical education of their peoples.[10]

I conclude this section with some personal reflections, partly in rebuttal and partly to emphasize the importance of some of the issues that have been argued in the course of the debate. We have devoted this much attention to the politics of music not because of the intrinsic excellence of the music produced under the influence of the Soviet ideology but because that ideology has reawakened interest in some of the most basic questions in the philosophy of music. No one who takes the trouble to think seriously about his role within musical society can afford to ignore the fundamental question—whether his decisions as an individual composer, performer, or teacher ought to be guided by the needs of his society, or whether they are entirely his own affair.

It is too easy and a little cheap to poke fun at Soviet tractor art, revolutionary ballets, and folksong suites. Undeniably the result of Socialist Realism has been the production of a lot of bad art, but bad art has flourished elsewhere in the world under a variety of political systems.

Among the positive accomplishments we may number the following: state support of composers and performers, high performance standards, technical competence on the part of the composer, the preservation of the Soviet Union's unique regional musical traditions, a successful program of music education and talent development, widespread enjoyment of the arts, and the maintenance of a thriving opera and ballet tradition. On the negative side we may point to an intellectual climate hostile to experiment and the free evolution of musical style, as well as a body of stuffy criticism that places more weight on content/message than upon the music itself.

No outside presentation, however sympathetic and impartial, is likely to do full justice to the Soviet aesthetic position, particularly with respect to some of the extremely subtle arguments. Nor should one lacking a first-hand knowledge of the real conditions in the parts of the world that Socialist Realism seeks to improve expect to be convinced by a summary of the main argument without the full context of Marxist thought. The scarcity of competent translations has imposed an unfortunate language barrier between the USSR and the Western world, greatly enhancing the opportunities for misunderstanding.

The quality of philosophic discourse invariably suffers in direct proportion to the use of code words, slogans, easy catch phrases, and similar devices of persuasive rhetoric. Labels such as *formalism, subjectivism,* and *Socialist Realism*—despite their popular appeal and their effectiveness in argument—have tended to lower the quality level of the debate.

The placement of music under state policy, now as throughout history, has predictable consequences: orthodoxy and stylistic conservatism. There is surely no reason why it is either desirable or undesirable for musical style to evolve or to remain essentially the same—the gap that has opened between composer and public in the West is more a matter of the *rate* of change than of the change itself. But political conditions that inhibit the development of the musical language and encourage conformity have had insidious effects. It seems inconsistent that those who argue that society should maintain a continuous revolutionary state should deny the same renewing impulse in their music.

The final sentence of Goebbels's letter is an admirably specific prescription for art. Few will fail to agree with him that art should be competent, although competence is not always easy to define. But a more thoughtful rebuttal might point out that art that seeks to be "combative" and is "self-conscious of its responsibilities" is more likely to be valued for its message than for its intrinsic properties, and that art that remains "close to the people" tends to set its standards by what will appeal to the lowest common denominator of musical taste. Viewers of American network television will find it hard to disagree.

These considerations bring up the general question of "detachment": is the ultimate value of music dependent upon socio-political theories and its usefulness in promoting desired social ends, or does it possess independent value? I would like to think the latter. The Soviet position poses a real danger for abstract music, implying that only music that conveys a concrete, extramusical message can serve its social purpose. This too denies independent existence to music.

If there is a tremendous potential for the social use of music, there is an equal potential for its abuse. My list of the possible abuses of music would include all techniques aimed at mass persuasion and mind control, the trivialization of music into a continuous, amorphous environment, the use of music as a narcotic or anesthetic (apart from legitimate therapeutic uses), the intrusion of music into the private sphere of one's life, and the determination of musical taste and standards by feedback techniques designed to manipulate and pander to a mass market.

Legitimate questions remain about music as an individual or a collective art. Music has traditionally been practiced within a social context, but the specific decisions—although influenced by group preferences—have generally been made by individuals. Only recently, in the People's Republic of China, has composition by committee become a practice. The "Great Man" theory of music history is undoubtedly an overstatement, yet it is difficult to deny that the greatest monuments in the heritage of Western music have arisen as the result of individual decisions.

Interchange of roles

Individual roles within the matrix of traditional musical society are usually thought to be quite unambiguous.[11] The standard nineteenth-century formula, which is still the model for public concert life, goes like this: the composer prescribes, the performer executes (or interprets), and the listener perceives—an oversimplification of a much more complicated relationship but adequate for our point. We note several interesting trends in recent music that cast members of the "social triad" in unfamiliar roles.

The composer as performer. This is not so much a new role as a reversion to a previous one. Prior to 1800 composers were almost invariably active performers and involved in one way or another with the performance of their own music. The dichotomy between the ivory-tower composer and the virtuoso is basically a creation of the Romantic century. But there are new twists. In some cases the composer now assumes full control over the performance and eliminates entirely the need for an executor or interpreter, as in some electronic or computer music or any music that can be recorded directly on magnetic tape. Composition and performance have thus merged into a single laboratory function.

In other cases the composer takes a hand in shaping the musical events during the performance—as director, collaborator, or even as "actor"—either because the musical script does not require high technical ability or because it is flexible enough to allow him to decide events during the course of the performance. Many composers are, of course, skilled performers and continue to function in the dual role that was typical in seventeenth- and eighteenth-century musical society.

The performer as composer. Performance and composition are not as separate functions as one might suppose: in musical cultures (India, jazz) and eras (the Baroque) which have maintained a tradition of improvisation, performers may more accurately be described as "spontaneous composers." But, more than this, performing music has always involved much more than the precise execution of a set of directions, however elaborate. Anyone who doubts this has but to compare any two recorded versions of the same composition. Even composers such as Gustav Mahler and Alban Berg, who filled their scores with verbal supplements to the standard notation, were unable to do more than minimize the deviation from their inner vision. Any composer and performer will readily admit that our notation is inherently too inexact to specify more than the outline of the composer's intent—until filled in by tradition, instruction, imitation, and instinct.

But recently certain composers have sought to increase the performer's role in their music and to capitalize on his flair for improvisation. Such a composer might see himself as a "planner" or a "designer" of a set of conditions under which something striking and beautiful—perhaps something unforeseen—could emerge. Scripts for this type of music may be minimal, so much so that the U.S. Office of Copyright has refused to grant copyright protection.[12] The actual piece may be more a projection of the performer's personality than of the composer's intent, or perhaps such was precisely the composer's intent!

This suggests some troublesome questions: Who should receive the credit (or the blame) for the piece—the composer or the performer? Who should be paid for it? If a composition exists in minimal form and differs to a high degree from performance to performance, is it the same piece? How much must it differ before it becomes a different piece? How can criticism deal with it as an entity? and so on.

The audience as performer. Music has not always been a spectator sport. In many non-Western musical cultures and in the tradition of amateur chamber music the roles of the performer and auditor are inseparable. The idea of a passive mass audience is again a creation of the nineteenth century and a fiction in that it has fostered many misconceptions about the nature of musical perception. And, in earlier centuries, the great tradition of sacred choral music, the general dance at the end of a court ballet, madrigal singing in Elizabethan England, and other musics that required audience participation give evidence that the role of the musical audience has not always been a passive one.

Recently, however, some composers have sought to involve the spectator more intimately in the musical process—by changing the configuration of the performing space to include the audience, by assigning various participatory roles (singing, percussion, noise) to the audience, and even by leaving certain performance decisions to the audience.[13]

The audience as composer. In an "ultimate" work such as John Cage's famous *4'33"* (of silence), the music is—in one possible interpretation—the growing self-awareness and resistance of the audience in the presence of controlled silence, the sound of one's own breathing, feelings of discomfort, coughs, snickers, growing irritation, and the like. Nothing can be less satisfying than a performance in which the entire audience knows what to expect and sits in polite silence. Perhaps the same purpose motivated Erik Satie's *Vieux Sequins et Vieilles Cuirasses,* in which the final eight-beat passage is to be repeated 380 times, and the even-more taxing *Vexations* which prescribes 840 repetitions of a very soft, slow module of fifty-two beats.

In these interchanges of role, many of which are admittedly intended more as philosophical demonstration than as formal music, one can detect what appears to be a healthy trend: toward a more holistic concept of music in which the functions of creation, performance, and perception are not kept in artificial separation.

Material

Romain Rolland, in his novel *Jean Christophe* (1904–1912), described his composer-hero's struggle with the limitations of traditional musical form and substance:

> The difficulty began when he tried to cast his ideas in the ordinary musical molds: he made the discovery that none of the ancient molds was suited to them; if he wished to fix his visions with fidelity he had to begin by forgetting all the music he had heard, all that he had written, to make a clean slate of all the formalism he had learned, of traditional technique, to throw away those crutches of impotency, that bed, all prepared for the laziness of those who, fleeing the fatigue of thinking for themselves, lie down in other men's thoughts.[14]

A fresh start, a "clean slate" (Locke's famous tabula rasa)[15]— these have been appealing images to many young composers who face the dismaying prospect of writing in a language still imperfectly understood or whose grammar and syntax they find hostile or restrictive to their thought. But should the slate already be ruled with musical staff-lines? Or should it be truly blank? Should what one writes thereon be predetermined in any way? Or should one bother with a slate in the first place?

An artist requires raw material—a substance he can act upon. The poet must begin with words: he has a wide selection, but his choices retain the determinate meanings and connotations of his language. What—and how determinate—are the composer's words? How "raw" is his raw material? It is probably a romantic notion to suggest, as Rolland does, that the sounds a composer imagines could somehow be independent of his previous experience, as if his subconscious could somehow be purged of its contents. And it seems inescapable that the act of imagining and prescribing specific sounds must be preceded by an elaborate (although largely unconscious) program of preselection, based on a number of assumptions—which sounds the composer (or his tradition) considers appropriate, beautiful, or useful; their potential relationship to one another, whether expressed in terms of a functional "system" or as thematic content; what sort of a gestalt they may ultimately form; and perhaps even the more mundane matter of which sounds are playable! No composer can claim acquaintance with the full range of acoustic matter available, nor will every composer consider this whole range appropriate for music; some, for example, will rule out those sounds whose vibratory patterns are nonperiodic, i.e., noise.

Edgard Varèse's answer to these questions was unequivocal: "The raw material of music is sound." And in a 1939 lecture he called for a machine that would give the composer total access to his acoustical material:

> Here are the advantages I anticipate from such a machine: liberation from the arbitrary, paralyzing tempered system; the possibility of obtaining any number of cycles or, if still desired, subdivisions of the octave, and consequently the formation of any desired scale; unsuspected range in low and high registers; new harmonic splendors obtainable from the use of sub-harmonic combinations now impossible; the possibility of obtaining any differentiation of timbre, of sound-combinations; new dynamics far beyond the present human-powered orchestra; a sense of sound-projection in space by means of the emission of sound in any part or in many parts of the hall. . . .[16]

Varèse lived to compose on such a machine, and the results were extraordinarily beautiful. But not all composers regard limitations as "paralyzing," nor are they inhibited by the "arbitrariness" of the traditional musical system. When Igor Stravinsky was once asked what he thought of new media and new resources, he replied: "I am not convinced that greater resources are what is needed. It seems to me that the possibilities are already rich enough, or too rich. A good artist will not be stopped by a want of resources, which are in the man himself, in any case, and which time makes new every day. The so-called crisis of means is interior."[17]

Here are some ways in which recent music reflects the desire for additional sound resources:

1   the demand for as complete a sound spectrum as possible— complete with respect to range (high/low), continuity (glissandi, availability of sound in "bits" smaller than the human thresholds of pitch- and time-discrimination permit us to discern), density (tone clusters, sound-masses, cross-rhythms), and assortment of timbres

2   electronic technology: tone generation and synthesis, sound recording techniques (on disc and magnetic tape), computer applications

3   the invention of new instruments, the use of traditional instruments in nontraditional ways, and the use of "noninstruments"

4   new vocal sounds, abstract use of phonetic material, new styles of musical declamation (such as *Sprechstimme*)[18]

5   ignoring the traditional distinction between musical sounds and noise

6   natural sounds (bird songs, whales) and environmental sounds

7   non-Western scales, rhythms, and instruments

8   transformations of pre-existent music: citation, allusion, borrowing, parody, and other types of "music about music"[19]

9   altered spatial arrangements, altered contexts or environments for music, various blendings of music with dance, literature, theater, and even architecture

We have the advantage of hindsight: many of these trends are apparent in music from the early nineteenth century, and the urge to become free of "limitations" is an obvious consequence of the aesthetics of Romanticism. It is also becoming clear that some composers prefer not to recognize music as an independent category of sound, i.e., detachable from the full context of environmental sound.

It is our job now to pose some of the aesthetic questions implied by these trends in the selection of sound material, supporting some with relevant quotations, arguing others briefly. To maintain proper perspective, it is a good idea to keep in mind that our concentration on new sound material tends to obscure the overwhelming statistical preference for traditional sound selection. If these questions dwell on the aesthetics of experimental music, it is because the experimental "establishment"—with John Cage as its most eloquent spokesman— has articulated with great clarity important issues for the philosophy of music, issues that will not go away.

Some of the following questions are asked from the composer's viewpoint and begin with the word *should*. These must not be taken in the sense of moral imperatives: philosophy is a means of producing change by persuasion, not legislation. Their meaning, when asked by a particular composer, might range from the relatively neutral "Shall this be the case?" to one based on certain aesthetic assumptions: "Will it be artistically productive if. . . ."

Can (should) sounds be detached from ideas about them? In other words, can sounds be regarded as meaningless, devoid of any symbolic content? Cage argues such a point of view:

> I imagine that as contemporary music goes on changing in the way that I'm changing it what will be done is to more and more completely liberate sounds from abstract ideas about them and more and more exactly to let them be physically uniquely themselves. This means for me: knowing more and more not what I think a sound is but what it actually is in all of its acoustical details and then letting this sound exist, itself, changing in a changing sonorous environment.[20]

And Morton Feldman adds, "Only by 'unfixing' the elements traditionally used to construct a piece of music could the sounds exist in themselves—not as symbols, or memories which were memories of other music to begin with."[21]

These statements raise thorny problems and deserve serious consideration. Each specification of an abstract sound, each mediation by the mind or an instrument, imposes symbolic meaning upon that sound, and it is doubtful that any composer or listener is able to disregard this train of meaning. On the other hand, the value of considering sounds as detachable objects lies in the attitude it implies: an attitude in which the ears and mind are more open to the savor of the unique properties of sounds, including the sounds around us as well as the sounds of formal music. To appreciate more fully the vividness of sound must be one of the main goals of the musical experience.

On the other hand, music consists of relationships—foreseen by the composer and perceived (although often subconsciously) by the listener. Some will argue (and, in my opinion, correctly) that it is the composer's business not to *let* sounds be but to *make* sounds be, guided by his superior power of imagination and his knowledge of what is possible and potentially pleasing within the realm of the audible. Just as the color red, or—more specifically—a crimson brush stroke in oil pigment, is inescapably a memory of a similar brush stroke, the same hue, or the category of "redness" itself, some will assert that sounds must inevitably be perceived as memories of other sounds—some vivid and specific, others more general. From this viewpoint every musical decision (even at times the decisions that one leaves for others to make) carries certain meanings along with it, whether the sound is produced by a violin bow drawn across a taut string or ice scraped from a metal surface. This brings us to a second question:

What specific meanings or values do particular sounds hold for us? We may regard certain sounds as "natural" or "musical," based on previous experience. We may find the sounds of the human voice intrinsically pleasing and/or meaningful, and it is unlikely that we can perceive human sounds without retaining some sense of their human origin. Various instrumental sounds may carry equally specific meanings, some of them peculiarly personal memories and associations, others more general associations (such as for the sound of the flute) that seem to be a part of the common cultural experience of mankind.[22] The method of sound production and the various tonal properties influence our reaction to a sound, e.g., one cannot but react with tension to a sound with a high impact or an extremely short sound. Negative value is attached to certain sounds, such as a belch or a fart, and we may react negatively when we see and hear a traditional instrument struck with a mallet or scraped with a rasp. Many listeners regard an electronic tone as "artificial," while others, who have grown up with the amplified sounds of electronic instruments and synthesizers, may attach positive value to the same sound. Stravinsky was strongly repelled by early efforts in the field of electronic music and once remarked, "I do not see why a medium so rich in sound possibilities should sound so poor."[23]

Meanings such as these can get in the way of the music and represent real obstacles to aesthetic enjoyment. But it seems unrealistic to deny their influence on many composers and most, if not all, listeners. Recording technology has made a major contribution toward the detachment of sound from meaning, but it might be argued that the sound acquires an equally specific meaning in its new acoustic setting.

Are all sounds equally beautiful? Can a sound be beautiful in itself, or does it require a context? And what are the prevailing standards for beauty? Despite the present lack of consensus, it seems evident that the nineteenth-century concept of tonal beauty (a smooth, opulent, vibrant, intensely rich tone) has lost some of its force. And, in its place, we hear a shift in the direction of leaner, straighter, edgier, more sharply impacted sounds, which I take to be closer to the tonal values of Baroque music as well as a predictable reaction against the tonal preferences of the last century. But, at the same time, one must concede that certain genres (notably opera) have proved resistant to these trends, and that large segments of musical society hold the tonal values of Romanticism as tenaciously as ever. We can legitimately inquire what grounds for preference we may apply to the profusion of electronic and environmental sounds in recent music, other than (as always) our instincts and experience. To dismiss the question with "each in its own way" seems an evasion. I suggest that a new set of tonal values is gradually coalescing amidst what appears to be the chaos of seemingly limitless variety. These values may never be proclaimed by consensus, but they are now being demonstrated, and—when Atropos permits—we will recognize them for what they are.

Does the nature of the sound material determine in any way the organization of the music? In a word, are sounds *causal?* To what extent does a composer's selection (or preselection) determine his organization? Causation is as difficult a concept in music as it is in philosophy. Musical choices frequently entail other choices, especially within an established style; the difficulty arises when one tries to narrow the train of cause-and-effect into a specific 1 : 1 sequence and asserts that a single specific cause leads to a single specific effect. To the extent that traditional tonal music permits the listener to feel expectation and predict the resolution of tendencies, causation is thereby demonstrated.

Let me present a few obvious instances. It seems clear that the respective properties of the diatonic and whole-tone scales have had causal implications, the former tending to promote tonal focus and differentiation of pitch structure, the latter virtually precluding both. Practical considerations can also be causal—bowed string sounds can be sustained longer than wind sounds, and electronic sounds can be sustained indefinitely. It is virtually impossible to write lyrical music with short, staccato sounds. And the skilled composer knows that he must foresee the mental and muscular consequences that his prescribed sounds will have for his performers, e.g., a heavy accent will require some recovery time, a note difficult to reach had best be preceded by some preparation time.

For many composers the traditional implications of the sound material will operate in a causal way, while other composers will attempt to select sounds and means of sound production that are relatively free of such implications. Whichever the case, by the time a composer has acquired a "style," there is usually a clear relationship between his material and what he does with it.

I have delayed putting the question with which I began this section, since it follows naturally from the preceding: *To what extent should the sound material be subject to any limitations?* The question contains any number of provocative subquestions: Should the sound material be "ruled" and overlaid with pitch- and time-scales? Should the pitch and temporal spectra be striated or continuua? Is such a preselection of the sound material a discipline that a composer views as a necessary prelude to his activity or, as Varèse claimed, a means of paralysis?[24] Is economy of means a valid aesthetic criterion, or does it matter—in the long run—whether a composer selects from a small, preorganized set of choices or from every sound available in the world? We may admire thrift, but should it influence our judgment? Lippman presents a traditional point of view, when he speaks of a force destructive of musical values,

> which is again connected with electronic technology, is the multiplication of aesthetic materials and means: of artistic composites, of scales of pitch, and of types of sound in which pitch is unimportant or absent. . . . Here two conditions of artistic value are being set aside; one is the essential restriction that turns matter into material and provides a framework of limitation; the other—which is connected with the relative artificiality of the new material—is the essential relation to the past that gives significance to the present and future.[25]

The distinction Lippman draws between "matter" and "material" goes to the heart of the question. John Cage, in his essay "Rhythm etc.," argues against any such "framework of limitation," citing in particular the determinate effects of traditional instruments: "we must dispense with instruments altogether and get used to working with tools. Then, God willing, we'll get some work done. It can be put this way too: find ways of using instruments as though they were tools, i.e., so that they leave no traces. That's precisely what our tape-recorders, amplifiers, microphones, loud-speakers, photoelectric cells, etc. are: things to be used which don't necessarily determine the nature of what is done. . . ."[26] While Cage's point is clear enough, the distinction between instruments and "tools" is not altogether convincing: it now seems clear that the sound-transforming techniques of primitive electronic technology have had more of a determinate effect on recent music than has hitherto been realized.[27]

Should the selection of material (and, of course, also its organization) *take into account the limitations of human perception?* Is music still addressed to people? If so, can there be any value in ignoring the thresholds of human perception or in flaunting the laws of auditory perception? It takes no great amount of data to exceed one's capacity to process it. Musical composition can most obviously be considered a private activity, and in that case the composer has every reason to seek his own satisfaction above all such practical considerations. In his essay "Who Cares if You Listen?" Milton Babbitt pleads the case for "specialized music":

> I dare suggest that the composer would do himself and his music an immediate and ultimate service by total, resolute, and voluntary withdrawal from this public world to one of private performance and electronic media, with its very real possibility of complete elimination of the public and social aspects of musical composition. By so doing, the separation between the domains would be defined beyond any possibility of confusion of categories, and the composer would be free to pursue a private life of professional achievement, as opposed to a public life of unprofessional compromise and exhibitionism. . . . Such a private life is what the university provides the scholar and the scientist.[28]

Should music be regarded as permanent or disposable? The question of permanence is central to the philosophy of music. The dichotomy between the transience of the musical process and the permanence of the musical product has developed into a common theme in Western literature. Until quite recently, however, aesthetic analyses have tended to focus upon the musical object and its qualities of "thingness," thus according it the status of a virtual museum object. A newer aesthetic emphasizes music as process, a concept more in harmony with most folk and traditional musics of the non-Western world.

I will not elaborate here on the important distinctions between music as product and music as process, other than to note certain implications for the musical substance: at stake are such concepts as the status of musical sounds, the manner in which they may be preserved, and the degree to which a composition—or an individual performance thereof—may be specified. The Western European intellectual tradition has assumed that musical sounds constitute a special category. If such is not held to be the case, then it follows that music may be composed with ordinary, "found" sounds—like the visual art that employs "found" objects. And, to carry this line of reasoning a step further, music itself may be considered a "throw-away" process, existing in no fixed form but changing from performance to performance. If such is the case, is it not inconsistent—perhaps even inimical to the process—to make a recording of such a performance? John Cage wrote that a recording of such a work "has no more value than a postcard; it provides a knowledge of something that happened, whereas the action was a non-knowledge of something that had not yet happened."[29]

The philosophy of music is properly concerned with the being of music (product or process), its permanence, and its specification—whether the composer prefers to choose from traditional, preselected sound material or from any other acoustic matter he considers appropriate, and whether he specifies his work in elaborate detail or leaves a large number of choices for the performer. In weighing their respective contributions, we cannot avoid certain issues: what is the irreducible minimum for the composition (an idea, a plan, a script, a complete blueprint), how fixed is it, and how is it actualized in its multiple performance versions?

I would like to point out that the preceding seven questions are neither a random nor a trivial assortment: we have considered in turn problems of detachment, meaning, value, causation, being, knowledge, and permanence—all crucial issues in the philosophy of music. Together they demonstrate how completely the composers of experimental music have challenged the traditional assumptions of Western art music. In summary of the newer alternative aesthetic, here are assumptions that Barney Childs asserts are no longer valid:

the "masterpiece" idea
permanence as esthetic value
process as subservient to the product it realizes
hierarchical systematized non-random ordering
esthetic validity being partly dependent upon the extensive and careful making of choices
the "responsibility" of the artist
the esthetic value of historicity and the validity of historical succession
emphasis on the logical, the rational, and the analyzable
the esthetic response's highest form being feelings of profundity, awe, and the like.[30]

Organization

Adrian Leverkühn, who has been introduced in an earlier chapter as the composer-hero of Thomas Mann's novel *Doctor Faustus*, was attending Kolonat Nonnenmacher's lectures on early Greek philosophy at the University of Halle, in preparation for the first examination in theology, and writing music under the influence of the magic square he had hung over his rented piano:

On the wall above the piano was an arithmetical diagram fastened with drawing-pins, something he had found in a second-hand shop: a so-called magic square, such as appears also in Dürer's *Melancolia*, along with the hour-glass, the circle, the scale, the polyhedron, and other symbols. Here as there, the figure was divided into sixteen Arabic-numbered fields, in such a way that . . . the sum of these numerals, however you added them, straight down, crosswise, or diagonally, always came to thirty-four.[31]

Twenty years after the writing of *Doctor Faustus*, the publication of Anton Webern's sketches (1926–1945) revealed that Webern had been similarly preoccupied with a famous Latin word square:[32]

S	A	T	O	R
A	R	E	P	O
T	E	N	E	T
O	P	E	R	A
R	O	T	A	S

The coincidence is no trivial matter. For Mann, as well as for Webern and other serial composers, the magic square was a potent symbol of order and rigor in music: the control of the horizontal and vertical dimensions by the same principle and the quantification of the musical substance, both of which have profound implications for the compositional process—in Mann's words, "calculation raised to mystery."[33] A compulsive borrower of persons and ideas, Mann used Arnold Schoenberg as his model for the character of Adrian Leverkühn and allowed Leverkühn to "invent" Schoenberg's system of composing with twelve notes.[34] This serial principle, in which the twelve notes of the chromatic scale appear in a predetermined order, was applied first to pitch but subsequently (by other composers) extended to the control of other musical dimensions. It has proved to be the most influential organizing principle for music in this century.

Music has, in a sense, come full circle. This approach invokes the ancient idea of music as a mathematical discipline and the symbol of universal order and harmony. Mann explicitly draws the connection between Adrian's experiments in musical calculation and the inspiration of Nonnenmacher's brilliant lectures on

> this early cosmological conception of a stern and pious spirit [Pythagoras], who elevated his fundamental passion, mathematics, abstract proportion, number, to the principle of the origin and existence of the world; who, standing opposite All-Nature as an initiate, a dedicated one, first addressed her with a great gesture as "Cosmos," as order and harmony, as the interval-system of the spheres, sounding beyond the range of the senses. Number, and the relation of numbers, as constituting an all-embracing concept of being and moral value: it was highly impressive, how the beautiful, the exact, the moral, here solemnly flowed together to comprise the idea of authority which animated the Pythagorean order. . . .[35]

The word square held a similar richness of symbolic content for Webern, if on a less cosmic and more practical level. It represented his passion for palindromic structure (a tendency that is evident in most of his later music),

$$\xrightarrow{\hspace{2cm}}$$
SATOR AREPO TENET OPERA ROTAS
$$\xleftarrow{\hspace{2cm}}$$

as well as the reciprocal relationships between the four basic forms of a tone series,

and the complete matrix that includes all possible transpositions of the four basic row forms.[36] The sketches for his Concerto, Op. 24, show how Webern used the word square as a model for the unique trichordal construction of his twelve-note row,[37] which is in turn responsible for much of the rigor and finesse analysts have found in this composition.

The general question of organization in twentieth-century music may be posed in two versions—one extreme, the other more moderate. In the extreme: *Do we prefer to conceive of music as a web of elegant formal relationships* (the serialist position) *or as a delightful series of discrete sound-events* (the minimalist view)? Is the beauty more in the relationships or in the individual sounds?

To a more traditional composer, this is not an issue at all; the question for him is *To what degree, and by what means, is his composition to be organized?* If a piece of music is to hang together for the listener, he expects either to recognize and respond to relationships, or at least to be persuaded that they are there—whether they have been systematically and consciously contrived by the composer, or occur as the traditional outcome of the (largely) subconscious aspect of the composition process, or are imposed on the arriving sounds by that part of our perceiving mind that abhors apparent disorder.

If the magic square is the symbol of organization, the dice (Lat. *alea*) symbolize chance and indeterminacy. Serial and aleatoric music have been contraposed in most discussions of recent music, and their respective virtues have often been argued with the type of rhetoric usually reserved for moral issues. Composers who opt for the extreme positions of maximal or minimal organization do so as a practical consequence of their philosophical concept of music—as universal harmony or universal entropy—and in full knowledge that they are addressing a limited audience, not competing against more traditional composers for the affection of the musical public.[38] To appreciate the position of those who advocate rigorous order in their music, it is essential to realize that many composers find the same intense satisfaction in the play of intellect that generates a rich tapestry of musical relationships that the mathematician takes in constructing an intricate theorem. Advocates of indeterminacy write with contagious enthusiasm of the spontaneity that can be achieved by removing the element of arbitrary, subjective, personal intent from the composition of music. John Cage concluded a 1957 lecture on "Experimental Music" with this passage:

> And what is the purpose of writing music? One is, of course, not dealing with purposes but dealing with sounds. Or the answer must take the form of paradox: a purposeful purposelessness or a purposeless play. This play, however, is an affirmation of life— not an attempt to bring order out of chaos nor to suggest improvements in creation, but simply a way of waking up to the very life we're living, which is so excellent once one gets one's mind and one's desires out of its way and lets it act of its own accord.[39]

In rebuttal, proponents of order may argue that music is neither an affirmation of life nor a way of wakening to our acoustical surroundings—it is, rather, the creation of beautiful and meaningful patterns in sound. Some are more attractive, more moving, more logically convincing than others, and it is the composer's job to choose between them.

The question of organization in music raises a number of provocative side-issues. We take up two that seem particularly important:

Should the order in a musical work be apparent? (Should we be able to *hear* it?)

and

Does musical coherence require some kind of pitch focus, i.e., tonality?

Serial music—and indeed, all tightly organized music from any historical period: a medieval isorhythmic motet or a Bach fugue—is often dismissed as cold and cerebral because the process of composition involves a certain amount of calculation. The accusation is based in part upon romantic assumptions (e.g., that music comes from the heart, not the head),[40] and it can be argued that all such genetic criticisms fall into the "intentional fallacy" and are quite irrelevant to the results. The real issues in this case are complexity, lack of redundancy, and unfamiliarity of style—all genuine obstacles to perception. The sense of order is one of music's chief pleasures, but it must be clear that one can never hear *all* the order that analysis can reveal within a musical work. Even the composer cannot foresee the full consequences of his work and is often surprised when unsuspected relationships in his music are pointed out to him. In an earlier chapter we cited the famous Heraclitean fragment "The hidden harmony is better than the obvious." And when asked if he expected the order in his music to be heard, Adrian Leverkühn replied: "If by 'hearing' you understand the precise realization in detail of the means by which the highest and strictest order is achieved, like the order of the planets, a cosmic order and legality—no, that way one would not hear it. But this order one will or would hear, and the perception of it would afford an unknown aesthetic satisfaction."[41]

The principle of tonality, in one version or another, has been the chief agent of coherence throughout the history of music—in the form of scalar modality until ca. 1600; followed by the great era of harmonic, triadic tonality (i.e., the system of major and minor keys), which is far from over; and, in the present century, an attenuated version of the principle that retains the preeminence of a central pitch (the *tonic*) but has discarded the supporting network of tonal relationships and implications. There is every reason to believe that tonality rests on strong and universal instincts, since it is a property of all known world musics.

Tonality is something that is strongly sensed by the listener who has been conditioned to respond to the particular "version" that prevails in his tradition, but its aural effects resist easy description. To illustrate the range of the concept, we present a conspectus of some of the metaphors that have been proposed. Traditional metaphors include: *focus*, as in optics; *homing*, as in pigeons; *attraction*, as in magnetics; *vectoring*, as in airport approaches; and *vanishing point*, as in perspective. Newer, more abstract descriptive labels include *centricity*, *priority*, and *referentiality*.

A complete tonal system displays these properties: (1) a "tonic" pitch—priority, centricity, stability, finality; (2) a supporting hierarchy (of tones or chords) with specific functions; (3) directionality—toward, away from, neutral; (4) authorized and unauthorized successions, approved pathways; with the possibility of (5) movement to competing tonal centers (modulation), involving exchange of functions; (6) ambiguity of function; and (7) secondary functions with their own satellite relationships.

These properties were first implemented in the melodic relationships between single tones and subsequently, in a most remarkable achievement, transferred to the more complex harmonic relationships between chords. Tonal motion—of single tones and of chords—occurs along several related axes: from "far" to "near" to "here," from weak to strong, unstable to stable, and from implication to confirmation. The members of a tonal system are assigned station and function, much like the members of any society. In fact, there is a superb Indian analogy that grasps neatly the idea of tonal "function" in terms of the mutual relations and obligations of feudal society:

the ruler—the tonic as goal and ultimate stability
his generals and ministers—strong, prominent, stable tones
his vassals—weak, neutral, and/or unstable tones
his enemies—foreign tones[42]

Tonality, like feudalism, was not created overnight: the sense of tonal legality has developed at a geologic pace over millennia. In the music of so-called primitives, tonality usually appears in the form of a limited set of tones clustering around a "nuclear" tone. In the more cultivated musics of the non-Western world, the resulting scales often serve as matrices for improvised variations (the *maqam* principle). It is perhaps unnecessary to point out that there is no reason why one pitch should be assigned priority over another or display any "tendency"—apart from the influence of certain basic human instincts: to go from a beginning through a middle to an end, to deviate from and return to stability, and to approach strong, stable tones by the smallest authorized interval.

Perle points out some of the ambiguities involved in discussing the status of tonality in twentieth-century music: "Contemporary musical developments have made it evident that triadic structure does not necessarily generate a tone center, that nontriadic harmonic formations may be made to function as referential elements, and that the assumption of a twelve-tone complex does not preclude the existence of tone centers."[43] And just as twelve-tone music may be tonal, atonal music may display certain referential properties. In sum, whatever properties of tension, attraction, stability, directed motion, priority, centricity, or referentiality one finds in atonal music are the result of the composer's decisions and properties of the individual work (or, if he is consistent, his style)—not inherent properties of the system.

To continue with the analogy of a society: most twentieth-century tonal music (e.g., that of Stravinsky or Bartók)—while it may and often does retain certain elements from traditional tonality—suggests a model of society in which all members have equal access to a strong ruler, with few if any specialized functions and reciprocal obligations. In contrast to this model, atonal music may be compared to a truly classless society in which all members perform all functions, obligation is a consequence of assigned position, and in which the ruler (if any) is *primus inter pares*. In theory, if not in practice, this sounds like an elected parliament.

It is always appropriate to hesitate modestly before proclaiming the end of "civilization as we know it," but the possibility of atonal music has existed for only an infinitesimal fraction of human history. Nevertheless, large numbers of composers have been writing atonal music for most of this century, and their efforts have demonstrated (perhaps not to everyone) that unity can be achieved in music without the aid of a tonal center or the more specific relationships of traditional harmonic tonality. Whether the musical experience of the general listener will eventually be conditioned to the point where he is able to respond affectively to the new music must remain an open question.

New models: For many composers, selecting a formal model is one of the first and most crucial of the precompositional decisions: it can range from a vague idea to a detailed concept, and it may be serious or trivial. It may serve merely as a stimulus to get his creative imagination started, or it may guide him every step of the way. Many new models for musical structure have been explored in recent years; perhaps the best generalization that can be made about them is that they are extramusical. It may be argued that most of the traditional musical schema (strophic, rondo, variations, et al.) were originally based on models extrinsic to music, but in time each of these schema became dependent upon the forces and tendencies of tonality. There is, of course, no reason why a composer need apply traditional schema in a traditional way: filling an old vessel with new content is often an extremely successful way of demonstrating the vitality of a familiar structure and maintaining what many composers believe to be an essential relationship with the past. We present an assortment of the new structural models, some with testimony from their composers; no attempt has been made to place them in an order that reflects their significance or popularity. It is too soon to predict what potential the various new models hold for the future: some may flourish, others may remain as curiosities. Taken as a group—and it is far from complete—they demonstrate the range of what is defined as music today.

1   The collage, a kaleidoscopic assembly of diverse material, often including quotations from other music. This model reflects the influence of the visual arts ("found" objects), the film montage, and the stream-of-consciousness novel. Perhaps there is also an inner model—the associative imagery of the dream state or the contents of the artistic subconscious before the jumble of ideas and connotations is consciously organized by the censoring intellect and will. This technique, pioneered in America by Charles Ives and in France (to a lesser extent) by Claude Debussy, has emerged as one of the important streams in contemporary music, particularly in the music of George Rochberg. As an example of the model, the second movement of Ives's Symphony No. 4.

The "stream-of-consciousness" model, with its discontinuities, flashbacks, and associations, was used in a slightly different way by Elliott Carter in his First Quartet (1951):

The general plan was suggested by Jean Cocteau's film *Le Sang d'un poète,* in which the entire dream-like action is framed by an interrupted slow-motion shot of a tall brick chimney in an empty lot being dynamited. Just as the chimney begins to fall apart, the shot is broken off and the entire movie follows, after which the shot of the chimney is resumed at the point it left off. . . . A similar interrupted continuity is employed in this quartet's starting with a cadenza for cello alone that is continued by the first violin alone at the very end.[44]

2   The game model, usually featuring improvisation governed by a set of predetermined rules. As an example, *Duel* by Iannis Xenakis (1959), a work for two conductors and two orchestras that involves tactics, probabilities, and scoring.[45]

3   The labyrinth, as described by Pierre Boulez:

To me, the labyrinth notion in a work of art is rather like Kafka's idea in the short story called *The Burrow.* Everyone creates his own labyrinth. . . . One builds it exactly as the subterranean animal builds this burrow so admirably described by Kafka: resources are constantly shifted about so that everything can be kept secret, and new routes are forever being chosen to mislead. Similarly, the work must provide a certain number of possible routes . . . with chance playing a shunting role at the last moment.[46]

The labyrinth is not a new notion in music: J. S. Bach, Heinichen, and other eighteenth-century composers constructed harmonic labyrinths, primarily demonstration pieces that modulate systematically through the gamut of keys and return to the starting point. For a twentieth-century equivalent, see the arioso that appears in the *Praeludium* and *Postludium* of Paul Hindemith's *Ludus Tonalis* (1943); and for another interesting version of the labyrinth model, see Elliott Carter's ballet *The Minotaur* (1947).

4   Crystal structure, a model that Edgard Varèse favored for his music and described in this way: "There is an idea, the basis of an internal structure, expanded and split into different shapes or groups of sound constantly changing in shape, direction, and speed, attracted and repulsed by various forces. The form of the work is the conse-

quence of this interaction. Possible musical forms are as limitless as the exterior forms of crystals."[47]

5   Parody, not used in the sense of a burlesque but in the Renaissance sense of the word: a creative paraphrasing of existing compositions or the simulation of a historical style, as in Igor Stravinsky's *Pulcinella* (Pergolesi), *Le baiser de la fée* (Tschaikowsky), Chorale Variations on *Von Himmel hoch* (J. S. Bach), Mass (the style of Guillaume de Machaut), and the "Dumbarton Oaks" Concerto (Baroque style). In *Music, the Arts, and Ideas* Meyer has drawn careful distinctions between paraphrasing, borrowing, simulation, and modeling.[48]

6   Role-playing, a musical *conversazione* between different "personalities"—a procedure used by Elliott Carter in his Second Quartet (1959):

> To a certain extent, the instruments are type-cast, for each fairly consistently invents its material out of its own special expressive attitude and its own repertory of musical speeds and intervals. In a certain sense each instrument is like a character in an opera made up primarily of "quartets." . . . The individuals of this group are related to each other in what might be metaphorically termed three forms of responsiveness: discipleship, companionship, and confrontation. . . .[49]

7   The spatial model, as in Charles Ives's masterpiece *The Unanswered Question* (1908), one of the first modern compositions in which the spatial deployment of the performers (a solo trumpet, four flutes, and a body of strings) and their independence from one another serves as the main organizing idea of the work.[50]

8   The cosmological model, as in Luigi Dallapiccola's *Sicut Umbra*, in which the contours of the musical ideas follow the outlines of various constellations.

9   The model of the absurd, manifested in such dadaist activities as performing nude, sawing the legs off a grand piano, throwing pies, jumping into tubs of water, and other such buffooneries.

10   The phonetic model, using the sounds of the human voice and the syntactic features of language as the basis for structure. See such works as Luciano Berio's *Sequenza III* (1965), John Cage's *Aria* (1958), Iannis Xenakis' *Nuits* (1968), and Karlheinz Stockhausen's *Stimmung* (1968).

11   The environmental model, as in Max Neuhaus's *Listen* (1966), in which "an audience expecting a conventional concert or lecture is put on a bus, their palms are stamped with the word *listen* and they are taken to and around an existing sound environment such as a power station or an underground railway system."[51]

12   The Muzak model, as in Erik Satie's proposal for a *musique d'ameublement* ("furniture music") to be played during concert intermissions: "We urgently beg you not to attach any importance to it and to act during the intermission as if the music did not exist. . . . We want to establish a music designed to satisfy 'useful' needs. Art has no part in such needs. Furniture music creates a vibration; it has no other goal; it fills the same role as light and heat—as *comfort* in every form."[52]

13   The mathematical model, of which any number of versions may be constructed. Joseph Schillinger, in *The Schillinger System of Musical Composition* (1941), suggested an array of procedures for deriving new scales, rhythms, and structures by applying various mathematical transformations and permutations. His approach was enormously popular at the time, perhaps because he could claim George Gershwin as one of his students, but more recent composer-mathematicians have devised more sophisticated means of generating music on the basis of mathematical models. In a critique of the Schillinger method, Carter wrote:

> The basic philosophical fallacy of the Schillinger point of view is of course the assumption that the "correspondences" between patterns of art and patterns of the natural world can be mechanically translated from one to the other by the use of geometry or numbers. . . . It comes from a Pythagoreanism that is quite out of place as a primary consideration in art music. Wherever this system has been successfully used, it has been by composers who were already well trained enough to distinguish the musical results from the non-musical ones.[53]

14   The statistical model, described by Pierre Boulez with the elegant analogy of a "Brownian movement"—the random motions of particles suspended in a gas or fluid as they are bombarded by the molecules of the medium, whose mass remains unchanged.[54] In musical versions of this model—the so-called sound mass pieces—the mass of the sound remains constant even though the position of any of the

individual pitches is indeterminate. Composition with dense sound masses has become an extremely important stream in recent music, as in Krzysztof Penderecki's *Threnody for the Victims of Hiroshima* (1960), Witold Lutosławski's *Jeux vénitiens* (1961), and György Ligeti's *Atmospheres* (1962). Xenakis coined the term *stochastic music* for his version of the model, governed by the laws of probability: "sonic events are made out of thousands of isolated sounds; . . . This mass event is articulated and forms a plastic mold of time, which itself follows aleatory and stochastic laws. . . . They are the laws of the passage from complete order to total disorder in a continuous or explosive manner."[55]

15 The architectural model, as in Xenakis' *Concret P-H*, written for the 1958 Brussels Exhibition and modeled upon the structure of Le Corbusier's Philips Pavilion. *P-H* signifies the "hyperbolic paraboloid" internal contours of the pavilion, which the architect fancifully likened to the shape of a cow's stomach. This work and its companion, Edgard Varèse's controversial *Poème Électronique*, were channeled and transmitted by means of 400 loudspeakers that lined the pavilion's inner surfaces. Xenakis chose the discharge of smoldering charcoal as his sound source and described the effect of the music as "lines of sound moving in complex paths from point to point in space, like needles darting from everywhere."[56]

16 The repetition model ("trance music" or "process music"), as realized in Steve Reich's *Come out* (1966), Terry Riley's *A Rainbow in Curved Air* (1969), and Phil Glass's *Music with Changing Parts* (1971)—and earlier in Ravel's *Bolero* (1928). Music has traditionally tolerated—perhaps even demanded—more repetition than any of the other temporal arts. The distinctive feature of this model is that continuous, hypnotic repetition has become the principal agent of musical structure, frequently suggesting the influence of Indian and other non-Western musics. Because repetition itself is merely a device, the actual models may be any of the following: the mantra (ritual incantation), a state of trance, drug-induced expanded consciousness—a continuous "now," the pulsating cellular vibration of lower organisms and the idea of regression to an earlier evolutionary state, or the Elizabethan vision of continuous music and dance in heaven.[57]

Ut pictura poesis?[58] Is a piece of music really like a painting or a poem? Not even the magic of the composer can translate ideas directly into music: he can only devise analogous patterns, motions, densities, connections, shapes, and interactions. Understanding how a musical work manages to realize an external model may satisfy one's curiosity, but it fails as a basis for criticism. If any of the cited compositions convinces us that it is a work of excellence, it does so by meeting our criteria for excellence—not because of the composer's skill in modeling.

What seems more important is the set of philosophical attitudes that the sixteen models demonstrate. We have seen music conceived as an *object*, stressing its traditional qualities of "thingness," permanence, and structure; as a *process*, emphasizing its dynamic properties—change, motion, and energy; as a *state*—music in the form of pure "being" with unity and stasis as its chief characteristics; as a *situation*, the spontaneous interaction of performing personalities; and as a *field*, a circumscribed terrain or domain in which events occur, regulated only by the laws of probability.[59] Perhaps still other possibilities will be suggested by future models.

Certain models seem to have been chosen more as philosophic demonstrations than as "music" in any of the generally accepted senses of the word: especially numbers 9, 11, and 12. Several imply that music is becoming less the willful product of a single imagining, selecting, shaping, editing intelligence and more the uncertain outcome of a set of circumstances or collective decisions. Taken as a group the models reveal a major shift in metaphorical thinking about music: away from the vegetative/organic metaphors popular during the nineteenth century and toward the abstract/inorganic and the personal/interactive. Music, these metaphors tell us, is no longer to be compared to the maturing of a tree or the living of a full human life—rather, it is to be likened to the physical processes of the inanimate universe or the unpredictable encounters and contingencies that contribute to the sense of existential tension in contemporary life.

Temporality: The idea of time in traditional Western music is rooted in a large number of related assumptions: that music is an art of directed motion; that it is teleological (aimed at a future goal) and hence irreversible; that it displays cumulative continuity; that it is laid out along a hierarchical scale of beats and periodicities; that it begins in a clear and decisive manner, proceeds through related parts, and ends with a sense of finality and fulfillment; that it follows a single time line that gradually passes from our future, through our present, into our past; that its ideal structure suggests a narrative interpretation of the dynamics of human life;[60] that it allows the listener to feel expectation and perceive by means of prediction and retrodiction; that its properties include causality, syntactic relationships, and connotations that invite and reward cross references between musical events that are separate in time. The time of music, in this interpretation, is singular, logical, predictable, continuous, and—above all—linear. Such a description applies equally to a Bach fugue, a Mozart quartet, or a Verdi opera. In this final section I present conflicting testimony on these assumptions, with brief comments.

Nothing could be more foreign to the traditional temporality of music than an aesthetic that attaches chief importance to the present moment, favors discontinuity over continuity, and denies the teleological view of music, thereby severing the moment of perception from both its past and its future. Rochberg outlines the philosophical basis for such a "particularist" aesthetic:

> The predominant philosophical mode of our time is acknowledged to be existentialism, a view of life which holds that the present moment is the nodal point of existence. It is in the present that existence is actual, most vital; before there can be being, there must be existence. One's sense of being derives from one's sense of existence. The way to sense one's existence is to charge each present moment with content and meaning. The present is reality. This view, though distinctly Western in origin, stemming from the thought of Nietzsche, Kierkegaard, Heidegger, Jaspers, and others, finds strong reverberations in Eastern Zen Buddhism, which also holds that the present moment is supreme reality.
>
> It is not at all strange, therefore, that composers of chance music, particularly, are drawn to Zen and imply in their attitude towards music an existential tendency; that is, to see music as the occurrence of unpredictable events, each moment of sound or silence freed of formal connection with the moment before or after, audible only as a present sensation. . . . In this form of existential music, the present erases the past by allowing no recall or return; and promises no future since the present happening is sufficient to itself, requiring no future event for its understanding. . . . All the listener can hope to do is grasp at each occurrence, just as he grasps at life's formless succession of events, hoping to derive some meaningful order. In the case of

chance music this is hardly likely; and, from the point of view of the composers of such music, highly undesirable. . . ."[61]

John Cage states what, in his opinion, is desirable: "The wisest thing to do is to open one's ears immediately and hear a sound suddenly before one's thinking has a chance to turn it into something logical, abstract, or symbolical."[62]

Discontinuity is a characteristic behavior in the contemporary arts, manifested in such diverse ways as the staccato contrast of extreme registers in the music of Anton Webern, Proust's flashback memories, the chaotic juxtaposition of citations in T. S. Eliot's *The Waste Land*, the stream-of-consciousness narrative in Joyce's *A Portrait of the Artist as a Young Man* and *Ulysses*, the rapid "cuts" made possible by splices in magnetic recording tape, the montage of superimposed film images in cinematography, the non sequiturs of the "theater of the absurd," as well as the sharp visual discontinuities of analytic and synthetic cubism. Although such techniques invite interpretation as disorder, their real significance is that order is asserted by *nonlinear* means. The implications of this revolution in artistic syntax have not yet been fully realized.

Not all artists are prepared to accept the consequences of this new orientation to musical structure. As Igor Stravinsky wrote a few years ago:

> Time, too, is a physical measure to me, and in music I must feel a physical here and there and not only a now, which is to say, movement from and toward. I do not always feel this sense of movement or location in, say, Boulez's *Structures* or those fascinating score-plans by Stockhausen . . . and though every element in those pieces may be organized to engender motion, the result often seems to me like the essence of the static. A time series may very well postulate a new parable about time, but that is not the same thing as a time experience, which for me is dynamic passage through time.[63]

And on another occasion: "I further admit to a need to go from a beginning to an end, through related parts. Perhaps in sympathy with my body's diminished mobility, my mind no longer seems to be willing or able to jump from isolated 'present' moments to other isolated 'present' moments."[64]

Meyer has called attention to the problems of perception and analysis of music that is projected as a series of discrete events, for which he coined the term *transcendental particularism:*

> When . . . attention is directed only to the uniqueness of things, then each and every attribute of an object or event is equally significant and necessary. There can be no degrees of connectedness within or between events. . . . An event which is without any redundancy whatsoever is its own simplest description. . . . Because in such a non-redundant world works of art cannot be described in simpler terms, criticism necessarily consists of: (a) an itemized list of the attributes of the art work, (b) a "translation" of such a list into a poetic-verbal analogue, (c) an account of the "rules" involved in the construction of the work, or (d) a discussion . . . of the cultural-ideological significance of the art work, rather than an analysis of its internal relationships and meanings.[65]

The new trends in the temporal concept and structure of music pose important questions for the psychology of perception: in particular, whether the experience of music is perceived as before in terms of the two traditional time series (Series A: before/after; Series B: past/present/future) or interpreted as the stasis of a perpetual "now." William James described the sensible present not as a "knife-edge" but as a "saddle-back" that appears to extend the limits of our consciousness of the present moment, perhaps to the duration of a motive, gesture, or phrase.[66] Various studies by gestalt psychologists have shown that the tendency to impose pattern upon apparently unconnected sense data is a characteristic of both our visual and auditory perception. One conclusion seems inescapable—that the laws of perception limit our ability to hear discretely.

Several provocative studies have examined the concept of temporality in recent music, particularly those of Childs, Kramer, and Stockhausen.[67] From their investigations, and especially relying on Kramer's elegant formulation of the problem, we pose a question that may help to clarify the diversity of temporalities in new music: *Can the temporal organization of a musical work—or of a section thereof—be best described as a single (linear) time, two or more simultaneous times, timeless, or one time moment after another?*

1   The teleological world of linear time, in which music is con-

ceived and perceived as directed motion, is our most familiar model, as in most of the music of Bartók, Berg, Britten, Copland, Hindemith, Prokofiev, and Schoenberg. Many of the traditional assumptions about time remain valid for this repertoire, particularly so for those works organized by the principle of tonality.

2   Music that separates into multiple, nonsynchronized time lines, as in Elliott Carter's Second and Third Quartets and Witold Lutosław-ski's Quartet (1964), suggests the existence of simultaneous times. The superimposed multiple images of cubism (as in Marcel Duchamp's 1911 *Nude Descending a Staircase*) and the fantastic spatial juxtapositions of Marc Chagall exhibit parallel tendencies in the visual arts.[68]

3   Most aleatoric and particularist music, music that is highly repetitive, most sound-mass pieces, and other works that feature the techniques of musical stasis outlined in chapter nine imply a state of timelessness.[69]

4   Stockhausen and Kramer have discussed "moment time"— music consisting of a set of discrete, self-contained modules, as illustrated by Stravinsky's *Symphonies of Wind Instruments* and Stockhausen's *Klavierstück XI*. According to Kramer, the attributes of moment time include (a) an absence of beginning and ending behaviors, (b) minimal connection of sections, (c) the order of sections appears to be arbitrary and not determined by any global logic, and (d) the structure of the work is defined by the relative proportions (as well as the number and order) of the "moments."[70]

To clarify the distinctions among these temporal modes, it may be useful to suggest examples from the music of one composer; and it seems particularly appropriate to cite from the works of Igor Stravinsky, generally acknowledged to be the outstanding composer of this century: as examples of traditional linear time, *Petrouchka* (1911) and many of the later Neo-Classic works—*Pulcinella* (1920) or the *Duo Concertante* (1932); in the loosely synchronized introduction to *The Rite of Spring* (1913), a musical representation of the chaos of primeval creation, the various instruments give the illusion of independent time lines;[71] in the slow, serene coda to the third movement of the *Symphony of Psalms* (1930), spun out over a hypnotic basso ostinato of three notes, time almost literally seems to stand still, suggesting a state of being rather than a process of becoming; and finally—although, as Kramer has pointed out, the *Symphonies of Wind Instruments* (1920) is clearly the best example of moment time in his catalog of works—there are strong hints of this mode of temporality in the second of his Three Pieces for String Quartet (1914) and in *The Wedding* (1917).

To demonstrate that the roots of the new temporal modes may be traced back well into the nineteenth century (perhaps even as far as Beethoven), here is a set of examples from the music of Richard Wagner. As examples of traditional linear time, one can cite the preludes to act 3 of *Lohengrin* and act 1 of *Tristan and Isolde*. To illustrate the phenomenon of simultaneous multiple times, I propose the final scene of the first act of *The Mastersingers of Nuremberg:* although the many independent rhythmic lines are synchronized within the structure of the prevailing meter, the control is minimal.[72] The prelude to *Parsifal* is so rhythmically ambiguous that it is virtually atemporal, with the long silences between events contributing to the general illusion of stasis. And the prelude to *Das Rheingold* is totally static with regard to both harmony and tonality, consisting of 136 measures of a sustained E-flat major triad with no articulation of the temporal flow apart from the steady growth in texture and volume. Passages that imply even a rudimentary mode of moment time are harder to locate, but I suggest that the tendency to encapsulate the musical flow may be heard in some of the long narrative monologues from the *Ring* cycle or Siegfried's funeral music from *Die Götterdämmerung*, organized into a dramatic and musical mosaic by the series of leitmotifs. Wagner intended the sequence of musical events to be as linear as the dramatic events they represent, but the distinctive individual rhythms, energies, and thematic contours of the successive motives hint at the possibility of the more discrete, self-sufficient "moments" heard in recent music. I do not suggest that all changes in the temporal modality of new music should be attributed to the influence of Wagner, but it seems evident that these changes are not entirely creations of the twentieth century.

Schuldt has summarized the variety of musical times:

Music can be driven by time or it can be static, a number of separate moments. It can develop as a life process, or it can be cyclic, returning to its starting point unchanged. It can head unswervingly toward a goal, or it can be labyrinthine and open-ended. It can be strongly physical in its accents and action, or it can suppress all regularity of pulsation, freeing mind from body. It can move in the dynamic time of Newton, in the four-dimensional space-time of Einstein, or in the unhurried time of the Orient.[73]

Prospect and retrospect

The changes observed in the temporal organization of music suggest not only new avenues for future exploration but also a possible framework of ideas with which we may interpret the recent past: just as the various stages in the evolution of tonality have provided a basis for identifying and interpreting long-range trends in the history of music, so may the evolving temporal structure of music provide a conceptual basis for assessing the succession and accelerating proliferation of styles since 1800. The stylistic course of music in the last two centuries may be described not only as the weakening and rejection of tonality as the main principle of organization, but also as the genesis and development of a new set of temporal modes, which may in time prove as influential a set of matrices for music as the modes, scales, and keys of traditional tonality.

The idea of music—and music is as much an "idea" as it is anything else—is no longer a single idea to which an entire culture can subscribe, but an array of alternative ideas, each supported by its own assumptions, prophets, scriptures, and values. To think one's way through the tangle of words and conflicting ideologies requires more than the guidance of competent criticism ("applied" philosophy)—it requires the aid of a body of basic thought on the nature of music ("pure" philosophy). The supply is dismayingly scarce.

I began by hesitating to define music, in the knowledge that postulating too convenient a working definition would have encouraged the reader to validate or challenge one particular concept of music, instead of the far more important task of surveying with an open mind the full dimensions of the idea of music—ancient, medieval, romantic, Asian, modern—in all its incredible variety. Looking back on this diversity, my preference is still to say "Let *music* signify anything that is normally called *music*."

The products of the New Music have denied, at one time or another, most if not all the traditional concepts of musical being, knowledge, and value—frequently by means of brilliant, mind-boggling "demonstrations" that compel listeners to examine their assumptions about music. No consensus on values is yet in sight, but I venture to suggest that the signs of some eventual clarification of the present confusion will be clearly evident in retrospect. I prefer to think that we are passing through a very important period of sifting ideas, questioning assumptions, and testing values—which in time will lead either to a new consensus (which I admit now seems unlikely) or to the consolidation of a parallel set of value systems, which may or may not have much in common. The extent to which music will remain an art that can be shared within a broad social context will depend on the consensus (or lack of consensus) that emerges. What seems certain is that both music and the idea of music will continue to evolve, perhaps in quite unexpected directions, adding new dimensions and sloughing off others, in a persistent development of what is surely one of the most ancient, complex, profound, and sensitive creations of the human intellect.

Notes

1 Introduction: terms and themes

1 Bertrand Russell, *The Problems of Philosophy*, p. 161.
2 Sylvia Angus, "It's Pretty, but Is It Art?," *Saturday Review of Literature*, 2 September 1967, p. 15.
3 Paul Weiss, *The World of Art*, p. 10.
4 Paul Weiss, *Nine Basic Arts*, p. 8.
5 *Aphorisms* 1.1. The author refers, of course, to the art of healing, but numerous later authors have quoted or paraphrased this saying in aesthetic contexts (Seneca, Chaucer, Browning, and Goethe, among others). See chap. 3 for the scope of the Greek word *techne* (art).
6 Bernard Berenson, "The Aesthetic Moment," in *Aesthetics and History*, p. 93.

2 Meditations on a menuet

1 For a review of the problem of dating this work and two excellent analyses (by Howard Boatwright and Ernst Oster) see Maury Yeston, ed., *Readings in Schenker Analysis and Other Approaches* (New Haven: Yale University Press, 1977), pp. 110–40.
2 *Metaphysics* Δ.2.
3 Monroe C. Beardsley, *Aesthetics: Problems in the Philosophy of Criticism*, p. 466.
4 Roman Jakobson, "Linguistics and Poetics," in *Style in Language*, ed. Thomas A. Sebeok (New York and London: The Technology Press of M.I.T. and John Wiley and Sons, 1960), pp. 350–77. I have adapted the model slightly from Jakobson's format.
5 Paul Hindemith, *A Composer's World*, pp. 15–22.
6 Blake Edwards's film *Ten*.

3 Music as art and artifact

1 *Nichomachean Ethics* 6.4.1140a.
2 Władysław Tatarkiewicz, "Classification of the Arts," p. 457.

3 Ibid., p. 460.
4 *Institutio oratoria* 2.18.1.
5 Max Dessoir, *Ästhetik und allgemeine Kunstwissenschaft* (Stuttgart, 1906), reproduced in Tatarkiewicz, "Classification of the Arts," p. 461.
6 Paul Weiss, *Nine Basic Arts*, pp. 34–38.
7 Ibid., pp. 124, 170–71.
8 For an excellent summary of Wagner's major treatises, see Beekman C. Cannon, Alvin H. Johnson, and William G. Waite, *The Art of Music*, pp. 378–84.
9 For a general exposition of the problem, see Monroe C. Beardsley, *Aesthetics: Problems in the Philosophy of Criticism*, pp. 339–48; for a set of more specialized studies, see Edward T. Cone, *The Composer's Voice.*
10 J. T. Fraser argues, in several recent works, that the (potential) global society of man may be considered as an emerging integrative level of nature, with its own distinctive temporality, causation, language, and unresolvable conflicts: "The Individual and Society," in *The Study of Time 3*, ed. J. T. Fraser, N. Lawrence, and D. Park (New York: Springer-Verlag, 1978), pp. 419–42; *Time as Conflict* (Basel: Birkhäuser, 1978), pp. 177–85, 263–80; and "Temporal Levels: Sociobiological Aspects of a Fundamental Synthesis," *Journal of Social and Biological Structures* 1 (1978): 339–55.
11 *Ars Poetica* (trans. H. R. Fairclough) 361–65.
12 See Wallis Dwight Braman, "The Use of Silence in the Instrumental Works of Representative Composers: Baroque, Classical, Romantic" (Ph.D. diss., Eastman School of Music of the University of Rochester, 1956); Gisèle Brelet, "Music and Silence," in *Reflections on Art*, ed. Susanne K. Langer, pp. 103–21; John Cage, "Lecture on Nothing" and "Lecture on Something," in John Cage, *Silence*, pp. 109–26, 129–40; Thomas Clifton, "The Poetics of Musical Silence," *Musical Quarterly* 62 (1976): 163–81; Zofia Lissa, "Aesthetic Functions of Silence and Rests in Music," trans. Eugenia Tarska, *Journal of Aesthetics and Art Criticism* 22 (1964): 443–54; Paul Weiss, *The World of Art*, pp. 109–10.
13 Grosvenor W. Cooper and Leonard B. Meyer, *The Rhythmic Structure of Music* (Chicago: University of Chicago Press, 1960), pp. 7–8.
14 For the background of this extremely important term, see Robert Christopher Ross, "'Ρυθμός: A History of Its Connotations" (Ph.D. diss., University of California, Berkeley, 1972).
15 For some examples and reasons see Lewis Rowell, "The Subconscious Language of Musical Time," esp. pp. 104–5.
16 Isaac Newton, "On Time," in *The Concepts of Space and Time: Their Structure and Their Development*, ed. Milič Čapek (Dordrecht: D. Reidel, 1976), pp. 209–10.
17 *Confessions* 11.14.
18 Victor Zuckerkandl, *Sound and Symbol*, pp. 168–212.
19 Ibid., p. 181.
20 Ibid., pp. 181–228; Zuckerkandl develops, and ultimately rejects, this

famous metaphor for time as "becoming," basing his arguments on Aristotle's essay on time in the *Physics* 4.3.

21 Henri Bergson, "Time as Lived Duration" (chap. 3 of his *Duration and Simultaneity*), trans. Leon Jacobson in *The Human Experience of Time*, ed. Charles M. Sherover, pp. 218–19.

22 See S. G. F. Brandon, "Time and the Destiny of Man," in *The Voices of Time*, ed. J. T. Fraser, pp. 140–57; this article will give the reader an entry into Brandon's more detailed works, especially his magisterial *History, Time and Deity* (Manchester: Manchester University Press, 1965); Jonathan D. Kramer discusses the concept of linear time in "New Temporalities in Music," pp. 539–41.

23 For a partial answer see Lewis Rowell, "The Creation of Audible Time."

24 Jonathan D. Kramer discusses this paradoxical concept of musical time in "New Temporalities," pp. 549–52.

25 Elliott Carter, *String Quartet No. 2* (1959) and *String Quartet No. 3* (1971), Columbia M 32738; Witold Lutosławski, *String Quartet* (1964), DGG 137 001.

26 *Nine Basic Arts*, pp. 171–81.

27 Eliseo Vivas and Murray Krieger, eds., *The Problems of Aesthetics*, p. 12.

28 See chap. 5.

4   Dionysus and Apollo

1   *Ion* (trans. Benjamin Jowett) 533e–534b.

2   *Timaeus* (trans. R. G. Bury) 47c–47d.

3   In *The Birth of Tragedy from the Spirit of Music* [*Die Geburt der Tragödie aus dem Geiste der Musik*] (1872); see "Apollonian and Dionysiac," *The Reader's Encyclopedia*, ed. William Rose Benét, 2d ed. (New York: Crowell, 1965).

4   *Politics* (trans. Benjamin Jowett) 8.6.1341a–1341b.

5   *Laws* (trans. A. E. Taylor) 669c–669e.

6   *Mathematica* (trans. E. Hiller) 1.

7   *Metaphysics* (trans. W. D. Ross) A.5.985b–986a.

8   Fragments 115–17 [in Diels's numbering: 48, 54, 51] (trans. Philip Wheelwright).

9   Edward Lippman, *Musical Thought in Ancient Greece*, pp. 10–11.

10 *Republic* (trans. Paul Shorey) 10.617b–617c.

11 See the famous study by Arthur O. Lovejoy, *The Great Chain of Being: A Study of the History of an Idea* (1936; reprint ed., New York: Harper and Row Torchbooks, 1960).

12 *De institutione musica* 1.2; for an English translation of this chapter, see Oliver Strunk, *Source Readings in Music History*, pp. 84–85.

13 Homer *Iliad* 18.468–617.

14 *Symposium* (trans. Benjamin Jowett) 210a–211b.

15 Władysław Tatarkiewicz, *History of Aesthetics*, 1:112.

16 *Poetics* (trans. Gerald F. Else) 1448b.

17 *Rhetoric* (trans. R. C. Jebb) 1.11.1371b.
18 Władysław Tatarkiewicz, "Mimesis," p. 226.
19 *Laws* (trans. R. G. Bury) 669a–669b.
20 *Politics* 8.7.1341b–1342b; see also Lippman, *Musical Thought*, pp. 128–32.
21 Translated by Kathleen Freeman, 37B6; see also Warren D. Anderson, *Ethos and Education in Greek Music*, pp. 38–42.
22 *Politics* (trans. Benjamin Jowett) 8.5.1340a–1340b, as quoted with minor changes in Julius Portnoy, *The Philosopher and Music*, p. 25.
23 *Republic* (trans. Benjamin Jowett) 4.424c.
24 *Politics* (trans. Ernest Barker) 8.7.1342a.
25 These issues are discussed more fully in Lewis Rowell, "Aristoxenus on Rhythm," pp. 68–70.
26 *On the Soul* 2.1.

5   The mythos of music

1 Northrop Frye, *Anatomy of Criticism*, pp. 131–62, 102.
2 *Poetics* 6.1450a.
3 For Lévi-Strauss's structural approach to the analysis of myth, see Claude Lévi-Strauss, "The Structural Study of Myth," in *Myth: A Symposium*, ed. Thomas A. Sebeok (Bloomington: Indiana University Press, 1958), pp. 81–106; *The Savage Mind* (Chicago: University of Chicago Press, 1966); and *The Raw and the Cooked: Introduction to a Science of Mythology*, vol. 1 (New York: Harper and Row, 1969).
4 G. S. Kirk, *Myth: Its Meaning and Functions in Ancient and Other Cultures* (Cambridge: Cambridge University Press, 1970), p. 7.
5 Frye, *Anatomy of Criticism*, p. 203.
6 Gen. 28: 10–12.
7 Martha Beckwith, *Hawaiian Mythology* (Honolulu: University of Hawaii Press, 1970), pp. 147–50.
8 Irwin Young, trans. and ed., *The "Practica Musicae" of Franchinus Gafurius* (Madison: University of Wisconsin Press, 1969), pp. xxvi–xxix, 1; for a fuller interpretation with numerous background references, see Edgar Wind, *Pagan Mysteries in the Renaissance*, 2d enlarged ed. (London: Faber and Faber, 1967), pp. 265–69 and fig. 20.
9 Excerpted from *Etymologiarum sive originum libri xx* 3.15-23, in Oliver Strunk, *Source Readings in Music History*, pp. 93–100.
10 Kathi Meyer-Baer, *Music of the Spheres and the Dance of Death*, pp. 219–336.
11 Strunk, *Source Readings*, pp. 62–63.
12 Rainer Maria Rilke, *Sonnets to Orpheus*, trans. M. D. Herter Norton (New York: W. W. Norton, 1942), bk. 1, sonnet 26.
13 Thomas Mann, *Joseph and His Brothers*, trans. H. T. Lowe-Porter (New York: Knopf, 1948), p. 436.
14 Gen. 4: 21.
15 1 Sam. 16: 14–23; 18: 10–13.

16 *De institutione musica* 1.33, in Strunk, *Source Readings*, pp. 85–86.

17 For a slightly different translation, see Warren Babb, trans., *Hucbald, Guido, and John on Music*, ed. Claude V. Palisca (New Haven: Yale University Press, 1978), p. 105; these are the first three lines of Guido's treatise *Regulae musicae rhythmicae*, in Martin Gerbert, *Scriptores ecclesiastici de musica*, 3 vols. (facs. ed., Hildesheim: Georg Olms, 1963), 2:25.

18 Kathi Meyer-Baer, "Saints of Music," p. 17.

19 Ibid., pp. 19–33.

20 Elaborated in Lewis Rowell, "The Lessons of *Faustus*."

21 Thomas Mann, *The Magic Mountain*, trans. H. T. Lowe-Porter (New York: Knopf, 1927), p. 113.

22 Ibid., p. 680.

23 *De institutione musica* 1.1, in Strunk, *Source Readings*, p. 82.

24 Marsilio Ficino, *Comm. in Tim.*, trans. D. P. Walker, in the latter's *Spiritual and Demonic Magic from Ficino to Campanella* (London: Warburg Institute, 1958), p. 9.

25 T. S. Eliot, *Four Quartets* (New York: Harcourt, Brace and World, 1943), p. 44.

26 See n. 9.

27 This is a term coined by Mircea Eliade in *The Myth of the Eternal Return*, trans. Willard R. Trask, Bollingen Series 46 (Princeton: Princeton University Press, 1954); see esp. p. 4.

28 Sir John Davies, "*Orchestra*" or "*A Poem of Dancing*" [ca. 1594], ed. E. M. W. Tillyard (London: Chatto and Windus, 1947), stanzas 17 and 95, pp. 19, 38.

29 Leo Spitzer, "Classical and Christian Ideas of World Harmony," pp. 324–27.

30 See Gretchen Ludke Finney, *Musical Backgrounds for English Literature*, pp. 1–20.

6 The European tradition to 1800

1 For Philodemus, see Warren D. Anderson, *Ethos and Education in Greek Music*, pp. 153–76, and L. P. Wilkinson, "Philodemus on Ethos in Music," *Classical Quarterly* 32 (1938): 174–81; for Sextus, see Sextus Empiricus, "Against the Musicians," in *Sextus Empiricus*, vol. 4, trans. R. G. Bury, Loeb Classical Library (Cambridge: Harvard University Press, 1949), pp. 372–405.

2 Władysław Tatarkiewicz, *History of Aesthetics*, 1: 230.

3 "Against the Musicians," p. 383.

4 Anderson, *Ethos and Education*, p. 167.

5 "Against the Musicians," pp. 396–99.

6 Longinus, *On the Sublime*, trans. W. Hamilton Fyfe, Loeb Classical Library (Cambridge: Harvard University Press, 1927), pp. 236–41.

7 See Monroe C. Beardsley, *Aesthetics from Classical Greece to the Present*, pp. 193–204, 218–22; see also Marjorie Hope Nicolson, "Sublime in External Nature," pp. 333–37.

8 See below and nn. 42, 43.

9 Plotinus, *The Enneads* (trans. Stephen MacKenna, rev. B. S. Page) 1.6.2; see also Beardsley, *Aesthetics from Classical Greece to the Present*, pp. 78–87.

10 *Enneads* 1.3.1–2; 5.8.1.

11 *Confessions* 10.49, quoted in Kathi Meyer-Baer, "Psychologic and Ontologic Ideas in Augustine's *De musica*," pp. 224–25.

12 *City of God* 19.13.

13 This point is amplified in Lewis Rowell, "Aristoxenus on Rhythm," pp. 63–79, esp. n. 36.

14 *De musica* 6.9.24. Throughout bk. 6 Augustine has arranged these rhythmic categories in various orders; this arrangement represents his final position. There is a serious misunderstanding on this point in Meyer-Baer's otherwise excellent "Psychologic and Ontologic Ideas in Augustine's *De musica*," pp. 226–27.

15 *De musica* 6.13.42; 6.12.35.

16 *De musica* 1.2.2; see also Paul Hindemith's exegesis in *A Composer's World*, pp. 1–13, 23–27.

17 *De musica* 6.12.35–36.

18 *Divine Providence and the Problem of Evil* [*De ordine*] 2.11.32, trans. Robert P. Russell (New York: Cosmopolitan Science and Art Service, 1942), pp. 133–35.

19 *De musica* 6.14.47.

20 *Confessions* 11.28.38.

21 *Summa theologica* (trans. by the Dominican Fathers) 1. Q. 27. art. 1.

22 Ibid. 1. Q. 39. art. 8.

23 *In sap.* 7.10, in Tatarkiewicz, *History of Aesthetics*, 2:237.

24 *Liber de summo bono* 2. tr. 3, c. 5, in Tatarkiewicz, *History of Aesthetics*, 2:244.

25 James Joyce, *A Portrait of the Artist as a Young Man* (New York: Viking Press, 1964), pp. 212–13.

26 In Manfred Bukofzer, "Speculative Thinking in Medieval Music," the author argues that the isorhythmic motet united the three main currents of speculative thinking in medieval music: the idea of music as an imitation of the *musica mundana*, the Pythagorean doctrine of numerical proportions, and the tendency toward interpolation as a commentary.

27 *De modo dicendi et meditandi*, in Tatarkiewicz, *History of Aesthetics*, 2:201.

28 Tatarkiewicz, *History of Aesthetics*, 2:202.

29 See Leon Plantinga, "Philippe de Vitry's *Ars nova*: A Translation," *Journal of Music Theory* 5 (1961): 204–23.

30 Dedication from the treatise *Proportionale musices* [ca. 1476], in Oliver Strunk, *Source Readings*, p. 195.

31 Dedication from the treatise *Liber de arte contrapuncti* [1477], in Strunk, *Source Readings*, p. 199.

32 René Descartes, *Compendium of Music*, trans. Walter Robert ([Rome]: American Institute of Musicology, 1961), pp. 11–13.

33   Tatarkiewicz, *History of Aesthetics*, 3:373.

34   See Joan Ferris, "The Evolution of Rameau's Harmonic Theories," *Journal of Music Theory* 3 (1959): 231–56, and Sister Michaela Maria Keane, "The Theoretical Writings of Jean-Philippe Rameau" (Ph.D. diss., Catholic University of America, 1961); Rameau's theories are argued at length in Matthew Shirlaw, *The Theory of Harmony* (1917; reprint ed., New York: Da Capo, 1979); for an English translation of Rameau's chef-d'oeuvre, see Jean-Philippe Rameau, *Treatise on Harmony*, trans. Philip Gossett (New York: Dover, 1971).

35   Quoted in Bernard Williams, "Rationalism," p. 73.

36   *An Essay Concerning Human Understanding*, p. 121; the idea of the mind as a tabula rasa (literally, a "scraped slate") goes back to Aristotle's *On the Soul* 3.4.430a and is echoed in Albert the Great and Thomas Aquinas. What Locke actually said was "white paper," but the expression *tabula rasa* has become linked with his brand of empiricism.

37   Francis Bacon, *Novum organum* 1.39.

38   Bertrand Russell, *Wisdom of the West*, p. 191.

39   David Hume, "Of the Standard of Taste," pp. 136, 137, 143.

40   Anthony Ashley Cooper, earl of Shaftesbury, "The Moralists," p. 137.

41   Shaftesbury, *Characteristics*, 1:296; for an exposition of this most important issue see chap. 8.

42   Nicolson, "Sublime in External Nature," pp. 333–37.

43   Edmund Burke, *A Philosophical Enquiry*, pp. 134, 149–50.

44   See George Buelow, "Rhetoric and Music," in *The New Grove's Dictionary of Music and Musicians*, ed. Stanley Sadie (London: Macmillan, 1980); also Hans Lenneberg, "Johann Mattheson on Affect and Rhetoric in Music," *Journal of Music Theory* 2 (1958): 47–84, 193–236.

45   Curt Sachs argues this thesis in *The Commonwealth of Art*, claiming that musical style has alternated between "ethos" (static/apollonian) and "pathos" (dynamic/dionysiac) cycles.

7   The Romantic synthesis

1   W. T. Jones, *The Romantic Syndrome*, p. 120.

2   Crane Brinton, "Romanticism," p. 209.

3   Frederick B. Artz, *From the Renaissance to Romanticism*, pp. 226–27.

4   Ibid., p. 226.

5   See Peter Salm, *The Poem as Plant: A Biological View of Goethe's "Faust"* (Cleveland: The Press of Case Western Reserve University, 1971).

6   Thomas Mann, "The Making of *Magic Mountain*," in *The Magic Mountain*, reprint ed. (New York: Random House, Vintage Books, 1969), pp. 717–27. This essay originally appeared in *Atlantic Monthly*, January 1953.

7   Alfred Einstein, *Music in the Romantic Era*, pp. 4–7.

8   See Shelley's "Ode to the West Wind" cited in chap. 5. See also Monroe C. Beardsley, *Aesthetics from Classical Greece to the Present*, p. 262.

9 Quoted in Artz, *From the Renaissance to Romanticism*, p. 227.
10 Friedrich Schiller, [*Letters*] *On the Aesthetic Education of Man*, trans. Reginald Snell (New Haven: Yale University Press, 1954), pp. 65–66.
11 R. T. Clark, *Herder's Life and Work* (Berkeley and Los Angeles: University of California Press, 1955), pp. 130–38, 249–62, 325–30.
12 Immanuel Kant, *Critique of Judgment*, pp. 172–73.
13 G. W. F. Hegel, *The Philosophy of Fine Art*, 1:118–19.
14 In an 1805 letter to J. H. Voss, in Georg Wilhelm Friedrich Hegel, *Sämtliche Werke* 27: *Briefe von und an Hegel*, ed. Johannes Hoffmeister (Hamburg: Felix Meiner, 1952), 1:100.
15 Arthur Schopenhauer, *The World as Will and Idea*, 1: 330–38.
16 Richard Wagner, *Das Kunstwerk der Zukunft*, in Oliver Strunk, *Source Readings*, pp. 880–84.
17 Eduard Hanslick, preface to the seventh [1885] edition of *The Beautiful in Music*, trans. Gustav Cohen (New York: Liberal Arts Press, 1957), p. 6.
18 Hanslick, *The Beautiful in Music*, pp. 21–25.
19 Schopenhauer, *The World as Will and Idea*, pp. 340–41.

8 Perception

1 Leonard B. Meyer, *Music, the Arts, and Ideas*, p. 271.
2 Edward T. Cone, *Musical Form and Musical Performance*, pp. 88–97.
3 Leonard B. Meyer, *Emotion and Meaning in Music*, p. 256.
4 Roger Sessions, "The Musical Impulse," in Elliott Schwartz and Barney Childs, eds., *Contemporary Composers on Contemporary Music*, pp. 185–86.
5 Paul Hindemith, *A Composer's World*, p. 16.
6 Immanuel Kant, *Critique of Judgment*, p. 45.
7 José Ortega y Gasset, *The Dehumanization of Art*, p. 10.
8 Edward Bullough, "Psychical Distance as a Factor in Art and an Aesthetic Principle," p. 401.
9 Ibid., p. 405.
10 The use of this piece in Blake Edwards's film *Ten* has been cited above in chap. 2, n. 6; the reader who has access to this film is invited to consider its implications for the concept of aesthetic "distance"!
11 Edward A. Lippman, *A Humanistic Philosophy of Music*, pp. 227–28.
12 Ibid., pp. 349–50.
13 See chap. 10.
14 P. A. Michelis, "Aesthetic Distance and the Charm of Contemporary Art," p. 12.
15 Immanuel Kant, *Critique of Pure Reason*, pp. 257–75.
16 A. Cutler Silliman, "Familiar Music and the a priori," *Journal of Music Theory* 20 (1976): 217–18.
17 For some answers see Thomas Clifton, "Music and the a priori," *Journal of Music Theory* 17 (1973): 66–85.
18 Monroe C. Beardsley, *Aesthetics: Problems in the Philosophy of Criticism*, p. 46.

19 Victor Zuckerkandl, *Sound and Symbol*, pp. 15–16.

20 The important issue of musical meaning is discussed in the following: Beardsley, *Aesthetics: Problems in the Philosophy of Criticism*, pp. 318–39; Wilson Coker, *Music and Meaning: A Theoretical Introduction to Musical Aesthetics*; Peter Kivy, *The Corded Shell: Reflections on Musical Expression*; Susanne K. Langer, *Philosophy in a New Key: A Study in the Symbolism of Reason, Rite, and Art* (1942; reprint ed. New York: Mentor Books, 1948), pp. 165–99; Lippman, *A Humanistic Philosophy of Music*, pp. 125–60; Meyer, *Emotion and Meaning in Music*; and Zuckerkandl, *Sound and Symbol*, pp. 66–70.

21 Morris R. Cohen, *A Preface to Logic* (New York: Holt, 1944), p. 47.

22 Meyer, *Emotion and Meaning*, pp. 34–35.

23 Beardsley, *Aesthetics*, pp. 321–22; some of the examples are mine.

24 Ibid., pp. 327–28.

25 Susanne K. Langer, *Feeling and Form*, p. 27.

26 Meyer, *Emotion and Meaning*, p. 40.

9 Values

1 See chap. 3 and the list of references in n. 11 of that chapter.

2 A bamboo flute carried by wandering (ex-samurai) priests during the Edo period; the instrument and its repertoire are described in William P. Malm, *Japanese Music and Musical Instruments*, pp. 151–64.

3 This is true for peculiar and highly technical reasons: this single pitch is the inevitable consequence and ultimate reduction of the preceding series of chords, a striking example of musical relationships that are totally convincing in their intellectual rigor yet beyond the aural comprehension of even the most expert listener. See Claudio Spies, "Notes on Stravinsky's Variations," *Perspectives of New Music* 4 (1965): 66–70, esp. ex. 6.

4 See chap. 7.

5 The chord is a staccato E-minor triad, scored for wind instruments, harp, piano, and low strings; its doubling and voicing violate the traditional "rules" by emphasizing the third of the chord (the pitch G) and by the close spacing at the top and bottom of the chord.

6 Richard Wagner was the first composer to expand these two "families" of brass instruments into complete choirs covering the full range from soprano to contrabass, especially in *The Ring of the Nibelung*.

7 The flute has a strong fundamental but virtually no overtones, while the oboe's more complex harmonic spectrum features an extremely strong first overtone and prominent upper partials.

8 Leonard B. Meyer, *Emotion and Meaning in Music*, pp. 222–29.

9 See Alfred Einstein, *Mozart: His Character, His Work* (London: Oxford University Press, 1945), esp. pp. 157–63.

10 See especially the passage beginning in measure 204 of Brahms's Second Symphony, mvt. 1.

11 Susanne K. Langer, *Feeling and Form*, p. 27.

12 Eero Tarasti, *Myth and Music*, pp. 71–129.

13 For musical versions of the traditional "four temperaments," see Carl Nielsen's Symphony No. 2 (1902) and Paul Hindemith's *Theme and Four Variations* (1947).

14 Barney Childs, "Time and Music," p. 195; see also the famous "Seven Ages of Man" speech in *As You Like It*, act 2, sc. 7: 139–66.

15 See Meyer, *Emotion and Meaning*, p. 32.

16 The reader may wish to refer to the discussion of time in chap. 3.

17 See Mantle Hood, *The Ethnomusicologist* (New York: McGraw-Hill, 1971), pp. 114–16.

18 Curt Sachs, *The Rise of Music in the Ancient World*, pp. 41–43.

19 For a fuller discussion of the free/strict archetype, see Lewis Rowell, "The Creation of Audible Time," pp. 204–9.

20 David Epstein develops this excellent analogy in his essay "On Musical Continuity," pp. 181–82.

21 I refer here to Mircea Eliade's concept of primordial time ["in illo tempore"] as set forth in *The Myth of the Eternal Return*, trans. Willard R. Trask, Bollingen Series 46 (Princeton: Princeton University Press, 1954).

22 Or "vertical time," as described in Jonathan D. Kramer, "New Temporalities in Music," pp. 549–52.

23 See chap. 11.

24 For additional background on these distinctions, see Lewis Rowell, "Aristoxenus on Rhythm," pp. 68–69.

25 I especially like Paul Weiss's treatment of this issue ("the prospect") in *The World of Art*.

26 Musical beginnings are discussed at greater length in Rowell, "The Creation of Audible Time."

27 Although, of course, various syntactical designs may be superimposed on a set of variations, as in the fourth movement of Brahms's Symphony No. 4, which includes a set of reprise variations.

28 Monroe C. Beardsley, *Aesthetics: Problems in the Philosophy of Criticism*, pp. 466–70.

29 Leonard B. Meyer, *Music, the Arts, and Ideas*, p. 34.

30 *Meditations* 4.20.

31 *Discourses* 2.18.

32 Beardsley, *Aesthetics*, p. 477.

33 In other words, *claritas*. For a novel and imaginative application of the canons of unity, complexity, and intensity, see Edward T. Cone, "Music: A View from Delft," pp. 57–71.

34 In his essay "Some Remarks on Value and Greatness in Music" (*Music, the Arts, and Ideas*, pp. 22–41), Meyer argues that a distinction may be drawn between "primitive music" (pop) and "sophisticated art music" (jazz) on the basis of whether the gratification of musical tendencies is immediate or delayed.

10   Comparative aesthetics: India and Japan

1   From the thirteenth-century *Saṅgīta-ratnākara* ["Jewel-mine of Music"] 1.3:1–2.

2   Ananda K. Coomaraswamy, "The Theory of Art in Asia," p. 39.

3   Zeami (1363–1443), *Shikwadō-sho* ["The Book of the Way of the Highest Flower"] 4, quoted in Eta Harich-Schneider, *A History of Japanese Music*, p. 427.

4   Donald Keene, "Japanese Aesthetics," pp. 293–306.

5   Kenkō, *Essays in Idleness*, p. 115.

6   Ibid., p. 70.

7   See Richard Lannoy, *The Speaking Tree*, p. 279.

8   See chap. 6.

9   *Shōtetsu Monogatari* (1430), quoted in Ryusaku Tsunoda, William Theodore de Bary, and Donald Keene, comps., *Sources of Japanese Tradition*, p. 285.

10   Tsunoda, de Bary, and Keene, *Sources of Japanese Tradition*, p. 287.

11   For biographical data and philosophical background, see Kanti Chandra Pandey, *Abhinavagupta*; for Abhinavagupta's aesthetic theories and, in particular, the theory of *rasa*, see the same author's *Comparative Aesthetics*, 1:151–256.

12   See chap. 6, n. 44.

13   Eliot Deutsch, "Reflections on Some Aspects of the Theory of *Rasa*," in *Studies in Comparative Aesthetics*, p. 16.

14   Pandey, *Comparative Aesthetics*, 1:162–165.

15   Ibid., pp. 166–78.

16   Ibid., pp. 178–80.

17   See Klaus Ebeling, *Ragamala Painting* (Basel and New Delhi: Ravi Kumar, 1973).

18   P. Sambamoorthy, *South Indian Music*, 2d ed., 6 vols. (Madras: Indian Music Publishing House, 1963), 5:167.

19   *Saṅgīta-ratnākara* 1.3:3–6.

20   See Lewis Rowell, "A Śikṣā for the Twiceborn," esp. pp. 72–75.

21   Wm. Theodore de Bary et al., *Sources of Indian Tradition*, p. 274.

11   Clotho and Atropos

1   *Republic* (trans. Paul Shorey) 10.617b–617c.

2   Robert Graves, *The Greek Myths*, 2 vols. (New York: Braziller, 1959), 1:48–49.

3   Walter Kaufmann, *Musical References in the Chinese Classics*, pp. 32–47.

4   Quoted by Theodore H. Van Laue in *Why Lenin? Why Stalin?* (New York: Lippincott, 1971), p. 90.

5   Quoted in Monroe C. Beardsley, *Aesthetics from Classical Greece to the Present*, p. 360.

6 As summarized by James Bakst in *A History of Russian-Soviet Music*, pp. 286–87.

7 In an open letter to the conductor Wilhelm Furtwängler, *Berliner Lokalanzeiger*, 11 April 1933.

8 Nikolai Shamota, "On Tastes in Art [The Soviet View]," in *Aesthetics Today*, ed. Morris Philipson, p. 28.

9 Nicolas Slonimsky, comp. and trans., *Music Since 1900*, pp. 1370–71.

10 Ibid., pp. 1378–79.

11 See chap. 3.

12 On the grounds that "ideas, plans, methods, systems, etc." are not subject to copyright as musical works in Class E; to be registered in Class E as a musical work the copy deposited must contain at least a minimal amount of original musical expression fixed in definite, concrete form (notations or other visible written expressions representing a succession of musical sounds)—Circular 96H, Copyright Office, Library of Congress.

13 As in the *Audience Pieces* of Ben Vautier, described in Michael Nyman, *Experimental Music*, p. 71.

14 Translated by Edgard Varèse and quoted in his 1939 lecture "Music as an Art-Science," in Elliott Schwartz and Barney Childs, eds., *Contemporary Composers on Contemporary Music*, p. 201.

15 See chap. 6 n. 36.

16 Varèse, "Music as an Art-Science," in Schwartz and Childs, *Contemporary Composers on Contemporary Music*, pp. 200–201.

17 Igor Stravinsky and Robert Craft, *Dialogues and a Diary*, pp. 68–69.

18 A style of vocal production halfway between speech and song, used with great effect in Alban Berg's opera *Wozzeck* and other dramatic works by Berg and Schoenberg.

19 A remark attributed to Rudolf Kolisch and applied scornfully to the music of Stravinsky by Theodor Adorno in *Philosophy of Modern Music*, pp. 182–84.

20 Quoted in Nyman, *Experimental Music*, p. 42.

21 Ibid.

22 See chap. 5.

23 Stravinsky and Craft, *Memories and Commentaries*, p. 100.

24 See n. 16.

25 Edward A. Lippman, *A Humanistic Philosophy of Music*, p. 350.

26 John Cage, "Rhythm etc.," p. 197.

27 A point made by Jonathan D. Kramer in "New Temporalities in Music," pp. 543–44, and elaborated in a paper on "The Impact of Technology on Musical Time," presented in a symposium on "Chronos and Mnemosyne: Time in Literature and the Arts," University of Southern California, 3 April 1982.

28 In Schwartz and Childs, *Contemporary Composers on Contemporary Music*, p. 249.

29 John Cage, "Composition as Process," in *Silence*, p. 39.

30 Barney Childs, "Time and Music," p. 197.

31 Thomas Mann, *Doctor Faustus*, p. 92.
32 See David Cohen, "Anton Webern and the Magic Square," *Perspectives of New Music* 13 (1974): 213–15; Dmitri A. Borgmann, *Language on Vacation* (New York: Scribner's, 1965), p. 208; and Anton von Webern, *Sketches (1926–1945)*, facs. ed. (New York: Carl Fischer, 1968), plate 34. The literal translation of the cryptic motto is "The sower Arepo keeps the work circling." See Willi Reich's postscript to Anton Webern, *The Path to the New Music* (Bryn Mawr, Pa.: Theodore Presser, 1963), p. 57.
33 *Doctor Faustus*, p. 379.
34 Mann did this to Schoenberg's extreme irritation; see the exchange of letters in *Saturday Review of Literature*, 1 January 1949, and subsequent letters in the *Letters of Thomas Mann*, trans. Richard and Clara Winston, 2 vols. (New York: Knopf, 1970).
35 *Doctor Faustus*, p. 93.
36 See Gary E. Wittlich, "Sets and Ordering Procedures in Twentieth-Century Music," in *Aspects of Twentieth-Century Music*, Gary E. Wittlich, coordinating ed. (Englewood Cliffs, N.J.: Prentice-Hall, 1975), pp. 392–93.
37 Webern, *Sketches (1926–1945)*, plate 34.
38 As Alvin Toffler claimed a few years ago in his popular *Future Shock*, it is questionable whether the concept of a "mass audience" is still valid.
39 John Cage, "Experimental Music," in *Silence*, p. 12.
40 See the Wagner quotation in chap. 7.
41 *Doctor Faustus*, p. 192.
42 Mukund Lath, *A Study of "Dattilam,"* p. 233.
43 George Perle, *Serial Composition and Atonality*, p. 8.
44 Elliott Carter, *The Writings of Elliott Carter*, pp. 276–77.
45 Analyzed in Iannis Xenakis, *Formalized Music*, pp. 113–22.
46 Pierre Boulez, "Sonate, que me veux-tu?," pp. 34–35.
47 Edgard Varèse, "The Liberation of Sound," in Schwartz and Childs, *Contemporary Composers on Contemporary Music*, p. 203.
48 Leonard B. Meyer, *Music, the Arts, and Ideas*, pp. 195–208.
49 *The Writings of Elliott Carter*, p. 278.
50 For an illuminating analysis of the trend toward spatial thinking in twentieth-century music, see George Rochberg, "The New Image of Music," pp. 1–10.
51 Nyman, *Experimental Music*, pp. 88–89.
52 Quoted in ibid., p. 31; see also John Cage, "Erik Satie," in *Silence*, pp. 76–82.
53 *The Writings of Elliott Carter*, pp. 120–21.
54 *Boulez on Music Today*, p. 67.
55 Xenakis, *Formalized Music*, p. 9.
56 Record jacket notes, Nonesuch H–71246.
57 See chap. 5 and esp. n. 28.
58 See chap. 3.
59 I have discussed these five possibilities in "The Creation of Audible Time," pp. 200–201, and suggested specific examples on p. 209, n. 8.
60 See chap. 9 and esp. n. 14.
61 George Rochberg, "Duration in Music," pp. 60–62.

264

62 Nyman, *Experimental Music*, p. 1.

63 Stravinsky and Craft, *Dialogues and a Diary*, pp. 127–28.

64 Stravinsky and Craft, *Retrospectives and Conclusions*, pp. 76–77.

65 Meyer, *Music, the Arts, and Ideas*, pp. 164–65.

66 William James, *The Principles of Psychology*, "The Perception of Time," chap. 15 in *The Human Experience of Time*, comp. and ed. Charles M. Sherover, pp. 370–74.

67 Barney Childs, "Time and Music: A Composer's View," pp. 194–219; Jonathan D. Kramer, "New Temporalities in Music," pp. 539–56; Karlheinz Stockhausen, ". . . how time passes . . . ," pp. 10–40.

68 Readers familiar with Kramer's excellent article "New Temporalities in Music" will note that we differ in terminology: Kramer uses the term *multiple time* for a reordered or "dislocated" version of linear time, as in his article "Multiple and Non-Linear Time in Beethoven's Opus 135," *Perspectives of New Music* 11 (1973): 122–45.

69 See chap. 9 and esp. n. 22.

70 Kramer, "New Temporalities," pp. 546–49.

71 The same effect, for quite different reasons, may be heard in the orchestral *Variations* (1964), dedicated to the memory of Aldous Huxley.

72 For an early example of multiple time, see the finale from act 1 of Mozart's *Don Giovanni*, the famous scene in which the two stage bands compete for our attention with the menuet played by the main pit orchestra, all three playing in different meters. Alban Berg parodied this scene brilliantly in act 2, sc. 4 of *Wozzeck*.

73 Agnes Crawford Schuldt, "The Voices of Time in Music," p. 549.

Bibliography

Adorno, Theodor W. *Philosophy of Modern Music.* Translated by Anne G. Mitchell and Wesley V. Blomster. New York: Seabury Press, 1973.

Anderson, Warren D. *Ethos and Education in Greek Music: The Evidence of Poetry and Philosophy.* Cambridge: Harvard University Press, 1966.

Artz, Frederick B. *From Renaissance to Romanticism: Trends in Style in Art, Literature, and Music, 1300–1830.* Chicago: University of Chicago Press, 1962.

Augustinus, Aurelius. *St. Augustine's "De Musica": A Synopsis.* By W. F. Jackson Knight. 1949. Reprint. Westport, Conn.: Hyperion Press, 1979.

Bake, Arnold. "The Music of India." In *Ancient and Oriental Music,* edited by Egon Wellesz, pp. 195–227. New Oxford History of Music, vol. 1. London: Oxford University Press, 1957.

Bakst, James. *A History of Russian-Soviet Music.* New York: Dodd, Mead, 1962.

Beardsley, Monroe C. *Aesthetics: Problems in the Philosophy of Criticism.* New York: Harcourt, Brace and World, 1958.

———. *Aesthetics from Classical Greece to the Present: A Short History.* 1966. Reprint. University, Ala.: University of Alabama Press, 1975.

———. "Theories of Beauty Since the Mid-Nineteenth Century." In *Dictionary of the History of Ideas: Studies of Selected Pivotal Ideas.* Philip P. Wiener, Editor in chief. Vol. 1, pp. 207–14. New York: Charles Scribner's Sons, 1968.

Beckwith, John, and Kasemets, Udo, eds. *The Modern Composer and His World.* Toronto: University of Toronto Press, 1961.

Berenson, Bernard. *Aesthetics and History.* 1948. Reprint. Garden City, N.Y.: Doubleday, Anchor Books, 1953.

Blacker, Carmen, and Loewe, Michael, eds. *Ancient Cosmologies.* London: George Allen and Unwin, 1975.

Blume, Friedrich. *Classic and Romantic Music: A Comprehensive Survey.* Translated by M. D. Herter Norton. New York: W. W. Norton, 1970.

———. *Renaissance and Baroque Music: A Comprehensive Survey.* Translated by M. D. Herter Norton. New York: W. W. Norton, 1967.

Boretz, Benjamin, and Cone, Edward T., eds. *Perspectives on Contemporary Music Theory.* New York: W. W. Norton, 1972.

Boulez, Pierre. "Alea." Translated by David Noakes and Paul Jacobs. *Perspectives of New Music* 3 (1964): 42–53.

———. *Boulez on Music Today.* Translated by Susan Bradshaw and Richard Rodney Bennett. Cambridge: Harvard University Press, 1971.

———. "Sonate, que me veux-tu?" Translated by David Noakes and Paul Jacobs. *Perspectives of New Music* 1 (1963): 32–44.

Brinton, Crane. "Romanticism." *The Encyclopedia of Philosophy.* Paul Edwards, Editor in chief. Vol. 7, pp. 206–9. New York: Macmillan, 1967.

Bukofzer, Manfred. "Speculative Thinking in Medieval Music." *Speculum* 17 (1942): 165–80.

Bullough, Edward. "Psychical Distance as a Factor in Art and an Aesthetic Principle," *British Journal of Psychology* 5 (1912): 87–98. Reprinted in *The Problems of Aesthetics*, edited by Eliseo Vivas and Murray Krieger, pp. 396–405. New York: Holt, Rinehart and Winston, 1960.

Burke, Edmund. *A Philosophical Enquiry into the Origin of our Ideas of the Sublime and the Beautiful* (1757). Edited by J. T. Boulton. New York: Columbia University Press, 1958.

Burkert, Walter. *Lore and Science in Ancient Pythagoreanism.* Translated by Edwin L. Minar, Jr. Cambridge: Harvard University Press, 1972.

Butler, Christopher. *Number Symbolism.* New York: Barnes and Noble, 1970.

Cage, John. "Rhythm etc." In *Module, Proportion, Symmetry, Rhythm*, edited by György Kepes, pp. 194–203. New York: Braziller, 1966.

———. *Silence.* Middletown, Conn.: Wesleyan University Press, 1961.

Cannon, Beekman C.; Johnson, Alvin H.; and Waite, William G. *The Art of Music.* New York: Crowell, 1960.

Carnegy, Patrick. *Faust as Musician: A Study of Thomas Mann's Novel "Doctor Faustus."* New York: New Directions, 1973.

Carpenter, Patricia. "The Musical Object." With responses by Leo Treitler, Rudolf Arnheim, Ruth Halle Rowen, Edward T. Cone, Bernard Stambler, and David Burrows. *Current Musicology* 5 (1967): 56–116.

Carter, Elliott. *The Writings of Elliott Carter: An American Composer Looks at Modern Music.* Compiled, edited, and annotated by Else Stone and Kurt Stone. Bloomington: Indiana University Press, 1977.

Chávez, Carlos. *Musical Thought.* Cambridge: Harvard University Press, 1961.

Childs, Barney. "Time and Music: A Composer's View." *Perspectives of New Music* 15 (1977): 194–219.

Coker, Wilson. *Music and Meaning: A Theoretical Introduction to Musical Aesthetics.* New York: The Free Press, 1972.

Cone, Edward T. *The Composer's Voice.* Berkeley and Los Angeles: University of California Press, 1974.

———. "Music: A View from Delft." In *Perspectives on Contemporary Music Theory*, edited by Benjamin Boretz and Edward T. Cone, pp. 57–71. New York: W. W. Norton, 1972.

———. *Musical Form and Musical Performance.* New York: W. W. Norton, 1968.

Coomaraswamy, Ananda K. "The Theory of Art in Asia." In *Aesthetics Today,* edited and compiled by Morris Philipson, pp. 33–63. New York: World Publishing Co., 1961.

Dahlhaus, Carl. *Esthetics of Music*. Translated by William W. Austin. Cambridge: Cambridge University Press, 1982.

de Bary, Wm. Theodore; Hay, Stephen N.; Weiler, Royal; and Yarrow, Andrew, comps. *Sources of Indian Tradition*. Records of Civilization: Sources and Studies 56. New York: Columbia University Press, 1958.

Deutsch, Eliot. *Studies in Comparative Aesthetics*. Monographs of the Society for Asian and Comparative Philosophy 2. Honolulu: University Press of Hawaii, 1975.

————, ed. "Symposium on Aesthetics East and West." *Philosophy East and West* 19 (July 1969).

Dieckmann, Herbert. "Theories of Beauty to the Mid-Nineteenth Century." In *Dictionary of the History of Ideas: Studies of Selected Pivotal Ideas*. Philip P. Wiener, Editor in chief. Vol. 1, pp. 195–206. New York: Charles Scribner's Sons, 1968.

Einstein, Alfred. *Music in the Romantic Era*. New York: W. W. Norton, 1947.

Ellinwood, Leonard. "Ars musica." *Speculum* 20 (1945): 290–99.

Epperson, Gordon. *The Musical Symbol: A Study of the Philosophic Theory of Music*. Ames: Iowa State University Press, 1967.

Epstein, David. "On Musical Continuity." In *The Study of Time 4*, edited by J. T. Fraser, N. Lawrence, and D. Park, pp. 180–97. New York: Springer-Verlag, 1981.

Finney, Gretchen Ludke. *Musical Backgrounds for English Literature: 1580–1650*. New Brunswick, N.J.: Rutgers University Press, n.d.

Fraser, J. T. *Of Time, Passion, and Knowledge: Reflections on the Strategy of Existence*. New York: Braziller, 1975.

————, ed. *The Voices of Time: A Cooperative Survey of Man's Views of Time as Expressed by the Sciences and by the Humanities*. 2d. ed. Amherst: University of Massachusetts Press, 1981.

Frye, Northrop. *Anatomy of Criticism*. Princeton: Princeton University Press, 1957.

Graham, John. "Ut pictura poesis." In *Dictionary of the History of Ideas: Studies of Selected Pivotal Ideas*. Philip P. Wiener, Editor in chief. Vol. 4, pp. 465–76. New York: Charles Scribner's Sons, 1968.

Hanslick, Eduard. *The Beautiful in Music* (1854). Translated by Gustav Cohen. New York: Liberal Arts Press, 1957.

Harich-Schneider, Eta. *A History of Japanese Music*. London: Oxford University Press, 1973.

Hegel, G. W. F. *The Philosophy of Fine Art* (1835). Translated by F. P. B. Osmaston. 4 vols. London: G. Bell, 1920.

Hindemith, Paul. *A Composer's World: Horizons and Limitations*. Cambridge: Harvard University Press, 1952.

Hofstadter, Albert, and Kuhns, Richard, eds. *Philosophies of Art and Beauty: Selected Readings in Aesthetics from Plato to Heidegger*. Chicago: University of Chicago Press, 1964.

Hollander, John. *The Untuning of the Sky: Ideas of Music in English Poetry, 1500–1700.* 1961. Reprint. New York: W. W. Norton, 1970.

Hopper, Vincent Foster. *Medieval Number Symbolism: Its Sources, Meaning, and Influence on Thought and Expression.* 1938. Reprint. New York: Cooper Square Publishers, 1969.

Hospers, John. *Understanding the Arts.* Englewood Cliffs, N.J.: Prentice-Hall, 1982.

Hume, David. "Of the Standard of Taste." In *Essays and Treatises on Several Subjects,* pp. 134–46. London: A. Millar, 1758.

Jones, W. T. *The Romantic Syndrome.* The Hague: Nijhoff, 1961.

Kant, Immanuel. *Critique of Judgment* (1790). Translated by J. H. Bernard. New York: Hafner, 1951.

———. *Immanuel Kant's "Critique of Pure Reason"* (1781). Translated by Norman Kemp Smith. London: Macmillan, 1929.

Kaufmann, Walter. *Musical References in the Chinese Classics.* Detroit Monographs in Musicology 5. Detroit: Information Coordinators, 1976.

Keene, Donald. "Japanese Aesthetics." With responses by Earle Ernst, Harold E. McCarthy, Stephen C. Pepper, and V. H. Viglielmo. *Philosophy East and West* 19 (1969): 293–326.

Kenkō. *Essays in Idleness: The "Tsurezuregusa" of Kenkō.* Translated by Donald Keene. New York: Columbia University Press, 1967.

Kivy, Peter. *The Corded Shell: Reflections on Musical Expression.* Princeton: Princeton University Press, 1980.

Kramer, Jonathan D. "New Temporalities in Music." *Critical Inquiry* 7 (1981): 539–56.

Krebs, Stanley D. *Soviet Composers and the Development of Soviet Music.* New York: W. W. Norton, 1970.

Langer, Susanne K. *Feeling and Form: A Theory of Art (Developed from Philosophy in a New Key).* New York: Charles Scribner's Sons, 1953.

———, ed. *Reflections on Art: A Source Book of Writings by Artists, Critics, and Philosophers.* Baltimore: Johns Hopkins Press, 1958.

Lannoy, Richard. *The Speaking Tree: A Study of Indian Culture and Society.* London: Oxford University Press, 1971.

Lath, Mukund. *A Study of "Dattilam": A Treatise on the Sacred Music of Ancient India.* New Delhi: Impex India, 1978.

Le Huray, Peter, and Day, James, eds. *Music and Aesthetics in the Eighteenth and Early-Nineteenth Centuries.* Cambridge Readings in the Literature of Music. Cambridge: Cambridge University Press, 1981.

Lippman, Edward A. *A Humanistic Philosophy of Music.* New York: New York University Press, 1977.

———. *Musical Thought in Ancient Greece.* New York: Columbia University Press, 1964.

Locke, John. *An Essay Concerning Human Understanding* (1690). Edited by Alexander Campbell Fraser. 2 vols. Oxford: Clarendon Press, 1894.

Malm, William P. *Japanese Music and Musical Instruments.* Rutland, Vt.: Tuttle, 1959.

Mann, Thomas. *Doctor Faustus: The Life of the German Composer Adrian Leverkühn as Told by a Friend.* Translated by H. T. Lowe-Porter. New York: Knopf, 1948.

Margolis, Joseph, ed. *Philosophy Looks at the Arts: Contemporary Readings in Aesthetics.* Rev. ed. Philadelphia: Temple University Press, 1978.

Meyer, Leonard B. *Emotion and Meaning in Music.* Chicago: University of Chicago Press, 1956.

———. *Music, the Arts, and Ideas: Patterns and Predictions in Twentieth-Century Culture.* Chicago: University of Chicago Press, 1967.

Meyer-Baer, Kathi. *Music of the Spheres and the Dance of Death: Studies in Musical Iconology.* Princeton: Princeton University Press, 1970.

———. "Psychologic and Ontologic Ideas in Augustine's *De musica.*" *Journal of Aesthetics and Art Criticism* 11 (1953): 224–30.

———. "Saints of Music." *Musica Disciplina* 9 (1955): 11–33.

Michaelides, Solon. *The Music of Ancient Greece: An Encyclopaedia.* London: Faber and Faber, 1978.

Michelis, P. A. "Aesthetic Distance and the Charm of Contemporary Art." *Journal of Aesthetics and Art Criticism* 18 (1959): 1–45.

Moore, Charles A., ed. *The Indian Mind: Essentials of Indian Philosophy and Culture.* Honolulu: East-West Center Press, 1967.

———, ed. *The Japanese Mind: Essentials of Japanese Philosophy and Culture.* Honolulu: East-West Center Press, 1967.

Morgan, Robert P. "Musical Time/Musical Space." *Critical Inquiry* 6 (1980): 527–38.

Murray, Henry A., ed. *Myth and Mythmaking.* New York: Braziller, 1960.

Nahm, Milton C., comp. *Readings in Philosophy of Art and Aesthetics.* Englewood Cliffs, N.J.: Prentice-Hall, 1975.

Nicolson, Marjorie Hope. "Sublime in External Nature." In *Dictionary of the History of Ideas: Studies of Selected Pivotal Ideas.* Philip P. Wiener, Editor in chief. Vol. 4, pp. 333–37. New York: Charles Scribner's Sons, 1968.

Nyman, Michael. *Experimental Music: Cage and Beyond.* New York: Schirmer Books, 1974.

Opper, Jacob. *Science and the Arts: A Study in Relationships from 1600–1900.* Rutherford, N.J.: Fairleigh Dickinson University Press, 1973.

Ortega y Gasset, José. *The Dehumanization of Art and Other Writings on Art and Culture.* Garden City, N.Y.: Doubleday, Anchor Books, 1956.

Palisca, Claude V. "Scientific Empiricism in Musical Thought." In *Seventeenth-Century Science and the Arts,* edited by Hedley H. Rhys, pp. 91–137. Princeton: Princeton University Press, 1961.

Pandey, Kanti Chandra. *Abhinavagupta: An Historical and Philosophical Study.* 2d ed. Varanasi: Chowkhamba Sanskrit Series Office, 1963.

———. *Comparative Aesthetics.* Vol. 1, *Indian Aesthetics.* 2d ed. Varanasi: Chowkhamba Sanskrit Series Office, 1959.

Perl, Carl Johann. "Augustine and Music." Translated by Alan Kriegsman. *Musical Quarterly* 41 (1955): 496–510.

Perle, George. *Serial Composition and Atonality: An Introduction to the Music of*

Schoenberg, Berg, and Webern. 4th ed. Berkeley and Los Angeles: University of California Press, 1977.

Philipson, Morris, ed. *Aesthetics Today.* New York: World Publishing Co., 1961.

Plato. *The Collected Dialogues of Plato.* Edited by Edith Hamilton and Huntington Cairns. Bollingen Series 71. Princeton: Princeton University Press, 1961.

Portnoy, Julius. *Music in the Life of Man.* New York: Holt, Rinehart and Winston, 1963.

———. *The Philosopher and Music: A Historical Outline.* New York: Humanities Press, 1954.

Radhakrishnan, Sarvepalli, and Moore, Charles A., eds. *A Source Book in Indian Philosophy.* Princeton: Princeton University Press, 1957.

Raghavan, V., and Nagendra, [?], eds. *An Introduction to Indian Poetics.* Madras: Macmillan, 1970.

Reese, Gustave. *Fourscore Classics of Music Literature.* New York: Liberal Arts Press, 1957.

Reynolds, Roger. *Mind Models: New Forms of Musical Experience.* New York: Praeger, 1975.

Rochberg, George. "Duration in Music." In *The Modern Composer and His World,* edited by John Beckwith and Udo Kasemets, pp. 56–64. Toronto: University of Toronto Press, 1961.

———. "The New Image of Music." *Perspectives of New Music* 2 (1963): 1–10.

———. "The Structure of Time in Music: Traditional and Contemporary Ramifications and Consequences." In *The Study of Time 2,* edited by J. T. Fraser and N. Lawrence, pp. 136–49. New York: Springer-Verlag, 1975.

Rowell, Lewis. "Aristoxenus on Rhythm." *Journal of Music Theory* 23 (1979): 63–79.

———. "The Creation of Audible Time: How Musics Begin." In *The Study of Time 4,* edited by J. T. Fraser, N. Lawrence, and D. Park, pp. 198–210. New York: Springer-Verlag, 1981.

———. "The Lessons of *Faustus.*" *College Music Symposium* 21, no. 2 (1981): 54–70.

———. "A Śikṣā for the Twiceborn." *Asian Music* 9, no. 1 (1977): 72–94.

———. "The Subconscious Language of Musical Time." *Music Theory Spectrum* 1 (1979): 96–106.

Russell, Bertrand. *A History of Western Philosophy.* New York: Simon and Schuster, 1945.

———. *The Problems of Philosophy.* 1912. Reprint. London: Oxford University Press, 1972.

———. *Wisdom of the West.* London: Rathbone, 1959.

Sachs, Curt. *The Commonwealth of Art: Style in the Fine Arts, Music, and the Dance.* New York: W. W. Norton, 1946.

———. *The Rise of Music in the Ancient World—East and West.* New York: W. W. Norton, 1943.

Śārṅgadeva. *"Saṅgīta-ratnākara" of Śārṅgadeva.* Translated by R. K. Shringy. Vol. 1. Delhi: Motilal Banarsidass, 1978.

Schopenhauer, Arthur. *The World as Will and Idea* (1819). Translated by R. B.

Haldane and J. B. Kemp. 4th ed. 2 vols. London: Kegan Paul, Trench, Trübner, 1896.

Schueller, Herbert M., ed. "Oriental Aesthetics." A special issue of *Journal of Aesthetics and Art Criticism* 24, no. 1 (Fall 1965).

Schuldt, Agnes Crawford. "The Voices of Time in Music." *American Scholar* 45 (1976): 549–59.

Schwartz, Elliott, and Childs, Barney, eds. *Contemporary Composers on Contemporary Music.* New York: Holt, Rinehart and Winston, 1967.

Shaftesbury, Anthony Ashley Cooper, earl of. "The Moralists (1709)." In *Characteristics of Men, Manners, Opinions, Times, etc.,* edited by J. M. Robertson, vol. 2. New York: Dutton, 1900.

Sharma, Prem Lata. "Traditional Indian Musical Aesthetics." *Journal of the Music Academy, Madras* 34 (1963): 83–98.

Sherover, Charles M. [comp. and ed.]. *The Human Experience of Time: The Development of Its Philosophic Meaning.* New York: New York University Press, 1975.

Skeris, Robert A. ΧΡΩΜΑ ΘΕΟΤ: *On the Origins and Theological Interpretation of the Musical Imagery used by the Ecclesiastical Writers of the First Three Centuries, with Special Reference to the Image of Orpheus.* Altötting: Verlag Alfred Coppenrath, 1976.

Slonimsky, Nicolas, comp. and trans. *Music Since 1900.* 4th ed. New York: Charles Scribner's Sons, 1971.

Spitzer, Leo. "Classical and Christian Ideas of World Harmony." In 2 pts. *Traditio* 2 (1944): 409–64; 3 (1945): 307–64.

Stockhausen, Karlheinz. ". . . how time passes . . ." Translated by Cornelius Cardew. *Die Reihe* [Musical Craftsmanship] 3 (1959): 10–40.

Strauss, Walter A. *Descent and Return: The Orphic Theme in Modern Literature.* Cambridge: Harvard University Press, 1971.

Stravinsky, Igor. *Poetics of Music in the Form of Six Lessons.* Translated by Arthur Knodel and Ingolf Dahl. 1947. Reprint. New York: Vintage Books, 1956.

Stravinsky, Igor, and Craft, Robert. *Conversations with Igor Stravinsky.* 1959. Reprint. Berkeley and Los Angeles: University of California Press, 1980.

———. *Dialogues and a Diary.* London: Faber and Faber, 1968.

———. *Expositions and Developments.* 1962. Reprint. Berkeley and Los Angeles: University of California Press, 1981.

———. *Memories and Commentaries.* 1960. Reprint. Berkeley and Los Angeles: University of California Press, 1981.

———. *Retrospectives and Conclusions.* New York: Knopf, 1969.

———. *Themes and Episodes.* New York: Knopf, 1966.

Strunk, Oliver, comp. and trans. *Source Readings in Music History: From Classical Antiquity through the Romantic Era.* New York: W. W. Norton, 1950.

Stuckenschmidt, H. H. *Twentieth Century Music.* Translated by Richard Deveson. New York: McGraw-Hill, 1969.

Tarasti, Eero. *Myth and Music: A Semiotic Approach to the Aesthetics of Myth in Music, especially that of Wagner, Sibelius, and Stravinsky.* The Hague: Mouton, 1979.

Tatarkiewicz, Władysław. "Classification of the Arts." In *Dictionary of the History of Ideas: Studies of Selected Pivotal Ideas*. Philip P. Wiener, Editor in chief. Vol. 1, pp. 456–62. New York: Charles Scribner's Sons, 1968.

———. "Form in the History of Aesthetics." In *Dictionary of the History of Ideas: Studies of Selected Pivotal Ideas*. Philip P. Wiener, Editor in chief. Vol. 2, pp. 216–25. New York: Charles Scribner's Sons, 1968.

———. *History of Aesthetics*. 3 vols. Vol. 1: *Ancient Aesthetics*. Edited by J. Harrell. Translated by Adam and Ann Czerniawski. 1962. Reprint. The Hague: Mouton, 1970. Vol. 2: *Medieval Aesthetics*. Edited by C. Barrett. Translated by R. M. Montgomery. 1962. Reprint. The Hague: Mouton, 1970. Vol. 3: *Modern Aesthetics*. Edited by D. Petsch. Translated by Chester A. Kisiel and John F. Besemeres. 1967. Reprint. The Hague: Mouton, 1974.

———. "Mimesis." In *Dictionary of the History of Ideas: Studies of Selected Pivotal Ideas*. Philip P. Wiener, Editor in chief. Vol. 3, pp. 225–30. New York: Charles Scribner's Sons, 1968.

Taylor, Henry Osborn. *The Medieval Mind: A History of the Development of Thought and Emotion in the Middle Ages*. 2 vols. 4th ed. Cambridge: Harvard University Press, 1959.

Tillman, Frank A., and Cahn, Steven M., eds. *Philosophy of Art and Aesthetics: From Plato to Wittgenstein*. New York: Harper and Row, 1969.

Tillyard, E. M. W. *The Elizabethan World Picture*. Reprint. New York: Random House, Vintage Books, n.d.

Tsunoda, Ryusaku; de Bary, Wm. Theodore; and Keene, Donald, comps. *Sources of Japanese Tradition*. Records of Civilization: Sources and Studies 54. New York: Columbia University Press, 1958.

Vivas, Eliseo, and Krieger, Murray, eds. *The Problems of Aesthetics: A Book of Readings*. New York: Holt, Rinehart and Winston, 1960.

Walker, D. P. *Spiritual and Demonic Magic: From Ficino to Campanella*. Studies of the Warburg Institute, vol. 22. Edited by G. Bing. 1958. Reprint. Nendeln/Liechtenstein: Kraus, 1969.

Webern, Anton. *The Path to the New Music*. Edited by Willi Reich. Translated by Leo Black. Bryn Mawr, Pa.: Theodore Presser, 1963.

Weiss, Paul. *Nine Basic Arts*. Carbondale: Southern Illinois University Press, 1961.

———. *The World of Art*. Carbondale: Southern Illinois University Press, 1961.

Whitrow, G. J. *The Natural Philosophy of Time*. 2d ed. Oxford: Clarendon Press, 1980.

Williams, Bernard. "Rationalism." *The Encyclopedia of Philosophy*. Paul Edwards, Editor in chief. Vol. 7, pp. 69–75. New York: Macmillan, 1967.

Xenakis, Iannis. *Formalized Music: Thought and Mathematics in Composition*. Translated by Christopher Butchers, G. W. Hopkins, and Mr. and Mrs. John Challifour. Bloomington: Indiana University Press, 1971.

Zimmer, Heinrich. *Philosophies of India*. Edited by Joseph Campbell. Bollingen Series 26. 1951. Reprint. Princeton: Princeton University Press, 1969.

Zuckerkandl, Victor. *Sound and Symbol: Music and the External World*. Translated by Willard R. Trask. Bollingen Series 44. Princeton: Princeton University Press, 1956.

Index

Abhinavagupta, 202, 204–5
Accent, 26, 151, 159, 168, 227
Acoustics: harmonic and arithmetic series, 41; of motion, 170; of musical tone, 31–32; in Rameau's harmonic speculations, 105–6; of timbre, 154–56
Aesthetic assumptions: of Greeks, 39–40; of Middle Ages, 94–95; of modern aesthetics, 102; on time in Western music, 242–43; of traditional Western art music, 230
Aesthetics: aesthetic attitude, 6, 194; aesthetic experience, 5–6, 49, 194, 203–7; aesthetic object, 5; aesthetic surface, 132–33, 155–56, 158–62, 201; aesthetic value, 150; Asian, 191; defined, 3–4. *See also* Beauty; Criticism; Perception; Valuation
Affektenlehre, 111–12, 124
Albert the Great, 93, 257 n. 36
Aleatoric music, 233, 243–44, 246
Ambiguity: as dynamic value, 166–67; in Japanese aesthetics, 199–200; as melodic value, 177; of minor mode, 157; as musical value in Romanticism, 118–19; as source of tension, 164–65; in Wagner's "Tristan" chord, 154
Amphion, 70
Angus, Sylvia, 4
Apollonian/Dionysiac, 37, 38, 40, 80–81, 116, 257 n. 45
Approach, as structural function, 176

A priori, the: defined, 103; in phenomenology, 142–43; in rationalism, 107
Aquinas, St. Thomas, 14, 88, 92–94, 184, 257 n. 36
Aristotle, 13, 20, 30, 38, 39, 41, 45, 47–48, 49–50, 51–55, 59, 88, 204, 257 n. 36
Art: Asian philosophy of, 191; definitions of, 4–5, 20; philosophy of, 3–4; Romantic view of, 122–23
Art-for-art's sake, 102, 121, 213, 215, 230
Artist and society, 14, 17; in Baroque, 112–13; Herder on, 123; interchange of roles in twentieth century, 218–21; in Marxist-Leninist aesthetics, 212–18; matrix of musical society, 32–34; in the Romantic century, 120–23. *See also* Role
Arts: classifications of, 20–24; common features of, 24–28; composite, 23; Hegel on, 125; major and minor, 21; seven liberal, 21, 78–79; of society (proposed), 23–24, 218. *See also* Art
Artz, Frederick B., 117, 118
Asafiev, Boris, 214
Athleticism as musical value, 165–66, 184; in concerto, 183; in Indian music, 193, 206
Augustine, St., 29, 30, 88–92, 256 n. 14

Babbitt, Milton, 228
Bach, J. S., 7, 110, 161, 181, 186, 238, 243

Acknowledgment is made to the following publishers for permission to reprint selections from material under copyright.

From Bernard Berenson, *Aesthetics and History in the Visual Arts*. Copyright 1948 Pantheon Books, Random House, Inc.

From Max Dessoir, *Äesthetick und allgemeine Kunstwissenschaft* (1906). Translated by W. Tatarkiewicz, in "Classification of the Arts," in *Dictionary of the History of Ideas*, vol. 1. Copyright 1968, 1973 Charles Scribner's Sons. Reprinted with permission of Charles Scribner's Sons.

From *The Problems of Aesthetics*, ed. Eliseo Vivas and Murray Krieger. Introductions copyright, 1953. Adapted by permission of Holt, Rinehart and Winston, CBS College Publishing.

From "East Coker" and "The Dry Salvages" from *Four Quartets* by T. S. Eliot. Copyright, 1943, by T. S. Eliot, renewed, 1971, by Esme Valerie Eliot. Reprinted by permission of Harcourt Brace Jovanovich, Inc. and Faber and Faber, Ltd.

From Thomas Mann, *Doctor Faustus*. Translated by H. T. Lowe-Porter. Copyright 1948 by Alfred A. Knopf, Inc. From John Updike, "The Music School," in *The Music School*. Copyright © 1962, 1963, 1964, 1965, 1966 by John Updike. From Wallace Stevens, "Peter Quince at the Clavier," from *The Collected Poems of Wallace Stevens*. Copyright 1954 by Wallace Stevens. Reprinted by permission of Alfred A. Knopf, Inc.

From James Joyce, *A Portrait of the Artist as a Young Man*. Copyright 1916 by B. W. Huebsch. Copyright renewed 1944 by Nora Joyce. Definitive text Copyright © 1964 by the Estate of James Joyce. Reprinted by permission of Viking Penguin Inc. and by the Society of Authors.

From René Descartes, *Compendium of Music* (Compendium Musicae). Copyright © 1961 by American Institute of Musicology. Hänssler-Verlag, D-7303 Neuhausen-Stuttgart. Order no. 68.708.

From Leonard B. Meyer, *Music, the Arts, and Ideas*, The University of Chicago Press, Copyright © 1967 by The University of Chicago Press.

From Roger Sessions, *The Musical Experience of Composer, Performer, Listener*. Copyright 1950 © renewed 1978 by Princeton University Press.

From José Ortega y Gasset, *The Dehumanization of Art*. Copyright 1948 © renewed by Princeton University Press.